D0349233

Praise for *The Killing in the Consulate*

'Compulsory reading. Grab this excellent book if you want to understand why and how Jamal Khashoggi was murdered – and the uneasy political triangle of Saudi Arabia, Turkey and the United States that is behind so many events in the Middle East. Rugman's book is fast-paced and brilliantly written, with chilling transcripts of bugged conversations as a Saudi hit squad killed a journalist – true crime, and high-level diplomatic analysis.'

Jeremy Bowen, BBC Middle East editor

'A murder mystery where the mystery is why the world has stayed silent. From the bride-to-be pacing the pavement outside, to the assassination squad inside with the bone-saw, Rugman has produced a gripping read revealing what really happened inside the Istanbul consulate in all its shocking detail. He has done any of us who believe in a free press and human rights an important service in making sure this cannot go forgotten.'

Christina Lamb, *Sunday Times* chief foreign correspondent

'Reads like a page-turning spy thriller. That it is true makes it all the more chilling. Engrossing and enthralling.'

Tim Marshall, bestselling author of *Prisoners of Geography*

THE KILLING
IN
THE CONSULATE

Investigating the Life
and Death of Jamal Khashoggi

JONATHAN RUGMAN

**SIMON &
SCHUSTER**

London · New York · Sydney · Toronto · New Delhi

A CBS COMPANY

First published in Great Britain by Simon & Schuster UK Ltd, 2019
A CBS COMPANY

Copyright © Jonathan Rugman, 2019

The right of Jonathan Rugman to be identified as the author
of this work has been asserted in accordance with
the Copyright, Designs and Patents Act, 1988.

1 3 5 7 9 10 8 6 4 2

Simon & Schuster UK Ltd
1st Floor
222 Gray's Inn Road
London WC1X 8HB

www.simonandschuster.co.uk
www.simonandschuster.com.au
www.simonandschuster.co.in

Simon & Schuster Australia, Sydney
Simon & Schuster India, New Delhi

The author and publishers have made all reasonable
efforts to contact copyright-holders for permission, and
apologise for any omissions or errors in the form of credits
given. Corrections may be made to future printings.

A CIP catalogue record for this book
is available from the British Library

Hardback ISBN: 978-1-4711-8474-1
Trade Paperback ISBN: 978-1-4711-8475-8
eBook ISBN: 978-1-4711-8476-5

Typeset in Perpetua by M Rules
Printed in the UK by CPI Group (UK) Ltd, Croydon, CR0 4YY

MIX
Paper from
responsible sources
FSC
www.fsc.org   FSC® C020471

In memory of Jamal Khashoggi, journalist
1958–2018

London Borough of Richmond Upon on Thames	
RTWH	
90710 000 413 508	
Askews & Holts	
953.805 RUG	£20.00
	9781471184741

DISCARDED FROM RICHMOND UPON THAMES LIBRARY SERVICE

'This one has caught the imagination of the world, unfortunately.'

President Donald Trump,
18 October 2018

CONTENTS

Introduction   1

1   The final journey   7

2   Walking the tightrope   18

3   Meet the crown prince   39

4   The fall from grace   59

5   Flight to Washington   68

6   The Ritz-Carlton affair   87

7   A woman in Istanbul   104

8   Last weekend in London   123

9   The killing in the consulate   133

10   Aftermath   148

11   Investigation   160

12   Trump and the House of Saud   188

13   Erdoğan and the House of Saud   215

14   The lonely Turk   228

15   Davos in the Desert   234

16   The Saudis vs the CIA   246

17   'Maybe he did, maybe he didn't!'   258

18   The crown prince comeback tour   266

19   One tragedy exposes another   272

20   The Faustian bargain   285

21   The story he did not complete   309

Acknowledgements   317

Notes   320

Bibliography   336

Index   337

INTRODUCTION

In October 2018, one of my editors at *Channel 4 News* asked me to fly to Istanbul. A journalist from Saudi Arabia named Jamal Khashoggi, who worked for one of the world's most famous newspapers, the *Washington Post*, walked into his country's consulate there to obtain the paperwork to get married. He was never seen again.

His Turkish fiancée, beside herself with worry as she waited for him on the pavement outside, had raised the alarm. The Saudi government furiously denied any involvement in the affair, even claiming their citizen had left the building. With the Turkish authorities demanding that Riyadh provide a full explanation, Khashoggi's disappearance was fast turning into an international crisis. His newspaper's chief executive later called it the 'most depraved and oppressive act against a journalist in modern history'.

On the day itself, Tuesday 2 October, I was away from my desk, giving a talk to sixth formers at a school in Kent. The talk was entitled 'Tales from the Front Line', an account of the perils of being a foreign correspondent in Iraq, Gaza and elsewhere. I had no idea that Jamal Khashoggi, a fellow journalist I'd never met, had been killed in Istanbul earlier that day.

For several days, I fended off my editor's request to go to

Turkey, arguing that I could cover the story from London. This was unusual: I lived in Istanbul during the 1990s and rarely turned down an opportunity to go back. In a faint echo of Khashoggi's story, I had also become engaged to my future wife in Turkey and was obliged to visit the British consulate in order to obtain the paperwork for us to get married there.

In my defence, my reluctance to return was based on an awareness that the diplomatic crisis engulfing the Saudi crown prince and the presidents of Turkey and the United States was not happening in Istanbul, but unfolding behind closed doors in Washington DC, Ankara and Riyadh.

I sometimes rail against the cosmetics of television news: the need to be seen relaying information from outside a building, even if a reporter can't see anything happening and the real drama is playing out elsewhere. This was one of those occasions.

The Saudis had denied Turkish police investigators entry to their consulate for almost two weeks and I reasoned that standing outside it all day with a pack of fellow journalists would therefore add little to my knowledge, or to that of our viewers on Channel 4.

Besides, sitting on my mantelpiece at home was an invitation to Saudi Arabia's national day in London the following week. The card from the ambassador, Prince Mohammed bin Nawwaf bin Abdulaziz, was embossed with a golden palm tree and two crossed swords and informed me that the Natural History Museum in South Kensington had been hired for the prince's party. Clearly, no expense had been spared.

When the evening came, I failed to show up, so angry at the disappearance of a fellow journalist that I had no wish to shake the ambassador's hand amid the museum's dinosaur skeletons and stuffed birds. Instead, I flew to Istanbul, as my editor had wanted: Turkish police, accompanied by sniffer dogs and a small drone, had finally been allowed inside the consulate. The building's iron-grey doors were, I noticed, also embossed with the national symbols of a golden palm tree and two crossed swords.

I checked into a hotel, the Mövenpick, where nine members of the Saudi hit squad sent to intercept Jamal Khashoggi had also stayed. On the first night, I barely slept. Instead, the story of what had happened kept turning over in my head. Flickering before me were the final surveillance-camera images of Khashoggi walking to his death; the images, too, of his fellow Saudis passing nonchalantly through the lobby of my hotel.

I thought of the torment of the woman Khashoggi was about to marry; and then of how he had become a silent pawn in a high-stakes political game: the Saudis concealing the crime while the Turks leaked astonishing if unverifiable details, making it harder for the Trump administration to defend Saudi Arabia – the world's biggest arms importer and biggest exporter of oil.

When daylight came, I learned little. Several Turkish contacts were too afraid to talk to me about the story on the record, given the sensitivity of the case. An audibly nervous adviser to President Recep Tayyip Erdoğan refrained from any background comment. Jamal Khashoggi's grief-stricken fiancée, Hatice Cengiz, was not giving interviews. If Turkish police had found anything of interest inside the consulate, then they weren't saying.

The flow of information on the case largely depended upon lurid and sensational leaks of excerpts from a transcript of an audio recording of the murder, given to the Turkish and American press. As these leaks had begun to dry up, and as the consulate itself had failed to give up its secrets, the killing was slipping from the headlines. After my cameraman had filmed the exterior of the building from every conceivable angle, we headed home to London, where I continued to cover the story.

For this book, I travelled back to Istanbul as well as to Ankara, Washington DC and beyond in an attempt to tell in full the story which I had failed to tell properly then.

It is the story of one man whose words would prove the death of him, a journalist killed by his fellow Saudis who regarded him as a traitor.

In 2018, the year of his murder, ninety-nine journalists were killed worldwide, the deadliest year ever recorded. If journalists now face a new front line, a new kind of harm in state-sanctioned murder, then Jamal Khashoggi's fate is a warning to us all. In ways his family and friends cannot have begun to imagine, his death also reverberated all the way to a real war zone, by calling into question the many tens if not hundreds of thousands of lives lost amid the bombing and starvation of Yemen.

Khashoggi's adult life was marked by the rise of Osama bin Laden at one end and the collapse of the Arab Spring at the other. It was a life therefore bookended by the major moments and failures of the Arab world in which he lived. In fact, Khashoggi seemed to embody that world, to reflect many of its own apparently contradictory aspirations, as an Arab intellectual, trying to reconcile his Western education with his belief in political Islam alongside his loyalty to his kingdom's rulers.

For a moment, his death caught the world's attention; and its imagination too, because of the chilling details which emerged afterwards. That moment also crystallised one of the major concerns of our age: what happens when the so-called 'rules-based order' breaks down, when the basic principles by which nation states are supposed to operate are ignored, when a proponent of freedom of speech is murdered with a shocking degree of impunity.

Perhaps above all, the killing of a journalist throws into sharp focus the choices our leaders often face in dealing with countries whose values are at odds with our own; the trade-offs between commercial and strategic advantage and the defence of basic human rights.

Hatice Cengiz has summarised the dilemma at the heart of her fiancé's murder well. 'I know that governments operate not on feelings but on mutual interests,' she wrote in the *Washington Post*. 'However, they must all ask themselves a fundamental question: if the democracies of the world do not take genuine steps to bring to justice the perpetrators of this brazen, callous act – one that has caused universal outrage among their citizens – what moral authority are they left with? Whose freedom and human rights can they credibly continue to defend?'[1]

Jamal Khashoggi was deprived of the freedom to say and write what he believed; deprived also of the freedom to marry the woman he loved. Only by this telling of his story, with the help of his fiancée and friends, can our leaders be held to account for the choices they make.

Jonathan Rugman
London, June 2019

I

THE FINAL JOURNEY

Istanbul, 2 October 2018

Hatice Cengiz didn't mind being woken by her alarm at 3.45 in the morning. She was meeting her fiancé, a Saudi journalist named Jamal Khashoggi, off his plane at Istanbul's Atatürk airport. She wanted to surprise him, to show him how much she cared, to see his careworn, bearded face beaming down at her affectionately again. Within a week or so, they would be married, although they hadn't chosen a firm date. What was the point of sleeping on a day which promised such happiness?

Khashoggi was flying back to her overnight, business class, on Turkish Airlines from London Heathrow. The sixty-year-old was one of the Arab world's best-known journalists, with over 1.5 million followers on Twitter and a column in the 'global opinions' section of the *Washington Post*. For more than a year, he had been living in lonely exile in the United States, wretched at his separation from his family, his stinging criticism of his homeland in his newspaper articles rendering his safe return there impossible. Istanbul, and Hatice Cengiz, augured happier times ahead.

Later that day, he planned to visit the Saudi consulate, to collect a copy of his birth certificate and a 'single status' document, confirming he was divorced; and then he would be free to marry her.

Earnest, bookish and religiously devout, Cengiz spoke fluent Arabic and was studying for a PhD in Gulf studies. She was also twenty-four years younger than he was. They had known each other for barely five months, having met at an academic conference in Istanbul earlier that year.

While she was dressing, Khashoggi texted her to say his plane had landed early. By 4.07 a.m., he had cleared passport control. She was just putting on her shoes when he phoned her to say he'd collected his luggage and she needn't come to the airport. He was already on his way.[1]

Long before the sun had risen over the mosques and minarets of the former Ottoman capital, he took one of the city's yellow taxis to the apartment the couple had bought only the previous week.

At 3.13 a.m., a privately hired Gulfstream jet from Saudi Arabia had touched down at the same airport carrying nine men. Its registration was marked on its twin engines as HZ-SK2 and the flight plan it filed before take-off from Riyadh showed it had official diplomatic clearance. The plane's passengers were less than an hour ahead of their prey.

All of them worked for what the CIA would later euphemistically call the 'Saudi Rapid Intervention Group', drawn from the ranks of the kingdom's military and intelligence services. One, Lieutenant Colonel Salah Mohammed al-Tubaigy, was a 47-year-old doctor at the Ministry of Interior and chairman of the Scientific Council of Forensic Medicine in Riyadh. His area of expertise was autopsy, the post-mortem examination of corpses to determine the cause of death.

The commander of the group was a brigadier general named Maher Abdulaziz Mutreb. Only six months earlier, he'd been photographed in the security detail of Crown Prince Mohammed bin Salman, the heir to the Saudi throne, on his official visit to Britain and the United States. Fifteen years earlier, he had worked at the Saudi embassy in London at the same time as Jamal Khashoggi himself. In fact, they had taken tea together in Mayfair. Now Mutreb was passing through Istanbul airport on a diplomatic passport, only twenty-nine minutes ahead of his former colleague.

'He always looked grumpy, like he was on the dark side,' a European surveillance expert who knew him said later.

The 47-year-old brigadier general was the most sombrely dressed, wearing a dark-grey jacket with a black T-shirt beneath it. His colleagues wore T-shirts and backpacks, with earphones draped around their necks, like tourists come to visit Istanbul's sights. Their hotel, the Mövenpick, was nowhere near the city's famous mosques and bazaars, but in the modern commercial district, only five minutes' drive away from the Saudi consulate. The men would not be sleeping much and once their business was over, they would not be staying long.

While Mutreb and his fellow Saudis were checking into their hotel, Jamal Khashoggi's taxi was taking him to his new home. The 'Europe Apartments' is a gated community of brand new flats near the E5 highway in Zeytinburnu, on the European side of this city of around 15 million people, as its name suggests.

When Khashoggi arrived, the guard on duty wouldn't let him past the security barrier without a key card, which had been issued to residents while he was away. As the journalist could not speak Turkish to explain himself, he called his fiancée for help. Hatice Cengiz, her head covered as usual in an Islamic headscarf, arrived with the key card just before 5 a.m.

Once they were inside what was due to be their first married home, Khashoggi said he was tired from his overnight journey and went to bed. Cengiz unpacked items she had bought to furnish the flat. The previous week, they had shopped for sofas and he had chosen a chair in which to write and watch television.

A refrigerator, washing machine and tumble dryer were also on order, though Khashoggi had texted her on the way to Heathrow to say that maybe a different model of fridge would fit the kitchen better.

When he woke up, they had breakfast together in a nearby café to discuss the day. They agreed to cancel the fridge; they would visit the shop later and choose a replacement: it was the kind of domestic dilemma any engaged couple might face – on one level, trivial; but on another, a nest-making ritual, the furnishing of their first home a statement of marital intent before the wedding day itself.

Khashoggi believed the final obstacle to their marriage could only be lifted if he visited the Saudi consulate to collect his documents. The journalist had been married at least three times, and his prospective Turkish father-in-law, who worried about the match, was insisting that he demonstrate on paper that he was now single. The marriage registry office required the documents, too: polygamy is illegal in Turkey, unlike in Saudi Arabia, where sharia law allows men to take up to four wives.

In a phone call before his flight from London, Khashoggi had told Cengiz that a friend would accompany him to the consulate, as he knew she had PhD classes to attend every Tuesday. Yet when she asked him over breakfast which friend he had in mind, he fell silent. She says that was his diffident way of requesting her company, without actually asking for it; and if this dangerously forthright critic of the Saudi kingdom was nervous about visiting its sovereign diplomatic territory, he certainly didn't show it.

'Okay. I'm not going to college, I'm coming with you,' she told him firmly.

'He wasn't tense,' she told me later. 'I wasn't tense. I thought: *he'll get the paper. He'll come out.* That would be it.'

~

At 9.55 a.m., Maher Abdulaziz Mutreb, the Rapid Intervention Group's commander, walked into the Saudi consulate. He was now wearing an open-necked white shirt and dark suit and holding his mobile phone. Discerning his state of mind from the security camera that filmed his entry is virtually impossible, but his attire was certainly businesslike, his jaw firmly set, and three other men followed in behind him.

That April, Mutreb had accompanied Crown Prince Mohammed to America, when he was visiting the rebuilding effort after Hurricane Harvey in Texas. He'd been standing at the back of the prince's entourage, keeping guard, sporting on the lapel of his suit a badge showing the US and Saudi flags intertwined. The month before that, he'd been photographed emerging from an official car in Downing Street, as part of the prince's delegation during his meeting with Britain's then prime minister, Theresa May.

Istanbul was different; a below-the-radar operation, while the prince was in his palace 1,500 miles away. Today, in his mind at least, Mutreb was on the defensive against an enemy of the state who had blackened the prince's reputation, though the boundaries between defence and attack had become blurred. Between 10.11 and 11.03 a.m., more of the Intervention Group arrived. The fifteen-man team had split into two groups: ten to the consulate, five to the residence nearby. The consulate team included Mustafa Mohammed al-Madani. At the age of fifty-seven, he was the oldest. In fact, his age and looks had helped him secure his place in the squad. Although he listed himself merely as a government employee on his Facebook page, he had been in New York just ahead of the crown prince's arrival there in March and was also a brigadier general in Saudi intelligence.

All the men entered the consulate's dull-grey metal front doors – the same doors that Jamal Khashoggi would disappear inside just over two hours later.

The consul general had earlier ordered any non-Saudi staff either to go home at noon or not to report for work at all. The Saudi staff who remained were called into an unscheduled meeting, which lasted for about an hour. In the meantime, those working at the consul's official residence, which is two minutes' drive away, were told they could not enter or leave because an engineer was coming to make repairs.

~

While the consulate's staff were in their meeting, three of the Saudi squad were in another room discussing what would happen next. Brigadier General Mutreb and Dr Salah al-Tubaigy did most of the talking.

The third Saudi present was believed by Turkish intelligence to be Thaar Ghaleb al-Harbi, a 39-year-old lieutenant in the Saudi Royal Guard. A year earlier, he had been promoted for his bravery in responding to a gunman who opened fire near the outer wall of the crown prince's al-Salam royal palace in Jeddah. The guardsman had visited the US in 2015, just ahead of Prince Mohammed's meeting with President Obama at his Camp David retreat.

The conversation began at 1.02 p.m.:

DR TUBAIGY: It will be easy hopefully.
MUTREB: Yes. (*He is heard yawning.*)
DR TUBAIGY: Joints will be separated. It is not a problem.

MUTREB: Will it be possible to put the body and hips into a bag this way?

DR TUBAIGY: No, too heavy. Jamal is tall, about 1.8 metres. He is very big. He has got buttocks like a horse. If we package as two plastic bags, it will be finished without leaving a sense of anything. We will wrap each of them.

A discussion about the use of 'leather bags' followed. The doctor complained that more information should have been provided ahead of a secret mission. He was also unhappy with the conditions in which he was expected to dismember a corpse – apparently on the floor:

DR TUBAIGY: This is the first time in my life that I will cut into pieces on the ground. Even if a butcher wants to cut, he hangs an animal up.

Dr Tubaigy's nerves were on edge. He told Brigadier General Mutreb how perilous this mission could be:

DR TUBAIGY: You are my manager. You have to protect me. There is nobody to protect me! I mean, Abdulaziz, they don't look after you!

Tubaigy had earned his Master's degree in forensic medicine at Glasgow University in 2004. In 2015, he spent three months in Australia as a visiting pathologist at the Victorian Institute of Forensic Medicine. The trip was paid for by the Saudi government. There's a photograph of him wearing green medical scrubs and rubber gloves in the institute's annual report, which proclaimed that 'death and injury investigations lie at the heart of any fair justice system'.

Today's assignment was unusual, to say the least, as Dr Tubaigy's speciality was determining the cause of death in mass-casualty accidents. In fact, he'd helped design an 18-metre-long mobile trailer which pathologists could use to examine bodies retrieved from fires, stampedes or terrorist attacks at Saudi Arabia's holy sites. In 2014, an Arabic newspaper described the scientist as a lieutenant colonel and claimed that he could perform an autopsy at a crime scene in no more than seven minutes.

Only one casualty was expected at the consulate that Tuesday, but maybe the doctor's speed explained why he had been chosen. At any rate, he was trying to put a brave face on his unexpected trip to Istanbul:

DR TUBAIGY: This is fun. Give me my headphones so I can forget myself while cutting. Normally, I would put my headphones on and listen to music. I'd also drink coffee and smoke my cigarette.

Perhaps the doctor's banter was meant to relax his fellow team members as Jamal Khashoggi's taxi approached. Perhaps he was merely revealing his own state of agitation. Or was he rendering the target of this operation already dead in his mind, like a corpse he would usually encounter in a morgue, so he could steel himself for what was to follow?

~

Time: 1.13 p.m.

MUTREB: Has the sacrificial animal arrived yet?
A VOICE: He has arrived.

In the Koran, Abraham is told by God to kill his son as a human sacrifice, as a test of his faith. He holds the blade of a knife to his son's neck, until an angel tells him he has already demonstrated his love for God, and so an animal can be substituted for sacrifice instead. There would be no substitution in Istanbul, no act of mercy, no sudden moment of reprieve. Four days of planning were about to reach their finale, even if their visitor's taxi was running slightly late for his appointment.

At 11.50 that morning, Khashoggi telephoned the Saudi consulate to tell them he was coming. A consular official told him they would call back. Forty minutes later, he was informed that his paperwork would be ready for 1 p.m.

At 12.42 p.m., he and his fiancée walked out of their apartment building into the street. A security camera filmed them, hand in hand, before he hailed the pair a cab. Their journey to the consulate was for the most part along multi-lane highways, through the ugly urban sprawl of the city's outskirts. Perhaps the journalist caught a glimpse, through the right-hand window of his taxi, of the gates of the old Byzantine city walls. The crumbling fortifications were flying red Turkish flags in celebration of Constantinople's conquest by the Ottomans over 500 years before.

It was here that Sultan Mehmet the Conqueror first entered the city in 1453. Khashoggi, a keen historian and of Ottoman descent himself, had visited Sultan Mehmet's tomb only the previous month. 'If I die now, would they bury me here?' he had joked afterwards.[2]

Their taxi crossed the Golden Horn waterway, its hills graced by the magnificent silhouettes of some of the finest mosques ever built. He told her about the warm weather he had left behind in England the previous day. However, the future, not the past, was for the most part on Jamal Khashoggi's mind that Tuesday. Once again, the couple discussed which fridge to buy. He responded to messages on his mobile phone.

The temperature in Istanbul on that afternoon of 2 October was in the low twenties and it was only partly sunny. The city's annual battle between the seasons had begun – its Mediterranean summer climate beginning to give way to the colder, northern climes of Asia. Istanbul's confluence of cultures, its peerless position as the crossroads between East and West, was mirrored in its weather that day.

It was a city which the journalist believed suited him perfectly; not just because of his relationship with Hatice Cengiz, but as a Western-educated writer who had fled from Saudi Arabia, a Muslim cast adrift from the country he loved, still looking for somewhere he could call home.

The taxi passed the tall office blocks of banks and telecoms companies. It passed the Wyndham Grand hotel, where six more members of the Intervention Group had spent the previous night. Three of them had arrived from Riyadh on a scheduled Saudi Arabian Airlines flight at around 4 p.m. the day before. A further three had arrived on Turkish Airlines at 1.40 a.m., while Khashoggi was himself still in the air.

The Saudi consulate is a two-storey building in Akasyali street, opposite a supermarket and a tennis club, down a relatively quiet hill. It is ochre-coloured and overlooked by fir trees. The green Saudi flag flies from its roof. Security cameras are mounted along its walls and there are two booths for the security guards stationed outside.

'See you soon, wait for me here,' Khashoggi told Hatice Cengiz.

'*Inshallah*, bring me good news,' his fiancée replied. She was wearing a purple headscarf and she looked up at his face for what neither of them knew would be the last time.

He handed her his two mobile phones and approached the consulate's outer ring of metal barricades. Exposing his paunch, he raised his arms in the air for a brief inspection by plainclothes security men.

At 1.13 p.m., Brigadier General Mutreb received a text on his mobile phone, informing him that the journalist had arrived.

Khashoggi then walked towards the building, his long strides betraying no hesitation or fear. At 1.14 p.m., a Turkish guard standing outside the building bowed his head in greeting. The grey consulate doors swung outwards to receive Jamal Khashoggi; and, as they did so, the golden swords embossed across them divided in two, before closing firmly behind him. His fiancée would never see him emerge as she'd expected, joy-fully waving at her the document they needed to get married. In fact, she would never see him again.

2

WALKING THE TIGHTROPE

'His life was a series of unexpected twists and turns . . .
not many people can say they got fired from the same
job twice, a few years apart.'

– Noha and Razan, Jamal Khashoggi's daughters,
Washington Post, 2 December 2018

Jamal Khashoggi's life as a journalist was one which required
frequent reinvention. It involved hitching the wagon of his
career to the right Saudi prince at the right time – but also
knowing when to decouple when he'd written or broadcast
what he shouldn't have. The game of journalism that he played
in Saudi Arabia was often postponed due to intolerant political weather.

In a country where most media organisations are controlled
by members of the Saudi royal family, and where senior
appointments require ministerial approval, the search for the
right royal patron was essential to surviving the whims, power
struggles and wrath of the royal court.

When journalists become well known to their readers or
viewers, it can lead them to believe that their jobs have become
more secure. In Khashoggi's case, the opposite was true. As his
reputation as an Arab writer grew, the more his career ran the

risk of ruination. Khashoggi's working life inside the kingdom ended when his opinions got the better of him and he ran out of patrons to defend him.

Jamal bin Ahmad Khashoggi, known to his friends as Abu Salah, was born in the holy city of Medina in 1958. In the accounts of his friends, he was an avuncular, warm-hearted and intellectually curious man. He was unfailingly polite and did not take himself too seriously. With a career in journalism as chequered as his, and a tangled series of marriages and relationships, perhaps he could not afford to. His passport says he entered the world on 22 January; his fiancée believed his birthday was 13 October; his family insist it was in March, during the Ramadan fast. In those days, birth records were not kept and official documents recording birthdays could not keep pace with variations in the Islamic lunar calendar. His last birthday was celebrated with chocolate cake in a Washington DC restaurant in March 2018. The journalist loved dining out and revelled in finding excuses for a party, but he told guests at that final birthday meal that the correct date was 23 March.

His parents, Ahmed and Esaaf, owned a date farm, where Khashoggi recalled using his feet to stamp the dates into tin cans when he was a child. His father then opened a small textile business in Medina. The city remained Khashoggi's spiritual home – bounded by hills and mountains, the capital of the Prophet Muhammad's first Muslim Empire, its ancient interior still out of bounds to non-believers.

He also much preferred the relative simplicity of Medina, the Prophet Muhammad's burial place, to Mecca, where Muslims believe that God ordered Abraham and his son to build the first house of worship. The journalist would later tell friends that Medina had shaped his personality: 'It was non-judgemental and optimistic,' he said. 'People were tolerant and open-minded.'

Tolerance in Saudi Arabia, however, had its limits. Khashoggi recalled that he didn't see a woman drive until he left the country to visit his sister in Tempe, Arizona, in 1976. The cinemas of his youth were makeshift affairs, he wrote in the *Washington Post*, with movies projected onto a wall while the organiser would keep a lookout for patrols by religious police. A friend of his had broken his leg while jumping off a wall to evade arrest.[1]

The journalist told Hatice Cengiz that his first contact with Turkey was when he accompanied his father to the textile markets of the port of Izmir. In fact, the family claimed Ottoman Turkish descent, having emigrated from the region of Kayseri in Anatolia 300 years earlier. The name Khashoggi is spelled 'Kaşikçi' in Turkish and means 'spoon maker'. The journalist hoped to visit Kayseri on one of his visits to Turkey, in search of distant relatives.

His father's cousin, Mohammed Khashoggi, had served as court physician to Ibn Saud, the first monarch and founder of Saudi Arabia; Adnan Khashoggi, the famously ostentatious arms dealer and billionaire, was Mohammed's son.

Obituaries of Adnan Khashoggi, who died in 2017, noted that he was allowed to become rich as long as he paid commissions into the Swiss bank accounts of his Saudi royal patrons.[2] The constant whiff of fraud and corruption eventually caught up with him; he was pursued by regulators, prosecutors and those to whom he owed money. His profligate lifestyle – his celebrity parties, his twelve homes, his 'pleasure wives', the models and call girls flown in from all over the world – earned him the embarrassment of the Saudi royal court.

Jamal Khashoggi would often be asked about his infamous second cousin and would play down the connection. 'He said they had chosen very different paths, because one was a businessman and one was a journalist,' his fiancée recalled.

'He would say he didn't agree with him on many things,' said Turan Kişlakçi, a Turkish journalist and friend for fifteen years. Turkish pop songs and television programmes about the arms dealer meant that the name was already well known in Turkey by the time the journalist disappeared in Istanbul.

The Khashoggi name was also well known to Donald Trump. In the 1980s, in need of cash as he faced extradition from Switzerland, Adnan Khashoggi sold his 281 ft yatcht, the *Nabila*, to the Sultan of Brunei, who then sold it on for a reported $29 million to the future American president. When it was built in 1980, the *Nabila* had been one of the biggest yachts in the world. It was so luxurious that it featured as the headquarters of the villain, Maximillian Largo, in the James Bond movie, *Never Say Never Again*.

Donald Trump renamed Khashoggi's vessel *Trump Princess*, but in 1991 the New York property tycoon, himself almost $900 million in debt from his casino projects, would go on to sell the boat via creditors to Alwaleed bin Talal, a Saudi prince, for $20 million.[3]

Prince Alwaleed would in turn become one of Jamal Khashoggi's friends and patrons, helping fund a television station he ran in 2015.[4] More importantly, Trump's purchase and then sale of Adnan Khashoggi's yacht was an early encounter with a world of Saudi wealth and influence; a world he so admired that it would prove critical in his response to the events of 2018.

~

Khashoggi studied at Taiba High School, where his favourite subjects were history and geography. As a teenager, he took a very different route to his second cousin by joining the Muslim Brotherhood, which had begun in colonial Egypt in the 1920s but was outlawed by Colonel Gamal Abdel Nasser's regime in 1954; Saudi Arabia hired many of these exiled Egyptians as teachers, influencing a whole generation of Saudi students.

'They brought with them new approaches to Islamic thought and law that were welcomed by many of us, including our leaders,' Khashoggi later explained in the *Washington Post*.[5]

Saudi Arabia's crown prince, Mohammed bin Salman, would say in 2018 that Saudi schools had been 'invaded' by Brotherhood teachers and that he wanted them 'eradicated completely'; but in the kingdom of the 1970s, their influence was profound.

'We were hoping to establish an Islamic state anywhere,' Khashoggi told the American writer Lawrence Wright.[6] 'We believed the first one would lead to another, and that would have a domino effect which would reverse the history of mankind.'

Khashoggi later recalled that one of his teachers at high school introduced him to Muslim Brotherhood books, and that he had known Osama bin Laden 'slightly' in the city of Jeddah through their Brotherhood connections.[7] The scion of the Saudi building conglomerate was only around eighteen months older than he was. Both men had joined the Brothers around the same time, but the journalist recalled that 'the only difference which set him apart from me and others' was the extent of his religiosity.

'He [bin Laden] would not listen to music. He would not shake hands with a woman. He would not smoke,' he told the American journalist Peter Bergen.[8]

There may have been family connections which stretched back further to the early childhoods of both men in Medina. In 1958, the bin Laden family briefly moved there, when Osama was six months old, as bin Laden's father had won the contract to triple the size of the Prophet's mosque. At any rate, both Saudis would talk about the city fondly when they met.

As bin Laden's notoriety grew and as the Muslim Brotherhood became increasingly unpopular with the Saudi monarchy – which outlawed it in 2014 – the more Khashoggi would be inclined to tell people he had never joined it.

'He told me he did not enter the Muslim Brotherhood but he read all their books,' was how Turan Kişlakçi put it.

Another friend, Khaled Saffuri, a Lebanese American businessman and political lobbyist living in Washington, said Khashoggi explained to him why he had left the group: 'He said he didn't think they were wise enough to be good politicians,' Saffuri told me.

His denials of ever having joined the Brotherhood were part of his survival strategy in a Saudi Arabia that had turned vehemently against the group – exposing him to the possible charge of being a traitor. The reverse of the official Saudi position was partly a belated response to bin Laden and many others morphing into jihadists, which threatened the kingdom; but more because of the perceived danger of Islamist politicians taking over much of the Middle East in the 2011 Arab Spring.

From 1977 to 1982, Khashoggi studied business administration at Indiana State University in Terre Haute, as one of thousands of Saudi students sent annually by their government to study across America.

'He told me he had a girlfriend,' an American friend said. 'He lived the typical "Saudi gets out of Medina" life. In other words, he had a good time.'

There is a photograph of him taken by the local newspaper, the *Tribune*, in the August of his first summer there. A thin, smiling freshman with thick curly hair sits between two friends on the lawn of the college quad. Laurie Elliott and her then boyfriend, Suleiman, are the friends flanking him in the photograph.

'I remember going to dinners at their house, where you would eat Saudi style,' she said, recalling how they sat on the floor and ate food laid out on newspapers.[9] Khashoggi and his friend Suleiman drove around Terre Haute in a British sports car, a TR7, a car he later described as an 'expensive mistake'; but the politics of the Middle East were never far away.

His student years coincided with the seismic shifts that have shaped the Middle East ever since. The Soviet invasion of Afghanistan in 1979; Iran's Islamic revolution the same year; and the seizure of the Grand Mosque in Mecca by extremist insurgents calling for the overthrow of the House of Saud. It was a time in which radical Islamic politics were spreading far and wide; even to Terre Haute, Indiana.

Khashoggi attended Islamic political meetings and later recalled meeting Abdullah Azzam, the Palestinian cleric who would become bin Laden's mentor. Khashoggi, like bin Laden, heard Azzam preach several times when he returned from the US to his home in Jeddah on the Red Sea.[10] In 1984, Azzam's religious declaration, 'Defending Muslim Lands', would serve as the clarion call for young Muslims to join a jihad in Afghanistan in the name of expelling the Soviet 'infidels'.[11]

Upon his return from Indiana, Khashoggi worked in the Tihama bookshop in Jeddah for about a year. In an interview in 2016, he recalled objecting to the store's decision to sell video cassettes.

'I can describe this as the radical period in my life,' he said. 'Now I think movies and cinema are very much part of people's lives,' he added, unapologetic that his beliefs as a devout Muslim had mellowed over thirty years.[12]

This radicalism not only shaped him as a young man, but along with his Muslim Brotherhood membership it would form the benchmark from which he measured how much his ideas changed over the decades and how much they stayed the same. Family members say his route into journalism was as a researcher in the library of the Saudi newspaper, *Okhaz*. By his own account, he was twenty-four or twenty-five and a religious-minded young man when he started writing economic reports for papers including the *Arab News*, the kingdom's first English language daily.

The first war a journalist covers often has a lifelong impact. In Khashoggi's case, there was a romance in the battle against Soviet occupation in Afghanistan, and an appeal to his youthful Islamic idealism which would never quite leave him.

The invitation to cover the conflict had come from Osama bin Laden himself. 'We are from the same generation, same background,' Khashoggi explained later.[13] The war was being waged by Islamic *mujahideen* (literally 'those who wage jihad') and backed by leading Islamic scholars.

Khashoggi wrote up the first of several interviews with bin Laden in an *Arab News* article in 1988. 'Muslims are one nation,' the piece began, before describing a 'unique brotherhood' fighting the Communists. In a photograph, Khashoggi posed confidently alongside a Saudi contingent of armed fighters, holding a rocket-propelled grenade launcher in his hands.

Khashoggi would go on to conclude that the war in Afghanistan had been a disaster after the Soviet pull-out, when different Afghan factions fought for power. He would also regret what he regarded as the folly of his youth: for example, an occasion when he and a group of Afghan fighters had sat in a hotel in Pakistan insisting that the window blinds be shut, so they could not see a bar which served alcohol. Khashoggi would later tell the story to an American friend, while the two of them were drinking glasses of wine. He had come to regard elements of his behaviour as ridiculous.

In his 1988 article, Khashoggi estimated that a thousand Arab youths had gone to Afghanistan to fight and carry out humanitarian work. His article read like a recruitment advertisement for the adventurous and devout.

'Muslims can be seen as supporting each other, like the bricks of a building,' he wrote. Bin Laden was, he continued, a business contractor from a famous Saudi family, playing a 'vital role' in the construction of a guerrilla camp. He quoted Jalaluddin Haqqani, an Afghan commander and later a revered ally of the Taliban, as praising the potential of Arab fighters 'as ambassadors of jihad in their own countries when they return'.

Those words turned out to be a good description of what would later become 'al-Qaeda'. As for Haqqani, his fighters would go on to kill thousands of people, mostly Afghans but also NATO troops, after the US-led invasion of 2001. No wonder Khashoggi's friendships in the Afghanistan of his youth would later raise questions as to whether he was involved in extremism himself.

'He was getting into trouble all the time because of his connections with al-Qaeda groups, but he was doing that as a journalist,' said Salameh Nematt, a Jordanian journalist who worked alongside him on the Saudi newspaper *Al Hayat* and remained a lifelong friend.[14] Nematt recalled that on one occasion in the early 2000s, he had to persuade Jordanian airport authorities not to deport Khashoggi because of his suspected terrorist links.

Yet Khashoggi's exuberant dispatch from Afghanistan was merely reflecting Saudi government policy. Saudi intelligence was heavily involved there, match-funding its partner, the CIA, in sending billions in either cash or arms to the *mujahideen*. In fact, Haqqani had once been a prized CIA asset. There's also evidence Khashoggi was nothing like as enthusiastic a supporter as his 1988 article suggested.[15]

Barnett Rubin, an Afghan expert at New York University's Center on International Cooperation, recalled meeting Khashoggi at the US consulate in Jeddah in 1989. The journalist criticised Prince Salman, the future monarch but then head of the Saudi committee supporting the Afghan fighters, for funding extremist groups in Afghanistan.

'It was typical Jamal,' Rubin said. 'We had just met for the first time and he began complaining about mistakes by the royal family.'[16]

This story of an early indiscretion illustrates a recurring element of his professional life: a Saudi patriot, often repeating the official government line, but also a jumble of contradictions who was unable to stop himself from airing the opposite point of view when given the chance.

His contacts in Afghanistan begged questions Khashoggi was asked throughout his life, as to whether he had begun working there as a Saudi spy. 'I asked him, "Please tell me, Jamal, tell me the truth,"' Turan Kişlakçi recalled. 'He said, "I know many of them, but really I didn't work for them."'

'He never had links with Saudi intelligence, even at a lower level,'[17] claimed Prince Turki al-Faisal, a long-time head of Saudi spying operations who had also funnelled money to the *mujahideen* in Afghanistan. The prince would become Khashoggi's friend and benefactor, until they fell out, Prince Turki said, over the journalist's sympathy for the Muslim Brotherhood.

In some ways the question may have been academic: how could a foreign correspondent living in an autocracy such as Saudi Arabia not 'report back' at the very minimum, should his government ask him to do so?

In 1992, Osama bin Laden moved to the Sudanese capital Khartoum, along with his four wives and seventeen children, at the invitation of Sudan's radical Islamist government. al-Qaeda had been formed three years earlier but, officially at least, the US still considered its leader a friendly *mujahideen* who had helped fight the Russians in Afghanistan. Bin Laden was grateful for America's financial assistance there. He was not yet the figure he would become after the bombings of the US embassies in Kenya and Tanzania in 1998 – America's most wanted terrorist.[18]

However, Algeria, Yemen and Egypt protested to King Fahd of Saudi Arabia that bin Laden was fomenting insurgency in their countries. The king cancelled his passport and sent several delegations to persuade him to return home, with bin Laden claiming he was offered money and a new passport if he abandoned jihad. Although he was homesick for Medina, nothing could bring the al-Qaeda leader to overcome his loathing of the Saudi king and pay homage to him as a good Muslim. One envoy, sent by one of bin Laden's cousins, was Jamal Khashoggi.[19]

They had a simple dinner of rice and lamb laid out on the floor of the al-Qaeda leader's terrace in Khartoum – Khashoggi with his tape recorder to hand, bin Laden his automatic weapon. At one point, the journalist heard his host denouncing violence for the first time. In Lawrence Wright's retelling of the story in his book *The Looming Tower*, Khashoggi asked him: 'Why don't you say that on the record?'

'Let's do that tomorrow night,' bin Laden replied. The next evening there was no denunciation of jihad as promised; instead, bin Laden boasted of his ambition to expel American forces from the Arabian peninsula.

'Osama, this is very dangerous,' Khashoggi replied. 'It is as if you are declaring war. You will give the right to the Americans to hunt for you.'

The following night, rice and lamb were once again on the menu on the floor of the terrace. As bin Laden reminisced about Khashoggi's home city of Medina and his wish to return, Khashoggi tried once more to get him to renounce violence.

'What will I get for that?' bin Laden asked.

'I don't know,' Khashoggi told him. 'I'm not representing the government. Just say something, break the ice! Maybe there will be a positive reaction. Don't forget you said a few nasty things about the kingdom.'

Bin Laden now said he wanted a full pardon from Riyadh and a timetable for American forces to withdraw. Khashoggi, beginning to give up, told his fellow Saudi to telephone him at his Khartoum hotel if he changed his mind about saying something conciliatory on the record. The telephone call never came. Jamal Khashoggi flew home, having played his own small part in failing to change the course of history, including al-Qaeda's attacks on Washington and New York.

The journalist spent most of the 1990s as a reporter for the London-based *Al Hayat*. 'Khashoggi said that many people consider Osama bin Laden the "Che Guevara" of the Arab world,' wrote a senior US diplomat who met him in Jeddah in 1998. 'The Saudi warned the Americans that the al-Qaeda leader was a popular resistance hero whom many would rather see die in battle than transported in handcuffs to the US.'[20] Nihad Awad, a campaigner for the rights of American Muslims, recalled meeting Khashoggi in his office in the city. What struck him first, apart from the journalist's smile and warmth, was a poster on the wall of a sole Chinese protester standing in front of a line of tanks in Tiananmen Square. It was the iconic image from the pro-reform demonstrations across China which were brutally crushed in 1989.

'In Saudi Arabia you always see pictures of the king or crown prince,' Awad told me. 'Not a picture which shows any defiance or protest. It surprised me, but that was Jamal Khashoggi the rebel.'

He wrote about the civil war in Algeria, which followed the army's decision to cancel elections that the Islamic Salvation Front looked poised to win in 1992. The conflict's terrible death toll of many tens of thousands spurred him to think more deeply about what would become a lasting preoccupation: the prospects for democracy in the Arab world.

Together with his friend Azzam Tamimi, a Palestinian academic and Muslim Brotherhood member, the journalist set up 'Friends of Democracy in Algeria', which later became 'Liberty for the Muslim World'. According to Tamimi, it was a PR project intended to alert the West to the dangers of cancelling democratisation. The organisation eventually folded in 1998. It was the first but certainly not the last Khashoggi project of its kind – begun with high hopes of political reform, but funded by wealthy Gulf businessmen who, Tamimi says, eventually stopped giving Khashoggi money.

~

He also charted with enthusiasm the rise of the Islamist Welfare Party in Turkey, which brought his first meeting with Recep Tayyip Erdoğan, then the party's mayor in Istanbul. Khashoggi's time in Turkey helped further his vision of Islamist parties holding power.

Although he could be accused of advocating an Arab utopia, Jamal Khashoggi's optimism endeared him to his friends.

'It was a constant for him that Arabs and Muslims deserved societies in which they could be heard,' a friend who had worked alongside him in Washington said.

In September 2001, al-Qaeda hijacked four passenger planes and ploughed them into buildings in Washington DC and New York as well as farmland in Pennsylvania, killing almost three thousand people. Fifteen of the nineteen hijackers were Saudis, and like many of his countrymen Jamal Khashoggi appeared to waver in his response to the actions of Osama bin Laden, a man he had known well.

A year later, on 10 September 2002, he wrote a condemnatory piece for the *Daily Star* in Beirut entitled 'A Saudi mea culpa'.

'The most pressing issue now', he wrote, 'is to ensure our children can never be influenced by extremist ideas, like those fifteen Saudis who were misled into hijacking four planes that fine September day, piloting them, and us, straight into the jaws of hell.'

The same year, he wrote in sympathy about his friend Daniel Pearl, the *Wall Street Journal* correspondent murdered by al-Qaeda in Pakistan. But in the same piece there was an element of mourning for the Osama bin Laden he'd once known.

'Anyone who knew Osama in those days never failed to be captivated by his sincerity,' he wrote. 'I really feel disappointed in how things turned out. Osama could have done great things for Islam had he maintained his moderate views.'[21]

Khashoggi's reluctance to face the horror of what his friend had done occasionally tipped into denial. His friend Turan Kişlakçi remembers the journalist telling him in around 2010 that maybe bin Laden was really a tool of a Western government or intelligence agency. Such views were not uncommon in the kingdom, reflecting a difficulty accepting Saudi culpability which was shared by senior members of the royal family: in the week after the attacks, Prince [now King] Salman insisted they were the work of the Israeli intelligence agency, Mossad.[22]

When the al-Qaeda leader was killed in a raid by American

troops on his compound in Pakistan in 2011, Khashoggi tweeted that he 'collapsed in tears', remembering how 'brave and beautiful' bin Laden had been in Afghanistan before 'succumbing to anger'.[23] It wasn't an endorsement of terrorism; more like a middle-aged man mourning that the rock band he'd idolised in his youth had gone off the rails. Only bin Laden's later life involved plotting mass-casualty attacks which killed thousands of civilians.

~

In 2003, Khashoggi was sacked as editor of the reformist Saudi newspaper *Al Watan*, even though it was owned by Prince Bandar bin Khalid al-Faisal, to whose family he had become close. He'd been dismissed just fifty-four days after being hired. There had been an argument between an *Al Watan* journalist and the interior minister, Prince Nayef bin Abdulaziz, about an article criticising the country's Salafist religious establishment, which advocates returning to the fundamentals of Islam. Khashoggi was seen to have attacked a fourteenth-century fatwa that justified the killing of Muslims if they stood in the way of killing infidels. He had tried to stand against religious support for al-Qaeda and paid the price for printing the piece.

Another of the al-Faisal clan, the former intelligence chief Prince Turki, came to the rescue with another job. The journalist became de facto spokesman of the Saudi embassy in London from 2003, when Turki was appointed ambassador there. In 2005, both men moved to the embassy in Washington DC.

'Prince Turki took him under his wing,' said David Ignatius, a *Washington Post* columnist who met Khashoggi during that time. 'He was an ironic, sometimes whimsical part of Turki's entourage – an intellectual.'

Explaining Saudi Arabia to the West after the terrorist

outrages of 2001 was never going to be easy. What complicated the task further was that the kingdom's former ambassador, Prince Bandar bin Sultan – so close to President George W. Bush that he was nicknamed 'Bandar Bush' – was continuing to visit the White House secretly, undermining Prince Turki's own diplomatic mission and authority.

However, the job of official mouthpiece provided Khashoggi's family with more stability than journalism could. He moved to Virginia with his wife Rawiya al-Tunisi, whom he'd met and wed in Medina in the early 1980s in an arranged 'salon' marriage. Their four children, all born in the '80s and early '90s, would go to college in the US. The youngest, his daughters Noha and Razan, also attended high school there. The girls, along with their eldest brother Salah, acquired joint US-Saudi passports. Only his son Abdullah remained a sole Saudi passport holder.

Now on his government's payroll in Washington, Khashoggi attempted to tread the same fine line he'd often pursued in his journalism; giving insight into the thinking of the Saudi monarchy without daring to overly criticise it. However, outspoken commentators on the kingdom who encountered him then, including the London-based Professor Madawi al-Rasheed, accused him of being 'an insider who always took the official point of view'; and his closeness to Prince Turki inevitably renewed speculation that he was working for Saudi intelligence.

Azzam Tamimi recalled that in 2005 Khashoggi asked to be invited to a meeting Tamimi had arranged with the Islamist Palestinian group Hamas in Lebanon. 'I heard afterwards that the Saudi government wanted him to come,' he said. 'The Saudis knew of Jamal's Islamist leanings and thought he could be useful to them.'

Hamas is an offshoot of the Muslim Brotherhood and is notorious for carrying out suicide bombings and rocket attacks against Israelis. Khashoggi's past Brotherhood membership might have made an introduction to the group easier, but any prospect of the journalist operating as a diplomatic go-between with the Saudis did not, as far as we know, materialise.

His patron, Prince Turki al-Faisal, abruptly resigned as ambassador in 2006, after just fifteen months in Washington, allegedly fed up with unscheduled visits from Prince Bandar, his predecessor and brother-in-law.

Khashoggi followed the prince home to Saudi Arabia, back to the newspaper *Al Watan*, where as editor he was credited with turning it into an important progressive voice, for example claiming there was no contradiction between granting more rights to women and preserving the purity of Islam. 'Khashoggi said . . . he knows his limits,' the US ambassador reported back to Washington. Another American diplomat described him as a 'Muslim Brother in his youth' who had become 'a leading voice for reform'. He was almost sacked again for publishing an article criticising the Saudi religious police; then in 2010 he was finally forced out, after the paper ran an article disputing Salafists' belief that shrines and graves have no place in religion. 'It was human error,' Khashoggi said, explaining that he disagreed with the decision to run the article and was out of the country at the time.[24]

'I got fired from my job twice because I was pushing for reform in Saudi Arabia,' he would tell Al Jazeera television in 2018. 'It wasn't that easy, but people were not being put in jails. There was breathing space.'

'His strategy was to survive in the post, until an article that was just a tad too critical got him into trouble,' wrote the Middle East analyst Bill Law, describing the ups and downs of his friend's career. 'Then he would lay [*sic*] low before re-emerging. That takes a great deal of courage, especially in a country like Saudi Arabia.'[25]

Khashoggi's relationship with his wife, Rawiya, did not survive his return to the kingdom. She stayed in Virginia, so that their daughters could complete their education there. Friends said that without divorcing his first wife, he married again, though this relationship lasted little more than a year. The wedding to his third wife, Alaa Naseif, took place on the same day he was sacked from *Al Watan* in 2010.

January 2011 saw the beginning of the Arab Spring revolutions. The Saudi king, Abdullah, rushed home from holiday and announced he was spending $130 billion on pay bonuses and public building schemes, clearly intended to stave off any internal demonstrations or dissent. Meanwhile, Khashoggi frequently talked with admiration about Mohamed Bouazizi, the Tunisian vegetable seller who died after setting himself alight at the end of 2010 – the act that became the catalyst for uprisings across the region.

'This is what he had been dreaming of – the era in which people would find the courage to challenge oppressive governments,' said David Ignatius. 'Jamal said we had been waiting for this for 100 years. It was a period of great optimism – and when it stopped, I think that was a difficult time for him.'

The Arab Spring soon petered out. By 2014, Egypt's Muslim Brotherhood government had been deposed by the army; Libya was lawless and Yemen was at war with itself, as was Syria – where hundreds of thousands of people would be killed.

In June that year, Khashoggi texted his friend Barnett Rubin in New York: 'Hello Rubin, as you can see things going from bad to worst in the Arab world.'[26]

However, the military coup in Egypt enjoyed Saudi support,

with Riyadh the first Arab capital to endorse the takeover. A freely elected Islamic government in Egypt, the Arab world's most populous state, could have set a revolutionary example to its Arab neighbours. The Saudis unsurprisingly backed a return to the status quo which had existed since President Nasser's time, providing the new regime in Cairo with $5 billion of aid. The coup left Khashoggi on the opposite side to his own government and therefore dangerously exposed.

'The eradication of the Muslim Brotherhood is nothing less than an abolition of democracy,' he would write later, calling it 'the loss of a great opportunity to reform the entire Arab world and allow a historic change that might have freed the region from a thousand years of tyranny.'[27] Never mind that millions of Egyptians were happy to see a government widely viewed as incompetent removed from power. There was now an opinion-ated recklessness to what a *Der Spiegel* interviewer called 'one of the most progressive thinkers in the country'. 'The absolute monarchy is obsolete,' Khashoggi told the German magazine from his office in the Kingdom Tower, 300 metres above the city of Jeddah. 'Democracy is the only solution.' 'Others in Saudi Arabia would be interrogated and locked up for such words,' the interviewer noted. It was time to move on.

In search of a new job, after his latest dismissal from a news-paper, Khashoggi was appointed head of a new satellite television channel, Al-Arab, based at the World Trade Center in Bahrain. It was funded in part by the Saudi billionaire Prince Alwaleed bin Talal. On its first day on air, 1 February 2015, the channel featured an interview with a prominent Shiite politician who had criticised the regime's crackdown on anti-government protests four years earlier. The Bahraini authorities cancelled the broadcast 'for technical and administrative reasons' after only twenty-four hours, leaving Khashoggi casting around for a new host country.

His friend Maggie Mitchell Salem, a former US diplomat, was not surprised and told him so. 'Dude, what did you think was going to happen?' she asked him. Khashoggi told her all he had been trying to do was to show balance in his coverage, by giving the Shiite opposition a voice. Friends often described this naivety in him, a never-ending hope that the Arab world was on the cusp of change.

'He tried to do real journalism and every time he told the truth, he got fired,' said David Ignatius.

A phone message to Barnett Rubin revealed Khashoggi's disappointment. 'I [sic] been thinking if it's time I gave up and retire somewhere safe in the West just to be free and write freely . . . we will never have freedom in the Arab world without true democracy.'[28]

Khashoggi explored the possibility of moving the channel to Cyprus or to Qatar, but nothing worked out. He would later tell a friend in America that he'd raised $27 million from Qatar for his television venture, but another friend based in Doha said the deal was never completed.

Turan Kişlakçi, the Turkish journalist, claims the Saudi met President Erdoğan in 2015, to see whether he could reopen the Al-Arab channel there. Permission was politely turned down.

'The Turkish government understood that it would cause a problem with the Saudi government,' Kişlakçi said. It seemed nobody would dare host a channel run by Khashoggi: his belief in editorial independence risked provoking a diplomatic dispute between Saudi Arabia and any country that agreed to grant him a home for his journalism. Now back writing a column for *Al Hayat*, in December 2015 Khashoggi described his philosophy towards his work, forged by his own precarious 35-year career.

'In the Arab world, everyone thinks journalists cannot be independent, but I represent myself, which is the right thing to do,' he wrote. 'What would I be worth if I succumbed to pressure to change my opinions?'[29]

It was not a philosophy which he had consistently followed himself, given his work as a government spokesman. Jobs – and the sympathetic princes who funded them – had come and gone, but the Arab Spring, which began just before his fifty-third birthday, appeared to have brought a clarity to his thinking about the kind of Arab world in which he wished to live. The Muslim Brotherhood of his youth had briefly resurfaced in the first free parliamentary and presidential elections in Egypt, and the group once again inspired him.

Khashoggi had long speculated whom Saudi Arabia's future leader would be, which from the next generation of princes would have the power to transform the kingdom. 'What is so unsettling', he had said back in 2009, 'is that nobody knows.'

As it turned out, his espousal of an Islamist version of democracy, based on Brotherhood ideas, would set him on a collision course with his country's new crown prince: a ruthlessly ambitious monarch-in-waiting, determined that neither Saudi Arabia nor its neighbours should become the Arab Spring's next victims.

3

MEET THE CROWN PRINCE

In March 2018, the heir to the Saudi throne, Prince Mohammed bin Salman bin Abdulaziz bin Abdul Rahman bin Faisal bin Turki bin Abdullah bin Mohammed bin Saud – colloquially known by his first three initials, 'MbS' – embarked on a three-week, multi-city tour of the United States, including New York, Silicon Valley and Hollywood.

He met President Trump for lunch in the White House, followed by a dinner attended by the president's son-in-law, Jared Kushner. 'You are more than the crown prince now,' the president told his guest, as if to underline what everybody knew – that MbS, and not his elderly father, was already running the country, and doing so apparently unchallenged.

'We have become very good friends over a short period of time,' Trump said, brandishing in front of MbS and the news cameras a chart showing $12.5 billion worth of American military aircraft which he claimed had recently been sold to the Saudis. 'That's peanuts for you,' he added.

There was also a visit to One Franklin Square, the headquarters of the *Washington Post*, where the crown prince gave senior journalists an off-the-record briefing lasting some two hours. Jamal Khashoggi, by now a freelance columnist in the paper's 'global opinions section', was not among them. In his articles, he had accused the prince of locking up even mildly critical voices and plunging his country into a catastrophic quagmire of a conflict in Yemen.

The two men had avoided an encounter in Washington; but tracking the course of their relationship is an essential part of any investigation into the journalist's death in Istanbul six months later. The crown prince was hailed as a champion of reform until it emerged that it was strictly on his own brutal terms; and that he was prepared to silence his enemies whatever the consequences.

'Mohammed was animated and engaged,' wrote one of those who heard MbS's briefing at the *Post*, adding that he fielded questions on everything from the Middle East peace process to the issue of human rights.

The American tour was, in hindsight, the high watermark of the crown prince's attempt to present himself as the acceptable face of Saudi Arabia to his Western allies. In California, he was photographed with the tech titans Mark Zuckerberg of Facebook, Bill Gates of Microsoft and Tim Cook of Apple. At the Four Seasons hotel in Beverly Hills, his delegation booked all 285 rooms and luxury suites. A dinner at Rupert Murdoch's Bel Air mansion was attended by movie moguls and film stars, including Michael Douglas and Morgan Freeman. The *Hollywood Reporter* noted that members of MbS's entourage posed for photos with the famous actors.

We don't know whether a senior royal bodyguard, Brigadier General Maher Abdulaziz Mutreb, was among those taking selfies with Hollywood royalty. Mutreb was certainly photographed alongside the crown prince on the Houston, Boston and New York legs of his US tour; in Madrid and Paris too. As we have seen, he was also caught on closed-circuit security camera six months later, walking into the Saudi consulate in Istanbul, as commander of the Rapid Intervention Group targeting Jamal Khashoggi. It therefore follows that you need to understand the prince Mutreb ultimately served if you are to understand why the journalist disappeared.

In the spring of 2018, many of America's business and political elite were swooning over this deep-pocketed, reform-minded prince. America's biggest cinema chain, AMC, was about to open the first of thirty cinemas in the kingdom, ending a 35-year-old ban; in a few months, women, although still legally treated as minors, would be able to drive cars there for the first time.

Never mind that political parties and public protests were still banned in the kingdom. Never mind that labour unions were still illegal and the country remained an absolute rather than a constitutional monarchy, meting out jail sentences for criticism of the royal family. The fact remained that MbS was promoting inward and outward investment, trying to create 6 million new private-sector jobs and end his country's total dependency on oil.

Young and dynamic, unlike the geriatric monarchs who'd run the kingdom for decades, the 32-year-old heir to the throne was hailed as the man who might just pull off the tricky balancing act none of his predecessors had quite managed – embarking on social reform without enraging religious conservatives and then giving up.

Unlike his father, King Salman, and the five monarchs before him, he was not a son of Ibn Saud, Saudi Arabia's founder, but a grandson, and so poised to be the first of a new generation of Saudi leaders in sixty-five years. Yet a few months after his visit to Britain and America, the MbS brand would turn perhaps irredeemably toxic.

A warning flag on MbS's behaviour was raised back in

December 2015, not long after he was appointed deputy crown prince by his father, the king. Germany's Federal Intelligence Service, the BND, took the highly unusual step of sending selected German journalists a briefing paper on Prince Mohammed bin Salman. The paper claimed that the 'cautious diplomatic stance of the older leading members of the royal family is being replaced by an impulsive policy of intervention'.

The BND briefing paper also predicted of MbS that 'in trying to establish himself in the line of succession in his father's lifetime, he could overreach with expensive measures and reforms'.[1] This intelligence leak was denounced by officials in Berlin, who pointed out that a government intelligence document is for internal consumption and not representative of the official view. Nevertheless, the conclusion that the crown prince was an impulsive overreacher would prove prescient.

However, at the time of his lunch with Donald Trump in March 2018, the US president – something of a disruptor himself – was reportedly boasting that he had groomed Prince Mohammed bin Salman, that the kingdom's heir was the White House's man.

MbS was striking investment deals with American companies and quietly helping Jared Kushner develop the administration's peace plan for the Israeli-Palestinian conflict. He shared with Trump a mutual loathing of Iran, Saudi Arabia's long-standing regional rival, having compared its Supreme Leader, Ayatollah Khamenei, with Adolf Hitler.

'He wants to create his own project in the Middle East, very much like Hitler who wanted to expand at the time,' MbS told an American interviewer. 'Many countries around the world and in Europe did not realise how dangerous Hitler was until what happened, happened.'[2]

Trump's predecessor, Barack Obama, had also invested heavily in the Saudi relationship, travelling to the kingdom more often than his predecessors and even more often than he did to Israel; but the relationship soured after Obama supported Arab Spring reforms and reached out to Iran. Most sanctions against Iran were lifted after an agreement in 2015, signed by all the permanent members of the UN Security Council, plus Germany and the EU, in exchange for Iran dismantling major parts of its nuclear programme. Donald Trump, by contrast, was minded to pull out of the deal on the grounds that it did not go far enough in curbing Iran's regional and military ambitions.

'They were happy to see Obama go,' Bruce Riedel, a former CIA analyst, said of the Saudis during MbS's first trip to the Trump White House in March 2017. 'Trump has made it clear he is not worried about supporting human rights or freedom,' Riedel told the *New York Times*. 'As the Saudis look at Trump, they see they don't need to worry about any of that.'[3]

The prince's political career had begun as an adviser to his father, Prince Salman bin Abdulaziz, who had served as governor of Riyadh for forty-eight years.

Prince Salman was 'basically the sheriff of the royal family,' said Bob Jordan, the US ambassador to Saudi Arabia after the 11 September attacks. The kingdom, then as now, was populated with thousands of over-pampered and parasitic princes on the state payroll, so rich and spoiled that they were free to do no work at all. Salman's job was to keep them in line. By contrast, his own son, MbS, proved a quick learner with a strong work ethic.

'Whenever I went to meetings, MbS would be there,' recalled Sir John Jenkins, the British ambassador in Saudi Arabia from 2012. 'He was in control of the briefing. When his father ran out of things to say, MbS would come across with an iPad and prompt him.'

Although MbS's fortunes were always tied to those of his father, who himself became crown prince in 2012, his rise had not been entirely smooth. The young prince, who was tall and of stocky build, had developed a reputation for intimidating rivals, earning the displeasure of his uncle, King Abdullah. Diplomats said Abdullah was so angry that at one point the king had MbS temporarily removed from the royal court.

However, in January 2015 Abdullah died at the age of ninety, allowing his half-brother, Salman, to ascend to the throne at the age of seventy-nine. Salman's son, MbS, who was already a minister of state, was then appointed minister of defence and put in charge of running the royal court. He was aged just twenty-nine.

The country King Salman inherited had been unsettled by the Arab Spring, which began four years earlier. Nearly all the Arab revolutions had failed, ending in civil war or a return to autocratic rule. Amid an extraordinary degree of turbulence stretching from Libya to Syria and Yemen, the tempo of arrests of activists and dissidents in Saudi Arabia increased: the new king was making it clear from the beginning that he would not tolerate dissent.

Executions reached a level not seen in two decades, including forty-seven on a single day – 2 January 2016.[4] Convicted members of al-Qaeda were among those killed, most of them by beheading; but the group also included Sheikh Nimr Baqir al-Nimr, a cleric from Saudi Arabia's Shia minority, who had been a figurehead in anti-government protests inspired by the Arab Spring.

That month the American academic Barnett Rubin texted his friend Jamal Khashoggi. 'Maybe the real target of the executions was people like you,' Rubin suggested. A year into the new monarch's reign, the academic was warning the journalist to be careful about what he wrote and said. The Saudi texted back to his friend in New York his belief that he was safe: 'Thanks, my friend. I didn't read it that way, the gov . . . wants to appear tough against extremism.'[5]

In fact, Khashoggi spoke in support of the executions, describing Sheikh al-Nimr as someone who had committed treason. The journalist was fulfilling his familiar role as a royal court insider, explaining government policy. 'We target only terrorists or dissidents that call for violence,' he said. 'We do not execute political criminals.'[6]

Much as Khashoggi believed this, he also knew he needed to watch his step. A year earlier, after King Salman's accession to the throne, his television venture in neighbouring Bahrain had been taken off air for broadcasting an interview with a senior Shia politician. It was essential the journalist acclimatise himself to the strictures and senior management of a newly disciplinarian Saudi royal court if he was to carry on working as a journalist.

The month after the forty-seven executions, Sultan bin Turki, a Saudi prince living in exile, was flying from Paris to Cairo on what he thought was a visit to his father when his private jet – which had been provided by the Saudi government – was diverted to Riyadh. The flight attendants pulled out weapons and physically subdued him. The prince was dragged away, screaming, into an unmarked car and has been banned from leaving Saudi Arabia ever since.

Another prince, Turki bin Bandar, was similarly abducted during a business trip to Morocco the previous year. He had been living in Paris and posting videos on YouTube, calling for reform in his homeland. Prince Saud bin Saif al-Nasr, who had backed a call for a coup against King Salman, also disappeared after being lured onto a private plane in Italy in 2015.[7] As a veteran Saudi journalist with connections to Saudi intelligence, Khashoggi knew about these renditions, which were bound to induce a fear of flying in any critic of the Saudi government. 'Even if my best friend said, "Let's go on vacation", I wouldn't go by private jet,' he told his friend Turan Kişlakçi.[8]

He also viewed the rise of MbS with suspicion. King Salman had older, better-educated and urbane sons he could have favoured instead. Prince Faisal, for example, who has a doctorate from Oxford; or Prince Sultan, who was not only the first Arab but the first Muslim to become a NASA astronaut.

MbS had a law degree from King Saud University but, like his father, none of the international education to which several of his eleven full and half-brothers had been exposed. And that, of course, was part of his appeal to the king. Although MbS had not been on the radar of many foreign diplomats as a possible contender for the throne, he reminded his father of a younger, unpolished version of himself.

US intelligence officials had been wary of his rise to power, describing him as naive and inexperienced.[9] It was noted that he was prone to giving lectures and hated his halting English to be interrupted by foreign guests. Rough-hewn as he often appeared, with his English nothing like as advanced as some of his brothers', the prince was also observed playing Beethoven's *Moonlight Sonata* at a soirée in the Washington home of John Kerry, then US Secretary of State.

A *New Yorker* profile of MbS which reported this detail in 2018 also noted that his favourite pastime was the *Call of Duty* video game.[10] The thought of the crown prince glued to his screen appalled Jamal Khashoggi, who talked about it the day before he flew for the last time to Istanbul. 'He's just a PlayStation king, a WhatsApp ruler,' he dismissively told Saad

Djebbar, an Arab lawyer and long-standing friend, over coffee in London. 'We used to criticise the old rulers – but bring back the old days.'

As a Saudi intellectual who had travelled widely, perhaps snobbery was at play here, as well as anger at how very far out of favour he had fallen. For all Khashoggi's criticism of MbS, the prince actually looked like an embodiment of the very old days: tall and bearded, like an old-fashioned Saudi tribal chieftain of the early twentieth century. He was charismatic, assertive, technology savvy and, in a country with a median age under thirty, seemed to embody the new Saudi Arabia too.

$\sim$

Within a few weeks of his father appointing him defence minister in 2015, MbS hatched a plan with his closest Gulf ally, the United Arab Emirates, to oust from power the Houthis, a northern tribe from a Shia minority sect who had seized power in neighbouring Yemen. The Houthis opened direct civilian air traffic between the Yemeni capital, Sanaa, and Iran, while the Iranians promised to deliver cheap oil in return. The Houthis had captured the port of Hodeidah and began marching towards Aden, the biggest port on the Indian Ocean. As MbS saw it, Iran, the traditional arch-rival of his Sunni Islamic kingdom, was staging a takeover of Yemen, the poor Arab satellite state on his southern border.[11]

Operation 'Decisive Storm' was launched with air strikes and a naval blockade. Saudi Arabia considers Yemen its back-yard and has intervened there several times since the 1930s. Apart from a border war with the Houthis in 2009, 'Decisive Storm' was the first time that Saudi jets had bombed another country since 1991, during the military campaign to end Iraq's occupation of Kuwait.

The bombardment began without much internal or external

consultation – even the head of the National Guard wasn't informed.[12] The Americans, the kingdom's biggest supplier of weapons, were given a few hours' notice. Washington's military and strategic alliance in the Gulf was considered too important for the Obama White House to do anything other than support it, albeit reluctantly. MbS, who appeared on Saudi television meeting troops as the public face of the war, had no military experience – and yet he was making it clear that he and his kingdom would be taking decisions on their own from now on.

Although the crisis in relations with Yemen had been building for years – the Houthis were part of a national Arab Spring uprising in 2011 – several of the senior Saudi royals who were expert in handling the Yemen brief, including King Abdullah himself, had died. 'You had people making decisions in Riyadh who didn't know Yemen,' Gerald Feierstein, a former US ambassador to Yemen, told me. 'Nobody expected an open-ended conflict. Nobody ever does.'

Diplomats in Riyadh who had in the past been frustrated by the pace of 'desert wisdom' – the Saudi principle of making wise decisions slowly and through consensus – now complained about the dizzying speed instead. 'You had a guy who was young and impetuous and so people became concerned about the lack of careful forethought,' Feierstein said.

It was the people of Yemen who would live with the catastrophic consequences. The Houthis modelled themselves on the Viet Cong and Lebanese Hezbollah and proved surprisingly resilient. Both sides committed war crimes, with Saudi air strikes in particular drawing international condemnation. By 2018, the war had resulted in a bloody stalemate and turned into the world's worst humanitarian disaster, with 14 million Yemenis facing starvation.

Barely a month after the war began in March 2015, King

Salman sacked his brother, Prince Muqrin, as crown prince, an unprecedented move against an heir to the kingdom which was never explained. The *Washington Post* reported that Prince Muqrin's silence was obtained by giving him a luxury yacht and other perks.

The Saudi monarchy's usual practice of 'agnatic seniority' – the brother of the king taking priority over a son – was jettisoned. Instead, the king named his nephew, 55-year-old Prince Mohammed bin Nayef, as crown prince. It was the first time the role had been assigned to a prince who was not a son of the kingdom's founder. The king also elevated his son, MbS, to deputy crown prince, placing him in the direct line of succession to the throne. It looked as if the king, who was said to be suffering from Alzheimer's disease, was using his nephew to keep the number-two seat warm for his own son, who would learn 'on the job'.

The portfolio of this upstart deputy crown prince was enormous and unprecedented. As well as defence, economic planning and the running of the royal court, MbS now had control of Saudi Aramco, the giant state oil company. Aramco had talented executives of its own, but the prince had nominally been put in charge of 10 per cent of the world's oil supply. 'It was attributable to nepotism and a desire to consolidate power,' Ambassador Bob Jordan told me.

By the autumn of 2015, the royal family was in such inner turmoil about the Yemen war, along with MbS's promotion and Muqrin's demotion, that an unnamed senior Saudi prince anonymously wrote letters, which were published online, calling for the king to be overthrown. He asked that senior members of the royal family – specifically the princes Talal, Turki al-Faisal and Ahmed bin Abdulaziz – choose a new leader from within their ranks. Although the letters came to nothing, they provided an early indication of the enmity MbS faced in leapfrogging older rivals in his rise to power.[13]

MbS and his cousin, the new crown prince, were both grandsons of Hussa-al-Sudairi, the favourite wife of Ibn Saud, Saudi Arabia's founding king. Ibn Saud had at least forty-two sons from what he claimed were at least 135 wives. But his seven sons with Hussa, known as the 'Sudairi Seven', had become the most powerful dynasty within the Saudi royal family, producing three out of six Saudi kings, including King Salman.

As interior minister and counter-terrorism czar, Mohammed bin Nayef had long been earmarked by the Americans as a possible future king, so his promotion to crown prince was warmly greeted by Washington. Ambassador Bob Jordan, who knows him well, told me Nayef was 'probably the most knowledgeable counter-terrorism figure in the Middle East'.

In 2009, he'd been injured in an assassination attempt by an al-Qaeda suicide bomber, in revenge for his successful and ruthless campaign to eliminate al-Qaeda terrorist cells. It was the third time the group had tried to kill him. The crown prince had been accused of torturing activists and dissidents,[14] but Western diplomats said they saw no evidence of this. In 2010, he certainly proved his worth to the British and the Americans by tipping them off about another al-Qaeda plot, involving bombs hidden in printer cartridges smuggled onto cargo planes in Yemen, which were bound for the US. MbS, by contrast, was so young and inexperienced that he was barely on Washington's radar.

In February 2017, Mohammed bin Nayef was awarded the CIA's George Tenet medal by Mike Pompeo, travelling to Riyadh on his first foreign policy trip as then CIA director. The medal, part of an attempt to shore up the relationship after the Obama years, would turn out to be a consolation prize: America's long-standing investment in the man often regarded as a future monarch would end in June 2017, when King Salman sacked his nephew in favour of another crown prince, his third – his own son.

MbS was thirty-one, married with just one wife and four children, and the presumptive heir to the kingdom, even though the average age of new Saudi monarchs was sixty-four. His youth, combined with his father's age and ill health, meant he was likely to rule Saudi Arabia longer than any other king had.

'I will always need your guidance and advice,' the crown prince told his predecessor in a theatrical show of family unity, kissing his cousin's hand and thigh.[15] In reality, a power-hungry MbS had muscled Mohammed bin Nayef out of a job he'd coveted for years. US intelligence sources have claimed the internal palace coup was provoked in part by reports of two assassination attempts against the young prince, who felt he had to act in response to threats from elder rivals in the wider royal family.[16]

The New Yorker reported that the night before MbS's appointment, guards in King Salman's palace seized Mohammed bin Nayef's phone and demanded he abdicate. Nayef was not only removed from all his previous positions, but later reportedly placed under a version of house arrest.

A court official named Saud al-Qahtani proved his usefulness to the crown prince during the affair, allegedly threatening Nayef till he agreed to give up his claim to the throne; Qahtani is also believed to have been behind the rumours, spread on social media, that Nayef's departure had been caused by an alleged and unproven addiction to painkillers following his injury in 2009. As we will see later, Jamal Khashoggi accused Qahtani of attempting to silence him too; and his alleged involvement in the plot against the journalist in Istanbul would also implicate his boss, the new crown prince.

But in Riyadh that June, the main task was to make sure the previous crown prince kept quiet. A relative was quoted as saying that the Nayef family's bank accounts had been emptied of funds. He was clearly being prevented from staging a comeback. No new deputy crown prince was appointed beneath MbS either. Three sons of the previous king, Abdullah, were sacked, detained or fled into hiding.[17] MbS was unchallenged and in control, even if *The Economist* magazine warned that he was 'callow', 'hot headed' and 'dangerous'.[18]

The timing of his elevation may not have been unconnected to President Trump's first foreign visit, to Riyadh the previous month. Former senior White House officials claimed Jared Kushner had been cultivating the young prince and asking US officials about the Saudi succession process and whether the Trump administration could influence it. The effort reportedly began just a few months after Trump took office in 2016, though a White House official later denied that Kushner had made any such enquiry.

'We've put our man on top,' the president later claimed to friends, according to *Fire and Fury*, Michael Wolff's explosive account of the first few months of the Trump White House.[19]

That may well have been wishful thinking on the president's part. The House of Saud fiercely and understandably protects its right to choose its own monarch, although the White House may have encouraged King Salman in planning what he was going to do anyway, which was to appoint MbS as his heir.

It may have seemed natural for Jared Kushner to develop a 'bromance' with the young prince, given that the fresh-faced New York businessman was the closest the White House had to its own princeling and only four years older than MbS.

Kushner had met a Saudi government delegation in Washington in November 2016, the month Donald Trump was elected. In their early attempt to engage with the incoming administration, the Saudis took note of Kushner's lack of knowledge about Saudi Arabia, but decided that talking to him about peace between Israel and the Palestinians was the best way of gaining his attention. 'The inner circle is predominantly deal makers who lack familiarity with political customs and deep institutions, and they support Jared Kushner,' the Saudi delegation concluded in a slide presentation obtained by the *New York Times*.[20]

US officials would begin to worry that Kushner's friendship with MbS was operating outside usual diplomatic protocols, involving WhatsApp messages and one-on-one phone calls at which White House note-takers were not always present. *Vanity Fair* reported that Rex Tillerson, the then US Secretary of State, described Kushner as a 'rookie, he doesn't know the region'. Tillerson reportedly confronted him many times about his contacts with MbS – although the fact that Trump and Tillerson did not appoint an ambassador to Saudi Arabia until the end of 2018 meant that there was a vacuum which needed to be filled in terms of maintaining high-level contact with Riyadh.[21]

The White House has pushed back at suggestions that Kushner acted beyond the usual boundaries of diplomacy, saying the president's senior adviser had 'always meticulously followed protocols and guidelines regarding the relationship with MbS', without explaining what those guidelines were.[22] Kushner had reportedly sat up one night playing video games in Riyadh with MbS. The friendship, as he saw it, could help deliver to this White House a prize which had eluded every previous president – a lasting peace deal between Israel and the

Palestinians. This goal, along with selling more weapons and containing Iran, would prove central to the Trump administration's dealings with Saudi Arabia.

～

For young Saudis, some 200,000 of whom were annually studying on scholarships overseas, MbS was a breath of fresh air. In 2016, he reined in the kingdom's religious police, the *muttawa*, who were tasked with enforcing the strict morality code and gender segregation associated with the Wahhabi religious establishment in the kingdom.

Known officially as the Committee for the Promotion of Virtue and the Prevention of Vice, the police had the power to question and arrest those guilty of crimes, such as appearing in public with an unrelated member of the opposite sex. MbS had that power removed, arguing that the police should provide religious advice and confine themselves to reporting alleged crimes rather than carrying out arrests. Restaurants and cafés began playing music for the first time; the threat of being confronted or arrested on the street by police patrols was sharply reduced.[23] A year later, King Salman announced that the ban on women driving, the only one of its kind in the world, would be lifted. Sports arenas also began to admit women, and a new Entertainment Authority laid on concerts featuring both Arab and international singers.

The first film to be shown in a Saudi cinema in decades would be *Black Panther*, a Hollywood blockbuster about a young king who must decide whether to hide his jungle kingdom from the outside world or engage with it. It wasn't lost on observers, including Jamal Khashoggi, that Crown Prince Mohammed bin Salman was trying to do something similar in the Saudi desert. 'It's a huge step towards normalisation,' the journalist wrote approvingly later in the *Washington Post*. 'For too long, hard-line religious figures have preached that cinema would bring about the collapse of all moral values.'[24]

MbS's social reforms led to a wave of optimism in Western capitals that Saudi Arabia was changing at last. What this analysis failed to take into account was that individual 'rights' were not being recognised in the kingdom – but instead, more privileges and favours were being bestowed. 'He never said this was becoming a constitutional monarchy,' was how Gerald Feierstein put it. 'What he was doing was not intended to diminish the authority of the Al Sauds as the rulers of Saudi Arabia.'

In April 2016, MbS, reportedly an admirer of Margaret Thatcher,[25] had launched a plan known as 'Vision 2030' alongside his social and cultural reforms. Based on plans drawn up by the consulting firm McKinsey Global Institute, it involved pouring money into education and healthcare and opening up Saudi Arabia to tourism. The centrepiece was that the state would sell off 5 per cent of Aramco, in what would be the world's biggest market flotation, then use the proceeds to wean Saudi Arabia off its dependency on oil and build a free-market economy. GDP would double. Youth unemployment, running at 30 per cent, would finally fall. MbS envisaged a new city called 'NEOM' on the Red Sea coast, costing $500 billion, run on solar power, with passengers ferried about in self-driving cars.

MbS's ambition was on one level admirable and indeed vital, if Saudi Arabia was to avoid budget deficits caused by falling oil prices. On the other hand, it risked being hopelessly undeliverable. Successive five-year plans had come and gone. Projects dating back to the 1970s had ended up as white elephants or had never been built. 'He was trying to do something which had never been done,' a Western ambassador in Riyadh said. 'To change the fundamentals of an economy within a decade and create 6 million jobs.'

Saudi Arabia's notoriously sclerotic bureaucracy, experienced in nothing beyond oil, would find it impossible to cope without substantial foreign participation; yet, as we shall see later, the climate of political repression, which worsened from 2015, put that foreign involvement at risk.

MbS's valuation of Aramco, at over $2 trillion, earned the derision of some investors who demanded Western standards of transparency and disclosure on corporate governance, funding and estimates of Saudi oil reserves. As a result, a stock-exchange flotation which promised a bonanza for international banks and consultants was postponed.

While the crown prince cut state budgets, his own royal excesses were certainly not about to be curbed. In 2015 he bought a 440 ft super-yacht, the *Serene*, for around $500 million, after spotting it on holiday in the south of France. It was an impulse buy from Yuri Shefler, a Russian vodka tycoon, and equipped with a helipad and seven bathtubs and swimming pools.

The same year MbS spent another $300 million on a French château which sits in 57 acres at Louveciennes, near Versailles. The château was completed in 2009 but designed to look as if it belonged in the late seventeenth century, even if the moat surrounding it included an underwater viewing chamber from which to watch exotic fish swimming by. The property developer was Emad Khashoggi, who happened to be Jamal Khashoggi's cousin.

Both the château and the yacht were purchased through shell companies in France and Luxembourg, controlled by Eight Investment Company, which was in turn controlled by the head of the crown prince's investment foundation.[26]

MbS was also alleged to be the secret buyer of *Salvator Mundi*, a portrait of Christ attributed to Leonardo da Vinci. Controversially identified as one of only twenty Leonardo paintings, it became the world's most expensive picture when it was bought at Christie's auction house for over $450 million in 2017.

The *New York Times* reported that the anonymous buyer was Bader bin Abdullah bin Mohammed bin Farhan al-Saud, a little-known Saudi prince who happened to be a close friend of MbS.[27] The Louvre in Abu Dhabi announced it would display the work, but by early 2019 it had still not appeared. Amid speculation that the crown prince had decided to keep it for himself, the art industry website art.net reported that the alleged Leonardo had been transferred to MbS's yacht, the *Serene*. Perhaps the crown prince was waiting for the picture's provenance – and therefore worth – to be more positively established before transferring it to public view, either in the United Arab Emirates or, perhaps more likely, a new cultural complex he would build in Saudi Arabia.[28] Or he believed it was a display of ostentatious wealth too far.

'My personal life is something I'd like to keep to myself,' he said later. 'As far as my private expenses, I'm a rich person and not a poor person. I'm not Gandhi or Mandela . . . but what I do as a person is spend part of my personal income on charity. I spend at least 51 per cent on people and 49 per cent on myself.'[29]

From his home in Jeddah, Jamal Khashoggi watched events unfold in the kingdom at what seemed a dizzyingly fast rate. In the first two years of King Salman's reign, the monarch had switched crown prince three times. His relatively inexperienced son, MbS, had launched a war in Yemen and introduced bold social and economic reforms.

The question was whether Khashoggi's already precarious career in journalism would survive the darker side of the crown prince's character. Any Saudi journalist worthy of the job title can expect to be caught in the crossfire between freedom of expression and absolute monarchical rule. Now the battle risked becoming unsustainable, in an environment so paranoid that it ceased tolerating any shade of opinion at all; and evidence would soon emerge that the crown prince felt powerful enough to act anywhere in the world against those he felt had crossed him.

4

THE FALL FROM GRACE

It was, ironically, Khashoggi's mild criticism of President Trump, and not of his own Saudi rulers, that would lead to the journalist being banned from writing. In the week after the presidential election in November 2016, Khashoggi had spoken by video link to a conference at a think-tank, the Washington Institute, entitled 'A New President and the Middle East'.

It was, the journalist told the audience, 'wishful thinking' that Donald Trump would bring about regional peace. He argued that the Saudis had been 'caught off guard' by his victory and were nervous that if he did not take a tough line against President Assad of Syria, then it would be harder to contain Syria's ally, Iran.[1]

There was nothing particularly controversial in the journalist's remarks. At this stage, nobody knew what an untested and unpredictable president would do in office, and his victory over Hillary Clinton had indeed caught many foreign governments by surprise. However, Khashoggi's opinions had been aired in Washington, the seat of American power, at the very moment the Saudis were about to open the next chapter of their relationship there.

The journalist had done what he often did – mused aloud on the possible dynamics between Riyadh and its most important ally. This time the gadfly had unwittingly stung the Saudi authorities, if not the crown prince himself. Khashoggi appeared to have misjudged how much the royal court had changed under MbS, how much comment was even less free than before.

A few days later, the Saudi Press Agency quoted a source in the kingdom's Foreign Affairs Ministry as saying 'that the author Jamal Khashoggi does not represent the government of Saudi Arabia or its positions at any level, and that his opinions only represent his personal views, not that of the Kingdom of Saudi Arabia'.[2] Khashoggi's regular Saturday column in the newspaper *Al Hayat* was cancelled the next month, after seven years. He was also banned from tweeting or making any media appearances.

'The "Arab Spring" was not defeated in Tunisia,' he wrote on 18 November 2016, in his final posting on social media. Tunisia was the only Arab country roiled by revolution which could call itself a success. Khashoggi was clinging to the happy memory of it, at the very moment he was deprived of the freedom of speech the Arab Spring had once promised.

Khashoggi heard about the ban in a phone call from Saud al-Qahtani, the adviser to MbS who would go on to help him force Mohammed bid Nayef to step down as crown prince. He was an official who had risen to such prominence in the new royal court that falling foul of him would prove dangerous. 'I was ordered silent,' Khashoggi said afterwards. 'He said, "You are not allowed to tweet or write your column or give comments to foreign journalists."'[3]

He returned to his home in Jeddah, living under what friends described as virtual house arrest, in despair at the direction in which his country was heading and at his lack of freedom to write. 'It was basically like being locked up in his own mind,' said a friend in Washington, who kept in touch with him. 'He told me that all he had meant in his speech about Trump was that we should not get over-enthusiastic about him, as we had with Obama.'

If Khashoggi was to endure being unable to work, he would need emotional support. Yet the previous year he had divorced his third wife, Alaa Naseif. She was the American-educated chief of staff of a Saudi charity, the King Abdullah bin Abdulaziz International Centre for Interreligious and Intercultural Dialogue. Constructing churches and synagogues is illegal in Saudi Arabia, where it is also illegal to practise publicly any religion other than Islam; but the centre, founded in 2012, was based in Vienna, which Naseif visited frequently. She was well-connected within the Saudi royal court, where her charity, named after the previous king, continued to enjoy the royal family's backing.

Khashoggi had married Naseif seven years earlier, on the day he was sacked for the second time as editor of the *Al Watan* newspaper. He told a close friend that he blamed the break-down of the marriage in part on the unhappiness he'd caused by taking more than one wife: Not only was he still married to Rawiya al-Tunisi, the mother of his children, but to complicate the situation further, there was a brief, second marriage to a woman named Maha, which lasted little more than a year.

'He said it was a great mistake and he was dark and depressed about the whole thing,' a long-standing American friend of the journalist said, claiming that he had pledged never to marry concurrently again, even if it was his right as a Saudi citizen to do so.

At the end of 2016, with Khashoggi silenced and in dire need of company, he remarried Naseif. A friend of the journalist said that for the sake of her family's safety, his wife made the reunion conditional on the journalist agreeing not to express his opinions in any way the Saudi authorities might dislike. It seemed he was being muzzled twice – first by the Saudi state and then by the woman he loved but who was also trying to protect him.

Evidence of how much trouble the journalist was in soon followed. He flew to Abu Dhabi, the capital of the United Arab Emirates, for a conference and was told at the airport that he had to return to Saudi Arabia. The crown prince of Abu Dhabi, Mohammed bin Zayed, known as 'MbZ', was the UAE's de facto leader and the Saudi crown prince's closest regional ally. 'MbZ has a problem with me,' Khashoggi told a lawyer friend in London afterwards. It was a bad problem to have: Khashoggi's first wife and three of his children had made their homes in the UAE, so being able to travel there was of vital importance to him.

Khashoggi telephoned Saud al-Qahtani to see whether the ban on working and travelling could be lifted. 'It is *Wali al-Amr*,' Qahtani told him. That meant the ruling had come from on high and required his absolute obedience to the rulers of the Saudi state.

'Okay, I will respect it,' Khashoggi replied. 'But how long does it last?'

'I will come back to you,' Qahtani told him.

Khashoggi told friends that as he could not write, he was like a 'fish out of water' and emotionally dead. 'When they stopped me from writing, they killed my spirit,' he told Wadah Khanfar, a Palestinian journalist and former director of the Al Jazeera Arabic television network. After a few months, and with still no word from the crown prince's adviser, Khashoggi called him back. He was told sternly that he could now travel, but not write or make any media appearances.[4]

In June 2017 – the same month Mohammed bin Salman toppled his cousin Nayef as crown prince – Saudi Arabia led its allies, the United Arab Emirates, Egypt and Bahrain, in imposing a boycott on Qatar for 'instigating against the [Saudi] state' and 'adopting various terrorist and sectarian groups'.

This diplomatic row is important to understanding what happened to Jamal Khashoggi in Istanbul the following year; partly because Turkey earned Saudi Arabia's enmity by siding with Qatar in the dispute; but also because it formed the backdrop to a growing intolerance of domestic dissent, in which critics such as Khashoggi were regarded and described as Qatari agents and traitors. The crown prince's adviser, Saud al-Qahtani, would play a key role in disseminating the kingdom's aggressively nationalistic message – and policing those who dared contradict it.

A Saudi travel ban divided Arab families living across the Qatari border and was accompanied by the closure of air and shipping routes. Exceptions were made for Qataris making the pilgrimage to Mecca. Although 11,000 members of an anti-ISIS coalition were stationed at the Al Udeid air base in Qatar, which was America's largest military outpost in the region, the Americans took the Saudis' side in the dispute.

In fact, President Trump took credit for the blockade as a product of his visit to Riyadh only the month before, on his first official foreign trip as America's commander-in-chief. '[The Saudis] said they would take a hard line on funding extremism,' Trump tweeted appreciatively, 'and all reference was pointing to Qatar. Perhaps this will be the beginning of the end to horror of terrorism!'

Western countries had long accused Qatar of a permissive attitude to terrorist financing. It had openly hosted members of the Taliban and Hamas and, in the 1990s, Khalid Sheikh

Mohammed lived there. The al-Qaeda member was later captured by the Americans and accused of being the main architect of the 11 September attacks.

The troubled relationship between Riyadh and Doha stretched back decades, at least as far as 1996, when the Qataris accused the Saudis and their allies of plotting a coup against their emir; the Saudis in turn accused the Qataris of conspiring with Colonel Gaddafi of Libya in a 2003 assassination attempt against their future king, Abdullah.

The Saudis were angry that the emirate had reportedly paid a ransom of up to £1 billion in 2017, after several members of Qatar's royal family were held hostage during a hunting trip to Iraq.

The crown prince was de facto head of state of a country of some 30 million people; but he also saw the tiny emirate of some 300,000 Qataris as a rival which appeared to punch too far above its puny weight. Qatar possessed a sovereign wealth fund worth over $300 billion and had successfully bid for the 2022 World Cup. More importantly, it had used its wealth from offshore gas to support Islamist parties in at least three Arab states which might, in theory, threaten the monarchies of the Gulf – even though political parties were banned in the emirate itself.

However, the biggest issue was Qatar's support for the Muslim Brotherhood, which Saudi Arabia had outlawed during the aftermath of the Arab Spring. Ever since he had fled from Egypt in 1961, Sheikh Yusuf al-Qaradawi, a radical preacher widely regarded as spiritual leader of the Brotherhood, had resided in Doha, from where his sermons and TV shows were broadcast to millions of Muslims worldwide. He had been banned from travelling to the UK and USA in the past, because of his outspoken support for Palestinian suicide bombers. The Saudis said Qaradawi, now aged ninety-one, was a terrorist.

Not only had Qatar sheltered this Egyptian cleric, but it had backed the short-lived Muslim Brotherhood government in Egypt. Even though Doha dissolved its domestic Brotherhood chapter in 1999, it granted temporary refuge to some of the group's senior figures who fled from Egypt, giving them airtime on Al Jazeera television to promote their cause. It also provided financial support for Hamas rule in the Palestinian Gaza Strip; and it had developed a close economic relationship with neighbouring Iran, with which it shared the world's largest gas field.

Now the Saudis were demanding Qatar sever all ties to terrorist organisations, specifically the Muslim Brotherhood. The threat the Brotherhood really posed to the monarchies of the Gulf is hotly disputed – though in 2013, sixty-nine people were convicted of plotting a coup on behalf of a Brotherhood affiliate in the United Arab Emirates.

Tunisia, Morocco and Jordan had found ways of accommodating non-violent Brotherhood parties, while the UAE, Egypt and Saudi Arabia had outlawed them. MbS certainly took a far more intolerant view of the Muslim Brotherhood than his father did, and that meant that Jamal Khashoggi's former membership would arouse his immediate suspicion. The prince had once accused the Brotherhood of assassinating his uncle, King Faisal bin Abdulaziz, and believed the group lay at the root of terrorism. 'If you look at Osama bin Laden, you will find that he was a Muslim Brother,' he said. 'If you look at [ISIS leader] al-Baghdadi, you will find that he too was a Muslim Brother. In reality, if you look at any terrorist, you will find that they were a Muslim Brother.'

On top of his Brotherhood youth, Jamal Khashoggi had been a regular visitor to conferences in Qatar and a guest on its Al Jazeera television network. Al Jazeera was highly influential, state-funded, and had given voice to many of the protest movements of the Arab Spring. For any Arab journalist wanting to be heard across the Arab world, the Qataris provided the biggest media platform available. Yet now the Saudis were demanding the station was taken off air. The journalist told friends there that although he was now allowed to travel, he needed to distance himself from Doha. 'I don't want to appear anti-Saudi,' he said.

'He was trying to avoid going to Qatar or to receive any funds from Qatar, to avoid this perception of being too close,' said Nihad Awad, a Palestinian American friend in Washington.

Turkey had sided with Qatar by sending it troops during the dispute, on the grounds that if it did not then Saudi Arabia might invade its neighbour. To the Saudi authorities, this was unwarranted interference in Arab affairs and so relations with Ankara, already strained by the opposing sides they had taken in the Arab Spring, deteriorated further. This too would form part of the political backdrop to the crisis in Istanbul the following year.

While Western diplomats found themselves battling to preserve the peace between Doha and Riyadh, Khashoggi reportedly tried offering himself, via an intermediary, as an adviser to the crown prince. Perhaps he saw himself as a kindly uncle who could restrain his young charge, in contrast with courtiers who did what they were told – one of whom, Saud al-Qahtani, had silenced him. Perhaps he was looking for a way back 'in from the cold' to end his isolation in Jeddah, to return to his status as a critic of the Saudi system and royal court insider – the tightrope he had walked so many times before. Maybe he was merely trying to keep the channels of communication open for his own safety, to keep talking, like a modern-day Scheherazade, to a ruler who might otherwise turn against him.

The *Washington Post* reported that MbS rejected Khashoggi's offer to work for him outright, on the grounds that the journalist was tied to the Muslim Brotherhood and to Qatar. In other words, the journalist had, in the crown prince's mind, been classified as belonging to the enemy camp. Currying favour with MbS was apparently no longer an option open to him.

Khashoggi's past association with the Muslim Brotherhood, his support for the Arab Spring, his Al Jazeera broadcasts . . . all this meant that squaring the circle of loyal servant of the kingdom and independent-minded journalist, which had never been easy, would now prove impossible.[5] MbS's aide had not only banned him from any media work, but he had been accused of taking sides in a wider regional dispute. He needed to make a living and to breathe more freely. It was time to leave.

5

FLIGHT TO WASHINGTON

'As comfortable as he had made his surroundings, he still spoke about how he longed to see his home, his family and his loved ones. He also told us about the day he left Saudi Arabia, standing outside his doorstep, wondering if he would ever return.'

– Noha and Razan, daughters of Jamal Khashoggi, *Washington Post*, 2 December 2018

In July 2017, just after Mohammed bin Salman usurped his predecessor as crown prince and began blockading Qatar, Jamal Khashoggi decided to flee from his homeland, taking two suitcases with him.

In their rapidly sketched obituaries, his fellow journalists would summarise his life from then onwards as one of 'self-imposed exile'. That abbreviation, which was also used by the Saudi ambassador to the United States, seems unfair; Khashoggi had come to regard his own government as a very real threat. 'I began to feel whatever narrow space I had in Saudi Arabia was getting narrower,' Khashoggi said later. 'I thought it would be better to get out and be safe.'[1]

'He decided to leave without being noticed,' said Saad Djebbar, his Algerian lawyer friend based in the UK whom he'd known for over twenty years. 'He said he was worried about his country and its new leader.'

At the end of June, he messaged an old American friend, a former US diplomat, with his new US mobile phone number. 'He told me he had been tipped off that he was going to face a travel ban,' she said.

'Jamal said that Saud al-Qahtani, the guy who had banned him from writing, the guy who hated him – had asked him to write again,' another friend said. 'But Jamal didn't trust him.'

'I said you either have to get a job abroad, or you have to seek asylum,' Saad Djebbar advised Khashoggi, once he'd heard that Qahtani had renewed contact. The journalist didn't need to be told the safest thing would be to get out.

Saud al-Qahtani by now was the crown prince's social media czar and one of his most trusted advisers. It was Qahtani, the *New York Times* reported, who forced Arabic MBC television to stop airing Turkish soap operas because of Turkey's support for Qatar; and Qahtani who persuaded MbS to fund commercials denouncing Qatar on American television networks.[2] Now in his late thirties, he had worked his way up inside the royal court over the course of a decade, becoming MbS's *consigliere*, chief propagandist and head of social media campaigns in the so-called Centre for Studies and Information Affairs in Riyadh. David Ignatius, a friend of Khashoggi's, described Qahtani in Shakespearean terms as having 'played Iago to his headstrong, sometimes paranoid boss'.[3]

The go-to aide would denounce MbS's enemies and vigorously promote his pet projects through media offensives online. He commanded over 1.3 million followers on Twitter, where he had earned the nicknames 'Mr Hashtag' and 'Lord of the Flies' – references to his command of a vicious trolling operation in defence of the crown prince. Saudi officials said later that Qahtani had assembled a team of 3,000 people to monitor and intimidate online critics of the kingdom. Saudi Arabia is one of the world's most avid users of social media and it was Qahtani's job to dominate this vital 'information space', full of young Saudi consumers.[4]

In August 2017, he appealed to his fellow Saudis to compile a list containing the names and identities of anyone showing sympathy with Qatar under the Arabic hashtag #TheBlacklist. 'They will be sorted. They will be followed up on from now,' he tweeted. He then tweeted that anyone who 'conspires' against Saudi Arabia or its allies involved in the blockade against Qatar would be unable to escape 'trial'. A Saudi who saw Qahtani's list of those who might be arrested or detained said it was composed of twelve names. Khashoggi's was one of them.[5] We don't know how long he had been on the list, but it seems he had escaped to Washington just in time.

It was Qahtani who had ordered Khashoggi to stop using Twitter and cease writing because of his remarks about Donald Trump the previous autumn. On the same day he tweeted that sympathisers of Qatar would be 'followed up', he also boasted about where his orders were coming from. 'Do you think I make decisions without guidance?' Qahtani asked on Twitter in August 2017. 'I am an employee and an executor of the orders of the king and the crown prince.'

There was no reason to doubt he was telling the truth, and this confirmation of the chain of command would have serious implications for the presumptive heir to the Saudi throne. If Qahtani had banned Khashoggi from journalism on the crown prince's orders, to what extent was the crown prince also responsible for Qahtani's alleged involvement in the journalist's disappearance the following year in Istanbul?

After all, the *Washington Post* reported that in the spring of 2017, just before Khashoggi fled, Saud al-Qahtani worked in coordination with 'snatch' squads, known as Rapid Intervention Groups, in a secret programme of kidnapping dissidents and holding them at undisclosed sites.[6] If Khashoggi was on Qahtani's list of potential detainees, it might follow that he was on a kidnap list too. The journalist certainly assumed that he was.

'He always thought he could be kidnapped, but not killed,' said his friend Wadah Khanfar, who had lunch with Khashoggi at the Landmark hotel in London that summer. 'He said the worst that could happen was that they would put him on a plane – and then he would open his eyes and find himself in Riyadh.'

Khashoggi wasn't entirely sure in his own mind whether to move to Washington DC or to London, but after taking soundings from friends during a visit to the UK he decided that America was the safer haven – even though London, where he'd also lived and worked, is one of the Arab world's major political and cultural crossroads. The journalist still owned an apartment in northern Virginia, just half an hour's drive from the White House, which he'd bought when he worked at the Saudi embassy in Washington over a decade earlier. It was a bolt-hole which he could finally put to personal use.

However, claiming asylum in America was something Khashoggi did not want to contemplate. It would have made his departure from his homeland irreversible. He had also left his wife, Alaa Naseif, and family members back in Saudi Arabia. In his mind, asylum would be an act of betrayal against the country and the people he loved.

If his first dilemma was where he should live, the second was how outspoken should he become? 'I am just an independent writer,' he told Saad Djebbar, 'but if I start to write what I believe in, they will punish me.'

'Those people don't have the word "independent" in their software or hardware,' Djebbar replied, warning him that the space for free debate in Saudi Arabia had vanished.

A friend in Washington warned him that the crown prince, MbS, was incapable of seeing him as anything other than friend or foe; for him, there was no in-between, no halfway house. A glimmer of hope for reconciliation came that August, after the Saudi information minister, Awwad Alawwad, told Khashoggi that the media ban on him had been lifted, allowing the journalist to start tweeting again. 'The crown prince would like to see you,' the minister said, according to a Khashoggi associate who heard the phone call. It was an offer to return to Riyadh which the journalist did not dare take up, fearing it was a trap.

Khashoggi's American home was a modest two-bedroom condominium in Lillian Court, a modern development overlooking a convenient if soulless shopping mall in Tysons Corner, Virginia. It wasn't far from the palatial residence of Prince Turki al-Faisal, the former ambassador and head of Saudi intelligence, who lived near CIA headquarters whenever he visited Washington. Though by now Khashoggi's relationship with Turki, his former patron, had turned sour.

The prince later indicated that the two had fallen out a few years earlier. Turki said they'd argued about the Muslim Brotherhood. The prince had described it as a cult involved in terrorism; while Khashoggi saw the Islamist movement as the best hope for change in the Arab world.[7] Losing Turki as a sponsor and protector was one more reason to believe that he could not risk returning to Jeddah.

Many in Virginia's Arab dissident community did not know

whether to welcome the newcomer in their midst. Although the Saudi crown prince would later tell the White House that Khashoggi was guilty of a close association with the Brotherhood, the irony was that Brotherhood members in exile regarded him as a royal court insider who could not be trusted. His long-standing friendship with Prince Turki, his work as his embassy spokesman in London and Washington, had made sure of that. It only added to the loneliness of an essentially clubbable man, now far from home and struggling to find his feet in America.

In his first few weeks there, a friend he'd met at Washington's Middle East Institute would call or message him most mornings, all too aware of how lonely he was. 'He was a grown man crying all the time,' she told me. 'This was a man who loved being with his family. A whole group of us supported him, because we knew what it meant for him, living in exile.'

Another friend recalled Khashoggi giving him a bear hug when they met and then bursting into tears. 'I have given up my family and everything I know for freedom,' he said.

Such was his isolation that the journalist reverted to a pattern of behaviour seemingly at odds with his exile. The *Washington Post* obtained documents showing that in September 2017 he was trying to raise up to $2 million from the Saudi government for a new think-tank, the 'Saudi Research Council'. 'Jamal was still hoping something would happen in Saudi Arabia that would lead to reform, so he didn't want to sever his ties completely,' Azzam Tamimi, his Palestinian journalist friend in London, told me.

Another friend, Wadah Khanfar, recalls it differently. Khashoggi told him that a Saudi businessman, close to the crown prince, had first tried to persuade him to come home, and then told him that he could have his own think-tank, funded by the Saudi government, if only he would stop tweeting critically about the kingdom. 'I have a private jet. I could pick you up and take you back to our farm in Mexico, where we could spend a few days discussing it,' the Saudi businessman told him.

Khashoggi turned down the offer. 'I will wake up in Riyadh,' he told Khanfar.

In the event, the Saudi businessman met him in Washington. The offer of a think-tank was still on the table. He was told it could be used as a vehicle to 'correct' the poor image of Saudi Arabia in America. Khashoggi would later laugh about how he rejected the proposal. 'They want to recruit me again, but I want to do my own stuff now,' he said.

In November 2017, Saud al-Qahtani called him to say how happy the crown prince was to see Khashoggi posting a message on Twitter, welcoming a government announcement that the ban on women driving would be lifted. An eyewitness to the conversation told me Khashoggi asked him to record the phone call, in case it contained threats.

'He was terrified,' the friend said, adding that Khashoggi's hand was shaking as he held the phone. Instead of politely listening to the prince's aide, he reeled off a list of several recently arrested prisoners. 'When there are good things, I will acknowledge them, but when there are bad things, I will criticise,' Khashoggi told Qahtani. 'When the arrests started happening, I flipped,' Khashoggi said later. 'I decided it was time to speak.'[8]

The crown prince's clampdown on dissent – along with the personal ban on his writing and accusations that he was in league with the Muslim Brotherhood – had become another major factor in the journalist's decision to move to America.

Prisoners of Conscience, a Saudi group that tracks political prisoners, reckoned that more than 2,600 dissidents had been jailed. Most were convicted under counter-terrorism legislation for crimes such as 'criticising the royal court' and 'ridiculing religious figures'. Such crackdowns were nothing new, but they had become more severe.[9] Top of Khashoggi's list of prisoners was the economist Essam al-Zamil, who had been detained in September 2017 as part of a round-up of dozens of intellectuals and clerics. Zamil had suggested on social media that the crown prince's proposed $2 trillion valuation of Saudi Aramco, the state oil company, was excessive. Zamil was Khashoggi's friend, and he took his arrest more personally than any to date. 'He [Khashoggi] had called Zamil and warned him not to return home,' said Saad Djebbar, adding that the journalist felt guilty that his advice to stay away from Saudi Arabia had come too late.

In the week of Khashoggi's death, Zamil would be referred to a Saudi court on charges of 'meeting with foreign diplomats' and 'joining a terrorist organisation'.[10] The economist had been branded as a Qatari agent and member of the Muslim Brotherhood.

Although campaigning for political prisoners would further estrange him from Riyadh, Khashoggi now felt compelled to do so. 'He felt guilty that he'd kept quiet in the past,' a friend in Virginia said. 'He always talked about that.'

Several friends helped him obtain an 'O' visa. As an 'outstanding professional', it would grant him residency status, setting him on the path to citizenship if he wanted it. The television anchorwoman Christiane Amanpour, who had interviewed him many times on CNN, was one of those who wrote a letter in support of his application, claiming he had 'set the benchmark for reporting in the Arab press'.

'His expertise on Saudi Arabia is particularly helpful and useful especially at this current time,' she wrote. 'His reporting style can be characterised as relentless, original, in-depth and he thinks outside the box, giving vital perspectives his readers may have never even thought of.'

He applied for a fellowship at the Woodrow Wilson International Center for Scholars in Washington, proposing that he should write a book. Tentatively entitled *United States for Saudis* or *US Made Easy for Saudis*, it would demystify America for Saudi visitors. Khashoggi noted that at least 750,000 Saudis had graduated from American colleges already. His proposal was, however, unashamedly political, as the book would also argue the case for 'expanding the scope of democracy and independence of authorities' in the kingdom. In other words, he was hoping the book could help persuade the crown prince to fill the gaping hole in his Vision 2030 economic plan – the need for political reform. Not that there was any indication the prince would listen.[11]

That September, he texted his friend, Barnett Rubin, about how he feared MbS. 'This kid is dangerous. I'm under pressure . . . to be "wise" and stay silent,' he wrote. 'I think I should speak wisely.'[12]

Khashoggi would find it impossible to follow his own advice. Instead, he agreed to start writing for the *Washington Post* that very same month. The decision to work for one of the world's most famous newspapers, close to the heart of American power, would mean that there could be no turning back.

The *Post*'s Global Opinions editor, Karen Attiah, hired him, claiming that what made his journalism unique was 'his keen desire to demystify Saudi Arabia for a global audience'.[13] The paper's 'word rate' was modest – about $500 for each of the twenty columns he contributed – and the more controversially the Saudi wrote, the more unlikely any wealthy Saudi patrons would come to his financial assistance, as they had in the past. 'He was hoping his old friends would dig their hands in their pockets,' said Azzam Tamimi, 'but it didn't happen.'

Khashoggi's first email to his new editor was reprinted by the *New York Times*: 'Hello Karen, thanks for asking me to write. I'm under so much pressure from family members and friends to stay silent. But this isn't right. We have enough Arab failing states. I don't want my country to be one too. I hope this is what you are looking for. Excuse my not-so-good English, but I'm sure you can fix that. All the best, Jamal.'[14]

His first *Washington Post* column was published on 18 September, provocatively appearing at the height of the UN General Assembly meeting in New York. Khashoggi happened to be visiting the city at the time for an event at a think-tank. The article was headlined: 'Saudi Arabia wasn't always this repressive. Now it's unbearable.'

From his very first piece, Khashoggi felt compelled not to hold back. He wrote of how his friend Essam al-Zamil and some thirty others had been rounded up in the middle of the night by masked men, who stormed into their houses and confiscated their computers. 'That is how breathtakingly fast you can fall out of favour with Saudi Arabia,' he wrote, acknowledging to himself the decline in his own fortunes and his escape into self-exile to evade arrest.

He described being fired twice from the editorship of the same government-controlled newspaper; yet noted that he had also advised Prince Turki al-Faisal, the Saudi ambassador to the UK and then the US. 'Perhaps it seems odd to be fired by the government and then serve it abroad,' he wrote. 'Yet that truly is the Saudi paradox.'

It was also the paradox that dominated Jamal Khashoggi's

career; how to handle the contradiction between loyalty to the kingdom and speaking his mind. The longer he continued trying, the more likely he was to fail. Now he was failing for the last time, and spectacularly so, in the opinion section of the *Washington Post*.

He wrote that he cared deeply about his country, that it was the only home he wanted, even if it now considered him an enemy of the state; but that he would no longer keep quiet to protect his job and his family, as he had in the past. 'I have left my home, my family and my job, and I am raising my voice,' he wrote. 'To do otherwise would betray those who languish in prison. I can speak when so many cannot.'

If Jamal Khashoggi knew how dangerous this was, if not for himself then for his family, then the risks were no longer sufficient to stop him. He had reached a point of no return.

Long-term critics of Saudi Arabia were initially sceptical of his outspoken change of heart, pointing out that it was only after a change of monarch and the rise of a new crown prince that Khashoggi's inner contradictions became unsustainable and flared into outright dissent.

'He was part of the old guard who lost his footing,' said Professor Madawi al-Rasheed, an academic at the London School of Economics. 'He used to repeat the regime's narrative – that we need gradual change. He had never joined those civil society activists calling for a constitutional monarchy.'

Yahya Assiri, a Saudi dissident living in London, witnessed Khashoggi's evolution – if not quite conversion – first-hand. They had previously met in television studios, debating the future of Saudi Arabia on opposing sides. Over tea in the lobby of a London hotel, Khashoggi now confessed to Assiri that his opponent had been right all along. 'He said, "I am exactly like you,"' Assiri told *The Independent*.[15] Khashoggi continued: 'I want democracy and freedom. I wanted it to be done more smoothly. I wanted to do it from the inside. But it's not possible.'

~

Khashoggi asked Karen Attiah, his *Post* editor, to have his first piece translated into Arabic. When it was, a spike in the paper's online readership followed. One of his closest American friends believes it was this exposure and subsequent translations of his work for Arab audiences which convinced Saud al-Qahtani that Khashoggi's criticisms were now so loud and potentially damaging to the kingdom's reputation that he needed to be stopped. 'It was the translations which did him in,' she said.

Khashoggi was asked to write more. He replied: 'Really honoured to have this invitation to write for your great paper after I got banned from writing in *Al Hayat* where I had a weekly column for seven years. I'm also delighted to have you as colleagues and friends. I'll take you up on your offer and write as freely as I wish any Arab writer could write in his home country. I'm sure my words will be more powerful in the *Washington Post*.'

Karen Attiah recalled his pride in the press release in December 2017, announcing his appointment as a regular columnist. A tour of the *Post*'s headquarters prompted the admiring Saudi to say aloud to himself: 'I wish we could build this in the Middle East.'

'He was like a kid in a candy store,' said David Ignatius, the *Post* columnist. 'When you saw him walk around this newsroom, he was so happy.'

He would rely on a small group of friends, some of them fellow exiles in Washington, London and Istanbul, to help him develop and then transform his thoughts from Arabic. 'He did not write well in English,' one of those friends explained. 'He had not written for any major English language newspaper, ever.'

His coterie of friend-advisers included Maggie Mitchell Salem, a former US diplomat who works for Qatar Foundation International, which sponsors Arabic language teaching and cultural exchanges. The *Post* itself revealed in a later news piece that Salem was giving Khashoggi editorial advice, fuelling speculation that the journalist was indeed a paid pawn of the Qatari government. It appeared to cast doubt on his journalistic integrity, and gave Khashoggi's critics ammunition for the argument that there was some political justification for his murder. However, Salem pointed out that she had willingly shared her text messages to Khashoggi with the paper, and both she and the *Post* insist the writer remained editorially independent.

He was hoping his new employer would go one step beyond hiring him and publish a regular commentary section in Arabic, reaching millions who could not read English. Khashoggi's wish would eventually be granted, though only three months after his death.

'I ask him from time to time if he's okay, if he's feeling safe,' Karen Attiah wrote shortly after he disappeared, not knowing if he was alive or not. 'He insists that he feels the need to write, despite the pressures from the Saudi authorities.'[16]

Those pressures were surely all the greater because of a feeling of betrayal in Riyadh. Khashoggi had been considered close to the royal court for decades; and, as a spokesman at its embassies in Washington and London, a central figure in combating criticism in the heated aftermath of the 11 September terrorist attacks. 'The crown prince was spending millions of dollars on PR to improve his image – and then along comes

Jamal Khashoggi with his articles saying "don't listen",' was how Azzam Tamimi put it.

The day his first piece appeared, Khashoggi texted Attiah with this confession: 'It's so painful for me to publish this,' he wrote.[17] Yet in a column the following month, his attack on the crown prince continued, accusing him of 'going after the wrong people' in having locked up seventy-two intellectuals without charge. 'I never want to be labelled as an exiled dissident,' he would frequently tell Attiah[18] – as if the label still didn't quite fit, as if the truth of how ostracised he had become was too difficult to contemplate.

He was, by now, financially reliant on a Saudi government pension but joked with friends that the money would surely be cut off soon. He purchased a second-hand BMW in the US, but lived parsimoniously, often counting on the hospitality of friends to pay for meals in restaurants. He was also living with the guilt that his writing for the *Washington Post* would have a direct impact on those he loved.

It would spell the end of his marriage to Alaa Naseif back in Saudi Arabia, who, according to his friends, had warned him not to write or broadcast any more.

'She had done a deal with him: "You go to Washington, you keep quiet, you do not write,"' a close friend of Khashoggi's told me. 'They had talked of moving to the States together, but she was not happy that he had accelerated the timeline, because he had to get out. She did not want to live the rest of her life in exile.'

Khashoggi's articles also resulted in a travel ban on Naseif, which prevented her from joining him even if she had wanted to. Several of Khashoggi's friends told me she was forced to divorce her husband and informed him by telephone in the autumn of 2017. 'She called him when she was in the office of some senior official and she told him – it is divorce,' claimed Azzam Tamimi. 'He felt very wounded by her action.'

Another friend recalled accompanying Khashoggi on a car journey in Virginia, when a lawyer had called from Saudi Arabia to say that his 'Muslim Brotherhood leanings' would form part of the divorce proceedings. 'He lost it, he was totally furious,' the friend said. A close family friend in Saudi Arabia told me the divorce was triggered by Khashoggi's first article in the *Washington Post*. 'Naseif was not forced,' the friend said, claiming the Muslim Brotherhood smear had been introduced in court by a lawyer solely to speed up the court case. Khashoggi told others he was in agony over the effect his decision to write would have on his wife and others close to him. What choice did she really have but to separate from him?

In an echo of events at the consulate in Istanbul later, the journalist was told he would need to visit the Saudi embassy in Washington, to finish the paperwork relating to the divorce. An American friend recalled her concern about the trip in the early autumn of 2017. 'I am going to the embassy to sort out some paperwork,' he had told her.

'They kidnap people – they could throw you on a plane and take you home!' she replied.

Khashoggi told her she was being ridiculous, although he agreed to text her before he went inside the embassy, where he had once worked himself. It was a mark of his recognition of his fall from grace that he agreed to send her the text.

He told Wadah Khanfar that while he was sitting inside the embassy, a messenger came to tell him that the ambassador, Prince Khalid bin Salman, would like to see him. Khalid was no low-ranking prince, but MbS's younger brother. The ambassador would later claim the two had 'maintained regular contact' in Washington. 'He told me I was a son of Saudi Arabia and that if there was anything I needed, then to come back,' Khashoggi recalled later. 'He told me the crown prince liked my tweets.'

'I told him the guy is evil,' said Khaled Saffuri, the Lebanese American political lobbyist in Washington, in an attempt to make the journalist realise the crown prince was, in his view, incapable of real reform. 'He said, "No, I have to encourage him when he does the right thing, to compliment him when he's right."'

Khashoggi's daughters, Noha and Razan – both in their twenties – and his 33-year-old son, Abdullah, were living in Dubai along with their mother, Rawiya, when Khashoggi arrived in the United States. Abdullah, a graphic designer like his sisters, was the only one of his children without dual US-Saudi nationality; Khashoggi was terrified his son would be forced to return to Saudi Arabia to renew his passport, which would expire in 2019. He feared that once Abdullah had flown home, he might be banned from travelling again, in revenge for his father's journalism.

Not only was his third wife, Alaa Naseif, already banned from leaving the kingdom; but his eldest son, Salah, a banker in Jeddah, discovered that he would not be able to leave either, after being turned back at an airport that November.

The journalist told Salah about his first *Post* article before it was published. A family friend said Salah had pleaded with him not to go ahead, but Khashoggi had replied that it was too late. 'That's the path you have chosen,' Salah reportedly told his father. 'No matter what, I am proud of you.' Fearing that their phone conversations were being monitored, Khashoggi's contact with his eldest son would now be restricted to family news and questions of health – the more innocuous the better. Salah would never see his father again.

Khaled Saffuri would take Khashoggi for kebab lunches and smoke cigars with him on Sundays, in an attempt to make him feel less lonely.

'My sons talked to me, and I feel terrible,' Khashoggi told him. 'They blame me for not being able to travel. They say I am selfish, they say that I don't think of them, that I only think of myself.'

'There was pressure on Jamal from his family to stop writing, to stop speaking,' recalled Nihad Awad, a friend for twenty-five years. 'But Jamal could not be other than himself.'

~

Friends back in Saudi Arabia now excluded him from their WhatsApp chat groups, distancing themselves from him for their own protection. Even though Riyadh had given him permission to tweet again, his return to social media resulted in a hail of online abuse which compounded his loneliness and upset him deeply. The journalist had written the slogan 'say your word and leave' beneath his @JKhashoggi twitter handle. Leaving the kingdom was of course what the journalist had done, but the Saudi trolls continued pursuing him. The most common names hurled at him online were 'cancer', 'traitor', 'Zionist', 'rat', 'liar', 'disease' and 'dog'. 'You are a dog of the Qatari royals,' was a fairly typical Twitter response. 'You support the terrorist Muslim Brotherhood,' was another. 'You are a corrupt traitor and a fugitive,' another still.

'He was distraught when he went back on Twitter,' one American friend said. 'It was blistering, it was awful. He went through it every hour of every day.'

She added that Khashoggi would while away the evenings in Tysons Corner, listening to his favourite Arab singers, or smoking cigars on his balcony. Attending social events in

Washington, or seminars at think-tanks, helped distract him from his depression.

Nevertheless, neither his journalism nor his public persona descended into self-pity. In November 2017, he shared on social media a photo of himself at a Thanksgiving dinner, telling friends he was thankful 'I have become free, and can write freely'.[19]

Although Khashoggi enjoyed red wine or a gin and tonic on social occasions, he had also found a place of refuge in his Islamic faith. By 2017, Virginia was home to some 200,000 Muslims, its mosques full of exiles fleeing repression across the Islamic world, which had increased in the aftermath of the Arab Spring; and among them a Saudi journalist, finding some comfort in his religious identity now that he was over 6,000 miles from home.

The first mosque he attended for Friday prayers was a rented room in the basement of the US Congress on Capitol Hill. He also joined in prayers in a room at the Sheraton hotel, near his apartment. The Adams Center mosque in northern Virginia was a favourite; and close by in Falls Church was the Dar al-Hijrah Islamic centre, where two of the 11 September hijackers had once reportedly attended sermons. A friend said he would even keep a prayer mat in her office in downtown Washington, should he wish to worship there.

The need for solace would grow more acute the more Khashoggi wrote for the *Washington Post*. Because the more he wrote, the more he realised there would be no forgiveness and that his ostracism was permanent. As far as the Saudi authorities were concerned, his words were arrows aimed very publicly at them. He had known of the risks for decades, every time he had lost his job by publishing or broadcasting a point of view he shouldn't have. Now ideas he had been thinking about for years were blossoming into print.

His apartment block in Virginia looked out across a busy highway. Beyond it stood a four-star hotel, the Ritz-Carlton. Seeing it must have reminded him of another hotel he knew well from home, the Ritz-Carlton in Riyadh. Only that hotel had achieved notoriety by closing its doors to visitors, trapping its 'guests' inside. Many Saudis being held against their will there were prominent billionaires – the most dramatic proof yet that nobody in MbS's realm could consider themselves safe.

6

THE RITZ-CARLTON AFFAIR

November 2017 provided further and emphatic evidence
that Jamal Khashoggi had been right to flee Saudi Arabia, as
MbS carried out his second internal coup in the space of four
months. First, he had ousted his cousin, Prince Mohammed bin
Nayef, as presumptive heir. Then around 200 Saudi businessmen, princes and former officials were arrested and detained
in the luxury Ritz-Carlton hotel in Riyadh, amid claims by the
prince's advisers that up to $20 billion of government spending
was being lost to corruption, which meant that budget targets
couldn't be met.

'I assure you anyone involved in corruption will not be
spared, whether he's a prince or a minister, or anyone,' MbS
announced on social media. Later, he put it in even starker
terms. 'You have a body that has cancer everywhere, the cancer
of corruption,' he said. 'You need to have chemo, the shock of
chemo, or the cancer will eat the body.'[1]

The 'chemo' against corruption began just days after
Jared Kushner had paid the crown prince a private visit. The
Washington Post reported the pair had stayed up till almost
4 a.m. on several nights, discussing strategy; though what,
if anything, the White House princeling knew about plans
to turn the Ritz-Carlton into a gilded prison has not been

disclosed.[2] All the captives were held without due process in an attempt to recoup billions from those accused of being guilty of state embezzlement. Detainees were locked up and, in some cases, physically roughed up until they agreed to pay vast financial settlements.

The Ritz-Carlton was where Donald Trump had stayed on his first foreign visit as president, just a few months earlier. Now businessmen, including several members of the bin Laden construction dynasty, were held there against their will. The cheapest of its 492 rooms cost $650 a night and its 52 acres included a gentlemen-only spa, used by Prince Alwaleed bin Talal among others. A friend and former sponsor of Khashoggi's, Alwaleed was worth an estimated $17 billion. He'd bought Adnan Khashoggi's yacht almost three decades earlier. He'd also put up part of the money for Jamal Khashoggi's television station in Bahrain in 2015, until the authorities there pulled the plug on it.

'What happened was forgiven and forgotten,' Alwaleed said after his release from eighty-three days of captivity in the hotel. He said that although he was not allowed to talk to other detainees, he had meditated, prayed, watched the news, gone for swims and developed a taste for Mövenpick strawberry sorbet. 'I was never tortured,' he added brightly. 'Actually, I was given the best service, to be honest with you, by the Saudi government.'[3]

One of the world's richest men was sounding incredibly grateful for his captivity. It was a remarkable demonstration of MbS's power to silence his potential critics. The Ritz-Carlton 'shakedown' neutralised potential rivals too.

Alwaleed was MbS's cousin and just one of a dozen senior princes detained. Among them was another cousin: Prince Miteb bin Abdullah, the head of the National Guard and son of the previous king. Saudi officials disclosed that the price tag for his release had been more than $1 billion.[4] Publicising such an enormous figure was in itself a way of destroying a rival's reputation and with it perhaps his chances of ever acceding to the throne.

Another potential threat to MbS's accession was Miteb's brother, Prince Turki, who had trained as a fighter pilot and served as governor of Riyadh. He too was detained and reportedly still locked away a year later.[5] It was reported that Turki's top military aide, Major General Ali al-Qahtani, died after being beaten in custody, aged just fifty-five.

'I have great confidence in King Salman and the crown prince of Saudi Arabia, they know exactly what they are doing,' President Trump tweeted in support of the detentions on 6 November. 'Some of those they are harshly treating have been "milking" the country for years!'

The US president's tweet read like permission for MbS to carry on, regardless. It may not have been a coincidence that Trump's endorsement followed on from a telephone call a few days earlier, in which he had tried to persuade King Salman to hold the first listing of the Saudi state oil company, Aramco, on an American stock exchange.

Aside from Alwaleed, Jamal Khashoggi knew several of the businessmen well – including Waleed Ibrahim, chairman of the Middle East Broadcasting Center, and Saleh Kamel, another billionaire businessman and head of a multinational conglomerate. Networking with the Saudi elite was second nature to this well-known journalist – and he followed the news with grim fascination from Tysons Corner in Virginia. If billionaires were being locked up, it surely vindicated the decision of a journalist without the funds to protect himself to flee the kingdom just a few months earlier. 'It was tough. Some were insulted. Some were hit. Some claim they were electrocuted,' Khashoggi said of the Ritz-Carlton affair afterwards, though the Saudis denied any abuse or deaths had occurred.[6]

'Jamal said he received a phone call from one of the hotel guests to say he had paid $400 million,' recalled Saad Djebbar, his lawyer friend in London. 'The friend had handed over the money and he got no receipt!'

'It was very upsetting to him, the icing on the cake,' said Khaled Saffuri, a friend in Washington. 'He thought it was typical MbS thuggery, which was making Saudi Arabia an impossible place.'

Relatives of some of those detained would later thank him in person for writing about the affair in the *Washington Post*, where he called it the 'Night of the Long Knives'. 'Mohammed bin Salman is acting like Putin,' he wrote, accusing the prince of imposing selective justice to centralise his own power. He also pointed out that the prince had himself spent $500 million on a luxury yacht in 2015. 'The buck stops at the leader's door,' he concluded. 'We are a kingdom of silence no longer.'[7]

Eyewitnesses said among those working in the hotel were Brigadeer General Maher Abdulaziz Mutreb, the commander of the Rapid Intervention Group who later intercepted Jamal Khashoggi in Istanbul; and Saud al-Qahtani, MbS's social media czar, who took part in hotel interrogations and who had earlier banned the Saudi journalist from writing. Alan Bender, a Canadian businessman visiting the kingdom at the time of the Ritz-Carlton detentions, claimed to NBC News that Qahtani had 'bragged to me that they slapped and hung some detainees upside down'.[8] It was a chilling indication of what might happen to those who found themselves on the wrong side of the crown prince.

Most of the businessmen and royals were eventually released, though fifty-six were still in custody three months later. By the week of Khashoggi's disappearance, almost a year later, the crown prince said the number who had refused to reach a settlement had fallen to eight. A further eighty-seven had confessed to charges against them, the government said.

MbS had predicted the operation would result in cash and assets worth around $100 billion being transferred to the state coffers; a figure equivalent to $106 billion was later confirmed, though nobody knew the truth.[9] 'Is this also about sending a message that, as we say in America, there's a new sheriff in town?' Norah O'Donnell of CBS's 60 Minutes asked MbS the following March.[10]

'Absolutely, absolutely,' he replied.

'It was an opportunity for the crown prince to settle some scores and to fatten the coffers of the kingdom,' Bob Jordan, a former US ambassador to Saudi Arabia, told me. 'At the time they were bleeding money, largely due to the war in Yemen.'

The incident seemed to recall an episode from MbS's teenage years, reported by the New Yorker, when he had allegedly used his family status to cajole $30 million from wealthy businessmen for his personal investment fund: those he approached were apparently so fearful of disobeying him that they handed the young prince the money.

Around the same time that MbS raised the $30 million, a Saudi land registry official received an envelope with a bullet inside it, after refusing to co-operate with the prince on a property takeover. After that incident, diplomats confirmed to me that MbS had earned the nickname 'Abu Rasasa' or 'Father of the Bullet' – though the prince blamed others for corruption, by trying to exploit his name and connections during his late teens.

The royal family's abuse of its power was a subject Khashoggi referred to several times in his *Washington Post* columns. The journalist pointed out that fewer than 40 per cent of Saudis own their own homes, as Saudi royals monopolise land ownership, even confiscating property from those too powerless to stop them.[11] 'The princes constitute a financial and moral burden on the state,' he concluded, although he also applauded King Salman's decision to order all princes to pay their own water, electric and telephone bills.[12]

If 'Father of the Bullet' made MbS sound like an Italian mafia boss inside the kingdom, that reputation was further enhanced on the world stage by the apparent kidnapping of Saad Hariri, the prime minister of Lebanon – another royal initiative which suggested that the crown prince believed he could do whatever he liked and was beyond anyone's control.

On 3 November 2017, the day before the Ritz-Carlton round-ups began, Hariri had flown to Riyadh for talks after an apparent summons from King Salman. Hariri was a dual Lebanese-Saudi national, with a home in Riyadh, his Lebanese family having made its fortune in construction there. The prime minister had also been told he would accompany the Saudi crown prince on a camping trip to the desert the following day. There was no standard ceremonial greeting at Riyadh airport. Instead, Hariri was placed under Saudi guard, and his mobile phone was confiscated.

The camping trip into the desert with MbS was postponed until after Hariri agreed to read a resignation speech on Saudi television, in which he denounced Iran and its Lebanese ally, Hezbollah. Hariri said the Arab world would 'cut off the hands which wickedly extend to it', and that he feared for his life. The words he read, however, did not sound like his own. It was reported that two Saudi officials had interrogated and threatened him; and that one of them was Saud al-Qahtani. The

New York Times reported that Hariri had not been allowed to go home and change into a suit before delivering his farewell to the Lebanese people, having to ask guards to fetch the suit for him instead.[13]

Western diplomats concluded that, because Iranian-built missiles were being fired at Saudi Arabia from Yemen, MbS had decided to force Hariri out and replace him with a leader who would help curb Iranian influence wherever it appeared, including Lebanon. Hariri's elder brother, Bahaa, was reportedly the replacement MbS preferred. It took a hastily arranged visit to Riyadh by President Macron of France before Saad Hariri was released, and his resignation was rescinded a few weeks later.

In his *Washington Post* column, Jamal Khashoggi saw the incident as a product of the 'Trump effect' – MbS's strong bond with the American president over their shared hatred of Iran had encouraged impulsive decision-making in the royal palace. 'MbS's rash actions are deepening tensions and undermining the security of the Gulf states and the region as a whole,' he wrote. It was another remark which would have prompted fury in Riyadh.

Just before the Lebanese debacle, Khashoggi spoke anonymously to Thomas Friedman, foreign affairs columnist for the *New York Times*, about the crown prince's social reforms. In the interview, he still tried to emphasise the positives while noting the negatives, though MbS's autocratic behaviour both at home and abroad was leaving the positive ledger increasingly in debit. 'This guy saved Saudi Arabia from a slow death,' he said of MbS, 'but he needs to broaden his base. It is good he is freeing the House of Saud of the influence of the clergy, but he is also not allowing any second opinion of his political and economic decisions.'[14]

The arrest of the economist Essam al-Zamil continued to

weigh heavily on him. In fact, he feared that the high-profile detentions of eleven princes at the Ritz-Carlton hotel would divert attention from the intellectuals, journalists and religious scholars languishing in jail, some of them in solitary confinement. 'They had never met or demonstrated,' he wrote. 'Their only form of protest was their ideas.'[15]

Later, after Khashoggi's disappearance, Thomas Friedman would describe him as 'this big teddy bear of a man, who only wanted to see his government reform in a more inclusive, transparent way'.[16]

Another battle Khashoggi fought in his newspaper columns was for the right of women to drive in the kingdom, which the journalist had campaigned for as editor of *Al Watan* in 2007. Back then he had bypassed a Saudi ban on public debate over the issue by publishing articles about a woman riding a camel, a donkey or a bicycle instead.

The best-known women's rights activist was Loujain al-Hathloul, who was jailed for seventy-three days after attempting to drive her car into Saudi Arabia from the United Arab Emirates in 2014. In March 2018, she was detained again, this time by security men in the UAE itself. She was handcuffed and flown by private jet to a Saudi jail where she spent a few days. Then, in May, she was taken from her bed in her father's house in Riyadh and arrested again, just a month before the ban on driving was due to be lifted.

The month after her detention, Jamal Khashoggi told the *New Yorker* magazine of his fear that the Saudi crown prince was dangerously out of control. 'He can do whatever he wants now,' he said. 'All the checks and balances are gone.'[17]

The journalist was appalled that Hathloul and others were being punished and accused of treason for speaking to foreign media. From his exile he was saddened that he could not savour for himself a genuine moment of progress when women were allowed to drive, then appalled that the campaign's pioneers were being punished. 'The people who were arrested were not radicals,' he told *Vanity Fair*. 'The majority were reformers for women's rights and open society. He arrested them to spread fear. He is replacing religious intolerance with political closure.'[18]

If anyone was going to be allowed to claim credit for securing the right to drive, it would be the crown prince, and certainly not those women who campaigned for it. Loujain al-Hathloul's husband, Fahad al-Butairi, a Saudi actor and comedian, was also detained during a visit to Jordan, where he was handcuffed and blindfolded and then flown home. He deleted his Twitter account, with its millions of followers, and his marriage to Loujain ended in circumstances which he hasn't explained, but which suggested the couple's decision to part may not have been entirely theirs.

Human Rights Watch and Amnesty International alleged that Hathloul was just one of a dozen women's rights campaigners who were flogged, electrocuted and sexually harassed. The Associated Press quoted its sources as saying at least one was waterboarded and another attempted suicide.[19] The Saudi official press agency countered that they had made 'suspicious contact with foreign entities . . . providing financial support to hostile elements'.

In the meantime, Jamal Khashoggi, using his online pulpit at the *Washington Post*, called for the crown prince to release Hathloul and her fellow women drivers. 'They should be allowed to finally witness the results of their tears and toil,' he wrote.[20] When he tweeted about the Hathloul case, the online abuse aimed at him by Saudi trolls intensified. One critic said he was a Qatari spy, or even worse, a Turkish one: 'go and have your breakfast at the Turkish embassy in Washington,' his message read, 'and enjoy with them your achievements in the betrayal of your country.'

'You should correct your mistakes and return to your real home,' read another. 'Otherwise you will become a traitor to the state and to the people for ever.'

The Saudis naturally denied any mistreatment of Loujain al-Hathloul, but her sister Alia wrote in the *New York Times* that Saud al-Qahtani, MbS's media adviser, was 'present several times' when she was tortured and had threatened to kill her and throw her body into the Saudi sewage system.[21, 22] At least two women had seen him in the torture chamber. 'I will do whatever I like to you, and then I'll dissolve you and flush you down the toilet!' Qahtani was quoted as telling one female detainee.[23] 'He was the one giving all the orders for the torture and all the ideas for the torture,' said Lina al-Hathloul, another of Loujain's sisters.[24]

Saud al-Qahtani was also encouraging if not orchestrating the social media attacks on Jamal Khashoggi, and, it seemed, physical attacks on prisoners at the Ritz-Carlton in Riyadh. Now he was accused of threatening women who had campaigned for the right to drive.

Given that Brigadier General Mutreb, the head of the Istanbul hit squad, had also worked at the Ritz-Carlton, it seems likely that he and his men may have also been involved with Qahtani in the interrogation of women's rights activists. The women were reportedly held in an unused palace in Jeddah on the Red Sea coast before being moved to a jail, where conditions improved. When their trial opened in 2019, journalists and diplomats were forbidden from attending.

The journalist's own communications with MbS's media adviser had certainly not ceased. In May 2018, Qahtani invited him to return home safely from Washington. Khaled Saffuri said Khashoggi relayed the contents of the phone call just after it happened.

'Guess who called me today?' Khashoggi asked him. 'Saud al-Qahtani. He offered me to return to a high position. As adviser to the crown prince. He said you are our son, you are an asset.'

'Will you go?' Saffuri asked him.

The response was immediate: 'Are you kidding me? I don't trust them one bit. If they catch me, they will kill me.'[25]

Khashoggi had good reason to be afraid. In February 2018, he had taken the decision to denounce Qahtani in the pages of the *Washington Post*. He described how the crown prince used his aide to control all broadcast and digital content in Saudi Arabia, either by arresting critics or by rewarding compliant journalists with money and access to senior officials.

'Over the past 18 months,' he wrote, 'MbS's communications team within the Royal Court publicly has chastised, and worse, intimidated anyone who disagrees. Saud al-Qahtani, leader of that unit, has a blacklist and calls for Saudis to add names to it. Writers like me, whose criticism is offered respectfully, seem to be considered more dangerous than the more strident Saudi opposition based in London.'[26]

Had Khashoggi still lived in Saudi Arabia, such a broadside would have been unthinkable. 'Just think twice about sharing or liking whatever isn't fully in line with the official government groupthink,' Khashoggi warned his readers. Once again, the journalist was making a powerful enemy even more angry.

Qahtani revealed just how powerful he was in his own words. In a column for Al Arabiya News that April, he recalled his own first meeting with his boss, the Saudi crown prince. 'He discussed with me the sources he read and liked . . .

with the spirit of a colleague, not a superior,' Qahtani wrote admiringly.

MbS had ordered him to reorganise the palace's media unit. 'I want you to completely devote yourself to this task,' Qahtani quoted the prince as saying. 'He then lowered his voice and continued, "This is important to me personally, and I do not want anyone to know about it." He made me feel that it is a huge classified task.'[27]

Qahtani had revealed the beginning of his secret and intimate relationship with MbS; an intimacy which would make it harder for the crown prince to distance himself from his aide when Jamal Khashoggi disappeared in Istanbul six months later.

~

From his exile in America, the Saudi journalist was watching his country's descent into further repression with increasing despair. He complained that the Trump administration had 'zero interest' in inspiring Middle Eastern democracy, and he was horrified to discover that at the Riyadh international book fair a title called *Against the Arab Spring* had gone on display.

Khashoggi wrote that he still asked himself the same question when he woke up in Virginia every morning: whether he had been right to speak out; but any ambivalence about his need to escape had gone, in the face of yet more arrests at home. 'Religious fanaticism that had tarnished Saudi Arabia's image for decades has given way to a new and perhaps more pernicious fanaticism,' he wrote. 'A cult of blind loyalty to our leader. That is a Faustian bargain that I will not make.'[28]

To make matters worse, the crown prince was being given warm receptions in Europe and the United States. The month before his official visit to Washington, MbS invited David

Ignatius of the *Washington Post* into his palace for a late-night interview.

'We want to work with believers,' the prince explained, at the end of a day which saw reshuffles of government and military jobs by royal decree, including the appointment of a woman cabinet minister. Ignatius asked if human rights activists would be released ahead of the prince's trip to America.

'If it works, don't fix it,' came the reply, as MbS pointed out that American and Saudi standards were not the same.[29]

In a speech in April 2018, Khashoggi fondly recalled how long voting lines in Tunisia and Egypt following the Arab Spring had shown that Arabs were ready for democracy.[30] 'In Saudi Arabia there are serious reforms that Prince Mohammed is leading. Many of my Saudi colleagues are saying I should support them. I do support them,' he said, before adding: 'Saudi leaders are still not interested in democracy . . . they are saying that absolute monarchy is our preferred form of government.' When he criticised the record of the crown prince, the attacks by online trolls increased.

'I advise you to look for a funeral parlour in America and pay in advance,' read one. 'After this article, your return home is impossible.'

In August 2018, Canada's foreign minister, Chrystia Freeland, also became the target of abuse on Twitter. Her ministry had issued a call – in Arabic – for the release of Samar Badawi, the sister of Raif Badawi, an infamous blogger who had been sentenced to ten years in prison and lashed in a public square. Within hours, the Saudis announced that they were expelling the Canadian ambassador, withdrawing Saudi investments, cancelling flights, recalling home over 8,000 students and no longer buying wheat and barley from the Canadian prairies.

In an echo of the imagery of 9/11, a tweet allegedly linked

to the Saudi government showed an Air Canada jet heading towards Toronto's famous skyscraper, the CN Tower. 'Sticking one's nose where it doesn't belong,' the accompanying text said menacingly.

Inevitably, Jamal Khashoggi weighed into the debate from what he believed was a safe distance, warning the crown prince that he was destroying the reputation his overseas tour had sought to strengthen. 'Canada raised the flag against human rights abuses,' he wrote. 'We cannot arbitrarily arrest female activists and expect the world to turn a blind eye.'[31]

The same month, surveillance experts at Citizen Lab in the University of Toronto concluded that the Saudi government had infiltrated the mobile phone of Omar Abdulaziz, a 26-year-old Saudi dissident living in Montreal. He was well known for his criticism of the Saudi royal family on social media. More importantly, he was in regular contact with Jamal Khashoggi.

Abdulaziz claimed that in June 2017 he inadvertently down-loaded spyware, by clicking on a text message designed to look as if it was from a well-known courier company informing him about a delivery. The spyware allowed the hacker to discover which keys Abdulaziz had pressed on his phone. The hacker could listen to calls and turn the phone's camera and micro-phone into surveillance devices. Abdulaziz claimed that two of his brothers in Jeddah were arrested in a police raid as a result of this monitoring.

Jamal Khashoggi, unaware of any danger, had sent Abdulaziz's phone more than 400 WhatsApp messages from the autumn of 2017 onwards – and many of them were critical of the crown prince. 'Arrests are unjustified . . . but tyranny has no logic, but he loves force, oppression and needs to show them off,' Khashoggi had written to him in May 2018. 'He is like a beast "PacMan" – the more victims he eats, the more he wants. I will not be surprised that the oppression will reach even those who are cheering him, then others and others and so on. God knows.'

Abdulaziz believed the phone hack could have revealed Khashoggi's communications – and therefore played a role in prompting the operation against him in Istanbul. He later filed a lawsuit, claiming that an Israeli software company, the NSO Group, had spied on him. The company countered that its products were licensed solely to fight terrorism and crime and that their business contracts were vetted by the Israeli government. Israeli news reports said the Saudi government had paid $55 million for the use of 'Pegasus' spyware in 2017.[32]

Saudi Arabia had always firmly supported the Palestinian cause, but the use of Israeli technology suggested a different narrative: that MbS was prepared to do business with Tel Aviv to get what he wanted. Both Riyadh and Tel Aviv shared a view of Iran as a regional threat and both were talking to President Trump's son-in-law, Jared Kushner, about a peace plan for Israel and the Palestinians; but the main concern of Omar Abdulaziz in Canada in the summer of 2018 was his personal safety rather than Middle East politics.

In an echo of Khashoggi's own experience, Abdulaziz was visited by two Saudi emissaries who asked him to return home and work for MbS. The messengers said they had been sent by Saud al-Qahtani. They held out the promise that he could meet MbS the day after he returned, with a hotel in Jeddah already booked for him. They even told Abdulaziz that Khashoggi was thinking of returning home too; and they recommended that he visit the Saudi embassy in Ottawa to make arrangements. 'Omar is a loser because he is going to jail,' one of the Saudis told him, when he asked what would happen if he refused their offer to return. However, a friend advised him not to reject any such offer and only to meet Saudi government officials in public places. That friend was none other than Jamal Khashoggi, who would tragically fail to follow his own advice that autumn in Istanbul.

Faced with a well-organised Twitter campaign against them, the two Saudis had conceived plans for an 'electronic army' of their own on social media, an army they called the 'cyber bees', designed to debunk Saudi state propaganda. The plan involved sending foreign SIM cards to young Saudis, so that they could be free to criticise their rulers on social media, without the authorities making the connection between local Saudi phone numbers and their Twitter accounts. Some 200 cards were in use by the time Khashoggi was killed.[33]

Abdulaziz claimed that Khashoggi had given him $5,000 for the project and pledged up to $30,000, promising to find more money from rich donors; but in August 2018, Abdulaziz heard that Saudi officials had become aware of the 'cyber bees' plan. 'How did they know?' Khashoggi asked him in a text message.

'There must have been a gap,' Abdulaziz replied, fearing that someone in his network of contacts might have leaked the plan.

Three minutes later, Khashoggi wrote back: 'God help us.'[34]

Writing articles critical of the regime from thousands of miles away was one thing. Building what looked like a free-speech network inside the kingdom itself appeared to take Khashoggi's opposition to a new and precarious level – precarious because the Saudi authorities may have known about it from intercepting Abdulaziz's phone.

The 4 July American Independence Day celebrations in Washington that summer of 2018 were particularly difficult for Jamal Khashoggi. He'd been invited to brunch by Khaled Saffuri, but ended up staying all day, joining Saffuri's family at a firework display at a country club that evening. Saffuri says the journalist was so lonely that he didn't have the heart to tell him to go home.

The Saudi never turned down speaking invitations at universities, think-tanks and Silicon Valley firms, in what friends described as an attempt to keep himself busy, to distract himself from his estrangement from his homeland. On Khashoggi's last visit to the Washington office of another American friend that summer, he asked her: 'Can I just give this up? Can I just not do this any more? I'm thinking that for two years, I want to go to a faraway island.'[35]

'I said, "No, you can't,"' the friend replied. 'You are in a war.'

Instead of flying to a faraway island, Jamal Khashoggi flew to Istanbul.

7

A WOMAN IN ISTANBUL

'Mr Khashoggi was a complex man . . . his was a
compartmentalised life, perhaps necessarily so, and
no one claims to have known him in all of his life's
dimensions.'

— Agnes Callamard, UN special rapporteur on
extrajudicial executions, June 2019

On 10 September 2018, in the month before he disappeared,
the Saudi journalist flew to Istanbul, where he would stay for
over two weeks. Before the flight, he met his friend Nihad
Awad at a coffee shop in Virginia to discuss their joint project – a new human rights organisation called Democracy for
the Arab World Now, known as DAWN.

Awad was the founder of the Council on American–Islamic
Relations, which worked to combat prejudice and discrimi-
nation against Muslims in the United States; Khashoggi's idea
was to establish a similar organisation that focused on reporting
human rights abuses in the Middle East.

'The *Washington Post* was not enough for him,' Awad told
me. 'I was astonished by the amount of energy he had . . .
he had more energy to effect change in Saudi Arabia and the
Arab world.'

Awad had started paying Khashoggi to raise funds and find volunteers, but although the pair met to discuss the new venture two or three times a week, the journalist was struggling to drum up financial support. The plan was to give the project a soft launch upon his return from Istanbul; it would be necessarily low-key, because they expected the Saudi government and its allies to discredit the organisation with personal attacks on Khashoggi himself, which it was feared could in turn increase political pressure on his son, Salah, living in Jeddah.

The two had discussed the journalist's personal safety in a 'brainstorming session' on the potential obstacles DAWN might face. Physical harm was at the bottom of their list of concerns. 'You work for the *Washington Post*, you are a resident of Virginia and you are not violent,' Awad had told him. 'Why should anyone harm you physically? They try to drown your voice with smear campaigns and put pressure on your family, but you are under the protection of the United States. God forbid if anything happened to you, the world would be turned upside down.'

'Yeah, yeah, that makes sense,' Khashoggi had replied. The subject was dropped.

The journalist told him he would be flying to Istanbul to 'settle for a bit', to be closer to his family. 'Whenever family issues were mentioned, he was very sad,' Awad said. 'Many times, I would see tears in his eyes.'

He was an Arab intellectual living in exile; his wife had divorced him and both she and his eldest son were banned from leaving Saudi Arabia. In the meantime, some of his friends were in prison, his royal sponsors had deserted him and a vicious online trolling operation was blackening his reputation in response to his columns in the *Washington Post*. Khashoggi hoped that Istanbul, the gateway between East and West, might ease his sense of homelessness and provide a path to greater happiness. He checked into the Grand Hyatt hotel, on top of a hill on the European shore overlooking the Bosporus Strait, and began making arrangements to get married.

He had met Hatice Cengiz, a Turkish woman twenty-four years his junior, at a conference in the city four months earlier, on 6 May. The event was organised by the Al Sharq Forum, a think-tank backed by Qatari money with offices in London and Istanbul. Entitled 'Towards New Security Arrangements for the Middle East and North Africa Region', it was the kind of event Khashoggi had been attending for years in his capacity as an expert on the Gulf, and he was a speaker in the opening panel discussion.

When she met him, Cengiz was a 36-year-old academic, working on her doctorate in Gulf studies. A fluent Arabic speaker, she had obtained Khashoggi's phone number from a mutual friend, a Turkish journalist, and then asked him for an interview. 'He was a bit surprised by a Turk interested in Gulf countries,' she told me when we met less than four months after Khashoggi's disappearance. 'I knew he was a well-connected journalist. I did not know anything about his private life.'

Cengiz speaks Turkish quickly and there is a bookish intensity about her. Her desire to speak about her fiancé is occasionally held in check by an understandable suspicion of journalists prying into the details of what was her private life, before it fell apart. She did not choose to become the face of a campaign for justice and she's wary of the publicity. She wears a headscarf and wide-rimmed spectacles and the venue she has chosen for our meeting is the upstairs room of an empty café in Istanbul. For her safety, she declined to give me the address until the night beforehand and she's accompanied by Ahmet, a plainclothes Turkish police guard, assigned to her in the aftermath of the disappearance of the man she had been about to marry. She is both the guardian of Khashoggi's memory and, as with others close to him, possibly a potential target herself.

Cengiz had grown up as one of five children, the daughter of a successful self-made businessman who ran a bakery and imported cutlery. Her family is from Erzurum, a religiously conservative town near Turkey's far-eastern border. She was sent to a religious school in the town of Bursa. Her mother is, she says, a housewife. Cengiz herself comes across as a far more liberated woman than her family background might suggest.

She studied social sciences at Istanbul University and learned Arabic in Cairo, also studying in Jordan. She researched how the Sunni–Shia sectarian divide helped create ISIS and al-Qaeda; she was interested, too, in the role of the Gulf states in either encouraging or thwarting the Arab Spring uprisings of 2011; and she wrote her thesis on whether the Sultanate of Oman and its tradition of religious tolerance could serve as a role model for the Muslim world.

Khashoggi's age, sixty, what she calls his 'maturity', was part of what made him attractive to her. She says she was wary of conventional marriages and she liked the fact that he was well-travelled and well-read. Like the journalist himself, she was trying to find a balance between Western liberal ideas and her devout Muslim faith. To her, Khashoggi's defining character-istics seemed to be his open-heartedness and warmth, and his expressions of loneliness made her feel sorry for him.

At their first meeting at the academic conference in Istanbul, Khashoggi had not held back in his criticism of Mohammed bin Salman, the Saudi crown prince.

'He thinks he is the only person who can save Saudi Arabia from this ignorance and backwardness,' he told her. 'The prince never lends an ear to others. He thinks he is the only one who has the magic recipe to govern the country.'

She asked him if he had a plan to return to Saudi Arabia.

'No, I just want to speak my mind freely,' he said. 'I've seen what happened to most of my friends. They are in jail. I don't want the same fate as them.'

'Will your prince soon be king?'

'Yes, and he will rule the country for fifty years.'[1]

After interviewing him at the conference, they began exchanging text messages and emails. In mid-July she called Turan Kişlakçi, the Turkish journalist who had given her his phone number, with a request: the Saudi was returning to Istanbul to see her. She wanted them both to be invited to a concert of Turkish and Arabic traditional songs on a Friday night the following month. It would be their first date.

'He started to tell me how he was alone and how he was unhappy,' she said. 'I was very surprised. Suddenly I saw a completely different human being, and then a special, direct dialogue began.'[2]

The Saudi told friends in the middle of August that he wanted to marry her, but he also knew that a three-times-divorced Arab journalist who could no longer return home safely to Saudi Arabia – and who had known her just a few months – might have a problem gaining her Turkish father's consent.

'You have to talk with her father,' Khashoggi told Turan Kişlakçi, who agreed to host in his office and act as translator for the Saudi's first meeting with Mr Cengiz in Istanbul in mid-September. When Khashoggi asked for his daughter's hand in marriage, he encountered resistance.

'Hatice's father asked me many times if Jamal was married or not,' Kişlakçi recalls. 'Jamal told me he wasn't married. But the father said, "I know Arabs. I visited Saudi Arabia many times. Arabs cannot live with one woman. They must have two or three.'''

After that initial meeting, Kişlakçi says Cengiz's father was still resisting his daughter's choice. He called Kişlakçi, the go-between, to a private discussion about Khashoggi's suitability as a husband. 'He is an old man, my daughter is in her thirties, how is this going to work?' Kişlakçi recalls the father saying.

'Hatice loves him – and he loves her,' the Turkish journalist replied. 'So you can't do anything.'

Four days later, Mr Cengiz requested another meeting in a café. According to Kişlakçi's account, it was also attended by Hatice's brother and lasted for four hours. Mr Cengiz was demanding further financial guarantees for his daughter, beyond Khashoggi's pledge to buy a home in Istanbul. 'Leave the other things for Hatice and Jamal to decide, not you,' Kişlakçi said.

'She cannot think about the future herself because she is in love,' her father replied.

It was pointed out to Mr Cengiz that, as Khashoggi was living in exile, his new wife would not be permitted by the Saudi authorities to visit the holy sites at Mecca and Medina. This was not what worried him: what naturally concerned him was whether his daughter would be well looked after. The Turkish journalist tried to end the meeting by reading the Fatiha, the opening verses of the Koran, intended to mark the start of a new chapter in the couple's life together, but Mr Cengiz again objected.

Kişlakçi says it was first and foremost Hatice's father who demanded proof in writing of Khashoggi's divorce. He also says Khashoggi asked his fiancée to persuade her father to drop this requirement of proof, but that she 'shared her father's concern'. The Turkish journalist had no idea his friend would take the risk of going to the Saudi consulate to collect the paperwork required. 'If he had told me, I wouldn't have allowed him to go,' Kişlakçi said.

In the midst of these marriage negotiations, Khashoggi's youngest son, Abdullah, came to stay with his father for a week in Istanbul. Cengiz had been nagging her future husband to tell Abdullah about the marriage beforehand but Khashoggi had refused, telling her, 'At my age, I don't tell my family details about my private life.'

When Abdullah arrived, his father introduced his prospective new bride and the three of them went sightseeing. 'Maybe marrying a Turk was a bit strange for Abdullah,' Cengiz told me. 'But he welcomed it. I told him we would be like brother and sister because our ages are close. I really liked him very much.'

The couple were keen to marry quickly, though no date had been set. 'He was sixty years old . . . he had very limited time,' Cengiz said later. Both of them wanted children and he saw the marriage as a new beginning, a break with the most troubled period of his life.

'I miss my country very much,' he had told her. 'I miss my friends and family very much. I feel this pain every single moment.'

Her father's concern about multiple wives was more prescient than Mr Cengiz or his lovestruck daughter could know. For it turned out that Jamal Khashoggi had, in fact, married for a fourth time only a few months earlier. His love life was far more complicated than this Turkish family could have imagined.

~

On 2 June 2018, a month after he first met Hatice Cengiz, Jamal Khashoggi had got married in an Islamic wedding ceremony in Alexandria, Virginia, not far from his home in the suburbs of Washington DC. Earlier that morning he had given a wedding ring to a fifty-year-old woman he met off a plane at the city's Dulles airport. He had known Hanan el-Atr, who was Egyptian, for the past decade, and although she was now working as an air stewardess, she had formerly been a trainee on an Arab newspaper. El-Atr still counted several prominent Arab journalists as friends, many of whom were friends of Khashoggi too.

El-Atr told me the couple's friendship intensified after November 2016, when Khashoggi was living in Jeddah under virtual house arrest: he had been ordered by the crown prince's media adviser not to talk or write. The Egyptian phoned and texted him from her travels in the hope of providing emotional support.

The following year, Khashoggi flew to attend a conference in the United Arab Emirates but was denied entry to the country. The UAE is Saudi Arabia's closest ally and the ban was interpreted by friends, including el-Atr, as a final warning that maybe it was safest if he left the kingdom. In el-Atr's account, Khashoggi had been suffering from depression for several years, to the point of seeking professional help in London. His flight to America in the summer of 2017 liberated him as a journalist, but it also took an enormous toll on his mental health.

'His body was in America but his mind and heart were in Saudi Arabia,' el-Atr said, recalling that she would often call him from the Middle East at 7 a.m., Washington time. 'My job was to wake him up, to encourage him and to motivate him,' she told me.

In March 2018, el-Atr flew to Washington to attend a dinner thrown by friends in honour of Khashoggi's sixtieth birthday. A friend took a photograph of the couple smiling as they sat behind a large chocolate birthday cake. The following month she visited him for another two days and she says that this was when he asked her to marry him. However, a close friend of Khashoggi's told me he may have married her out of a sense of responsibility for what had befallen her: el-Atr had been questioned by the security service of a Middle Eastern country for ten days, because of her friendship with the dissident journalist. 'He was really upset and concerned for her,' the friend said. 'I think he married her out of respect and out of guilt.'

The question of where they would live was certainly left unanswered. The Egyptian didn't want to leave her job in the Middle East and had speculated about relocating to Qatar or Oman, but he told her that if he returned to live in the Gulf, it could anger Saudi Arabia and possibly lead to his forcible repatriation there.

El-Atr, like Hatice Cengiz a few months later, wanted to be sure Khashoggi was really single before she married him. 'I asked him, "Is it clear that you have no other woman?"' she told me. '"No, it is only you, Hanan," he said.'

One of the witnesses to the marriage was Khaled Saffuri. He says he had lined up two imams to conduct the ceremony but that Khashoggi rejected them both, because they insisted he attend marriage preparation classes first. 'Jamal said, "I don't want this headache, I want someone to do it quickly,"' Saffuri recalled.

The ceremony itself was kept secret. El-Atr says this was because she feared reprisals against her family for marrying the controversial Saudi journalist. The union was never legally registered with a certificate – and Saffuri says Khashoggi was in no hurry to sort out the paperwork.

Photographs taken on 2 June show the happy couple in Virginia beaming for the camera, el-Atr dressed and veiled in white, holding a bouquet of white flowers. Khashoggi's youngest son, Abdullah, did meet Hanan el-Atr after the journalist's death, when she informed him that she had married him; but the Khashoggi family have not formally recognised the Egyptian as his last wife.

The last time el-Atr says she saw him was an overnight stay in a hotel in New York on 6 September, less than a month before he disappeared. He had told her he was planning to buy a house in Turkey, in case he ever needed a Turkish passport; but he never told the Egyptian he was engaged to be married to a Turk. 'Jamal did not tell me about another woman,' she said. 'I felt he was hiding something. He believed in many wives – he was a Muslim, Saudi man.' Although el-Atr vehemently denies it, Khashoggi's friends claim he may have told her he was divorcing her during that final meeting in New York.

On 25 September, she called him to say she expected to be in Washington in about a month – she says Khashoggi agreed to meet her then. On 30 September, during his last weekend in London before he was killed, Khashoggi left two messages on her phone, wishing her a happy birthday, and it was the last she heard from him.

She learned about his disappearance in Istanbul from her Twitter feed two days later. 'I hope he went quickly, without any pain,' she told me, holding back the tears. 'Jamal never even put the security chain on the back of the door before we went to sleep. He used to laugh and say, "Why would they harm me here?"'

~

Hatice Cengiz knew nothing about el-Atr and neither did many of Khashoggi's friends. 'What does she want?' the Turkish fiancée asked the *Washington Post* later. 'I suspect that this is an attempt to discredit him and hurt his reputation.'

However, there was no doubt the Saudi had concealed a really important truth from his wife-to-be. His fourth marriage, to an Egyptian, risked making a mockery of what Khashoggi had told the Turk. 'Dear Hatice, I have my health and everything else, but I have nobody to share life with.'[3] It is possible, as several of Khashoggi's friends claimed, that he stumbled into the marriage with el-Atr in desperate need of company, and then told her he was divorcing her after his romance with Cengiz had made some progress; it is also possible that he considered living parallel lives in Washington and Istanbul.

Khashoggi's friend, the Palestinian journalist Azzam Tamimi, said it was common for Arabs to 'have a second wife and a third wife and the first wife doesn't know'.

'He didn't need to lie. He wasn't the type,' Cengiz told me. 'I think he would have divorced her.'

If the Saudi journalist wasn't living an emotional double life in his final months in Washington and Istanbul, he was certainly searching for rapid solutions to his loneliness. He had careered into one marriage so quickly that it was never legally certified, though Cengiz was certain that his subsequent engagement to her was serious for both of them. To use her own word, Khashoggi was 'broken', living in exile apart from his family, with the jailing of Saudi activists weighing increasingly on his mind.

'He was having nightmares,' his fiancée said, 'they were full of their voices and silhouettes. At times he couldn't sleep so he was taking pills, a sedative, because he was worried about what was happening to his country.'

Another question, apart from the divorce papers, was where the newlyweds were going to live. He told her he had applied for US citizenship, that he wanted to feel the world's political pulse from Washington DC, to become an influential journalist there. He had begun sending her his draft articles for the *Washington Post* and she would call him back with her thoughts.

Cengiz had never been to America and was only in her first year of her doctorate at Fatih Sultan Mehmet University in Istanbul; her father suggested they should stay in Turkey for the time being; but Khashoggi was planning to return to Virginia soon after the marriage.

'I told him to come and work with us on radio and television stations in Turkey,' said Turan Kişlakçi. 'He said we wouldn't pay him enough money, that he didn't want to leave the *Washington Post*.'

Fulfilling the wishes of his future father-in-law, he bought a flat in the 'Europe Apartments', a new luxury development close to the E5 highway on Istanbul's European side. It had a glass-fronted balcony overlooking a series of water fountains, with pass-only access for pedestrians, and a manned checkpoint for cars. By about 26 September, the paperwork was complete and they had begun to move basic furniture into the flat. 'Jamal thought this was a win-win for him,' Cengiz said. 'If he had a place, people from Saudi Arabia could come and visit him. He was feeling very, very safe in Turkey.'

The two discussed how they would obtain the documentation confirming his divorce from his ex-wife in Saudi Arabia. She asked him if he had been threatened since he had fled to America: he told her the relationship with his home country was not one of hatred, that if he was in serious trouble, his government pension would have been cut. It had not been. He had stayed away from Qatar since the summer of 2017, precisely to avoid allegations of complicity with a foreign power. She asked him if the Turkish politicians he knew could help obtain the paperwork. He said he didn't want to bother anyone with his private affairs.

'Could the Saudi ambassador in Ankara help?' she suggested.

'The ambassador is a friend of mine and we are from the same city,' Khashoggi told her. 'But I don't want to put him in a situation where he'd be under strain, or where he would have to say no.'[4]

Their first visit to a registry office in Istanbul's Fatih district was on 28 September, the last day of what had been an eighteen-day visit. Cengiz acted as his Turkish translator. She recalls his concern when a Turkish official asked him about his marital status. He enquired whether it would be easier if they married abroad but was told the same documents would be required from the Saudi authorities, wherever their union was registered. The meeting only lasted a few minutes. Closed-circuit television camera footage, leaked to the Turkish press, later showed them holding hands as they left.

'He was a bit tense about it,' she said. 'He saw that this visit to the consulate was the only way to get married. He turned around and said, "What shall we do?"'

'You know best what to do,' she replied.

'Shall we try it?' he then asked her.

He had tried to obtain the necessary paperwork online and in the United States. This was now his only option. Spontaneously, with no appointment or phone call to say they were coming, they took a taxi to the Saudi consulate, arriving at 11.50 a.m. 'Let's have a go,' he said, 'and, *inshallah*, nothing bad will happen and they will say it is not going to be a problem.'

Cengiz recalls no fear in him, just mild concern. He had on previous occasions talked about the possibility of being interrogated or detained, but she also knew him to be prone to emotional outbursts which quickly passed; in calmer moments, he had told her he did not fear for himself and claimed he did not fear the Saudi crown prince either.

'When I am not in my country, I don't think there's that kind of threat,' he told her. He added that he always felt he was in 'direct contact' with Saudi Arabia. 'Maybe it was wishful thinking,' she said, 'but he thought he had an open channel.'

That first Friday, 28 September, he left his two phones with her as he felt uncomfortable about handing them over to Saudi security inside. His personal safety was not his concern. She waited for him on the pavement and soon began to worry. She feared he might miss his plane to London and was on the point of asking a security guard where he was. It was forty-five minutes to one hour before Khashoggi emerged, safe and well. The Saudi staff had, he later told friends, 'panicked initially but they turned out to be very friendly. They promised to help me.'

He had enjoyed talking to his fellow countrymen, who recognised him as a Saudi media personality and told him they followed his posts on Twitter. It was agreed he should return the following Tuesday, when his paperwork would be ready.

Recordings of phone traffic between Riyadh and Istanbul show that the plot against Khashoggi began soon after he left the building, while he was waiting to board a 2.40 p.m. flight to London for the weekend.

'The enemy they had been looking for had arrived by foot,' Yasin Aktay, Khashoggi's friend and an adviser to President Erdoğan, explained to me. 'And then they started to plan.'

~

In at least two phone calls between Riyadh and the consulate that Friday, the future commander of the operation, Brigadier General Maher Abdulaziz Mutreb, spoke to a Saudi intelligence attaché in Istanbul, a man we will name 'SA'. We don't know who the 'Hatim' referred to here is:

Time: 2.22 p.m., Friday 28 September 2018

SA: I informed the communications office about the infor-
mation that Hatim gave.
MUTREB: Did you inform the communications office?
SA: Yes, I conveyed everything together with the videos.
MUTREB: Can you make sure it is closed, as normal?
Don't let anybody read it.
SA: Okay.
MUTREB: Thank you.
SA: Goodbye.

Turkish Intelligence, who recorded this conversation, are certain that the 'videos' SA referred to and sent back to Riyadh
were the closed-circuit camera footage of Khashoggi saying
goodbye to Cengiz and then entering the consulate earlier
that day. They would provide confirmation of the journalist's
appearance and identity.

SA talked about the 'communications office' again in a
second call. This is possibly a reference to the Saudi royal
court's media department – the so-called Centre for Studies
and Media Affairs, known as CSMARC. This was where Saud
al-Qahtani worked – the senior adviser to the crown prince
who had banned Khashoggi from writing and whom the journalist accused of intimidating the prince's critics.

In this call, the intelligence officer at the consulate was
beginning to sound anxious. Perhaps he was frightened of
getting involved in a clandestine operation against a fellow
countryman and media personality he had just enjoyed talking
to minutes earlier. SA needed to know whether Khashoggi
was a wanted man or not ('sought after'):

Time: 2.27 p.m.

SA: I talked to the communications office. He didn't want to give me full information. Do you understand me? I have not hidden it from you. He does not want to give me full information. Do you understand me?

MUTREB: Yes.

SA: Of course, I didn't tell him that I forwarded the letter. I just want to ask you a question.

MUTREB: Go ahead.

SA: Is Jamal, our brother who has just come to us, among the people sought by you?

MUTREB: There is nothing official, but it is known that he is among the people sought after.

SA: Though we did not receive any letter from our service regarding whether there is any problem or not on him.

MUTREB: What I mean is, even if you are going to chop off his head, he is not going to say anything.

SA: Yes, I have no doubt about it.

'Chop off his head': Brigadier General Mutreb had just made the shocking admission that there was carte blanche to do whatever they wanted with Khashoggi, even kill him. We don't know who the 'he' referred to in the next part of the conversation is:

MUTREB: But he is aware that he will come? Everything depends on time.

SA: What do you mean? I don't know that.

MUTREB: I am asking if he is aware that Khashoggi will reapply to the consulate on Tuesday?

SA: Oh, definitely. We are all shocked. I just spoke with him [Khashoggi]. I said 'How are you?'

MUTREB: Did you inform him at the time?

SA: Absolutely.

MUTREB: Did you give him information that Khashoggi will come back to the consulate on Tuesday?

SA: Yes, Tuesday ... we received information that Khashoggi will come on Tuesday. I gave the intelligence office the information that Khashoggi will come on Tuesday. In addition to this information, I added the videos.

MUTREB: May Allah be pleased.

SA: May Allah be pleased.

In a third call that Friday, a man we shall name AS, believed to be a senior official at the Ministry of Foreign Affairs in Riyadh, talked to the consul general, Mohammed al-Otaibi, in Istanbul:

Time: 7.08 p.m.

AS: I will tell you something. The head of state security called me.

AL-OTAIBI: Yes?

AS: They have got an assignment. I suppose they are asking for someone to be assigned from your delegation for a special issue – someone from your protocol staff.

Various names were then discussed for this special mission. They included the consulate's deputy head, a Saudi intelligence officer. The conversation continued:

AS: He wants him in Riyadh on Sunday or tomorrow. We are asking for the person responsible for your special and top-secret mission.

AL-OTAIBI: Our brother is trusted. No problem. Yes, sir.

AS: Send me his number now. I can send it to them an hour later so that they can call him. They will make the arrangements. Let him buy his ticket. Let him arrange it. Because there is a holiday, there is no time for correspondence. Otherwise this will drag on.

AL-OTAIBI: If this assignment is security-related, we have AR. Is he not useful?

AS: Yes, the assignment is security-related. The mission is a national duty. He is asking for him for just four to five days. It will remain between us. Both you and I will keep quiet for the sake of the consulate. Tell him that you gave me his number.

AL-OTAIBI: But the man's wife and children are here. Will it be a problem?

AS: How?

At 8.04 p.m., the consul general, Mohammed al-Otaibi, was heard talking to an intelligence officer we shall name AMA, one of his staff now being assigned the mission to fly to Riyadh. He was still concerned that his colleague might be exposed or compromised by leaving family members behind in Istanbul:

AMA: Is there anything?

AL-OTAIBI: Yes, there is an urgent training in Riyadh. They called me from Riyadh. They told me they asked for an official from protocol who was reliable and nationalist. The issue is very important. It is being developed rapidly . . . but the issue is top secret. Nobody should know at all. Even none of your friends will be informed.

Then later:

AL-OTAIBI: The best is you buy a ticket for yourself and family . . . the issue is top secret. Nobody should know at all, it is almost five days.

The Saudis had been given an unexpected opportunity to move against Jamal Khashoggi; but somebody who could be trusted was required to fly to the Saudi capital to help coordinate the operation, before the journalist returned to the consulate four days later. Blinded by love and desperate to get married, he was about to fall into their lap.

8

LAST WEEKEND IN LONDON

That Friday evening, while his fellow Saudis were plotting against him, Jamal Khashoggi flew to London for a long weekend.

'When I come back from London, this time there will be a home to go to,'[1] he told his fiancée excitedly before leaving Istanbul: with a newly purchased flat, and the Saudi consulate promising to provide the document he needed by the following Tuesday, the next phase of his life was rapidly falling into place.

On the Saturday morning he was due to speak at a conference, hosted by Middle East Monitor, a pro-Palestinian news website. The event was entitled 'Oslo at 25: A Legacy of Broken Promises'. The organiser, Daud Abdullah, had included Khashoggi as a late addition to the programme. He had suggested the journalist stay at a hotel, guaranteeing more anonymity than the Ambassadors in Euston, where most guests were staying.

'He had become a very prominent critic of the Saudi establishment,' Abdullah told me. 'I thought he should be more discreet.'

Khashoggi brushed away the concern and happily accepted the invitation to stay at the Ambassadors. 'He was not at all

paranoid or disturbed, he said he was looking forward to getting married,' Abdullah said.

The subject of his forthcoming marriage to Hatice Cengiz
would come up again over lunch, taken with a group of friends
including Wadah Khanfar, the former director general of Al
Jazeera television.

'You look different – this young lady has made you look ten
years younger!' Khanfar told him.

'It is true,' Khashoggi replied. 'Had I known, I would have
done this ten years earlier.'

They discussed whether he would become officially resident
in Istanbul after the wedding; Khashoggi said America would
still be his main base and indicated that he would not want to
cause a political problem between Turkey and Saudi Arabia
by moving to Istanbul permanently. He talked too about the
need to find a job for his youngest son, Abdullah, in either
the UK or US, somewhere safely outside the kingdom: the
Saudi government pressure his family faced as a result of his
journalism was never far from his mind.

His seven-minute conference address, which began just
before three o'clock, was a typical example of what he did
best – demystifying Saudi foreign policy, when the kingdom's
official representatives usually did a poor job of doing so, or
didn't bother at all.

He explained that the Saudi crown prince and Jared Kushner
had thrashed out the outline of a possible Middle East peace
deal which would confine a future Palestinian capital to Abu
Dis, a village outside Jerusalem. Until the Saudi king intervened over his son's head.

'The Saudis suddenly backed down,' Khashoggi told the audience in London. 'And a statement [has] come out, that the king
of Saudi Arabia, not the son, decided to revert back to the old

Saudi position. Which is a very smart position – which the Saudis always use – that we accept whatever the Palestinians accept. So it looked like Saudi Arabia has backed down.'

Khashoggi was not only endorsing the right of Palestinians to decide for themselves. Here was an explicit rejection of the 32-year-old crown prince's fledgling efforts at diplomacy.

'The Palestinian question is still a touchy issue in Saudi Arabia,' Khashoggi continued, adding darkly: '. . . even though the government is totally in control, people in jails, and silencing dissent, voices, clergies.'

~

At 3.15 p.m., just a few minutes after Khashoggi had finished speaking, two security attachés from the Saudi consulate took off from Istanbul for Riyadh on a top-secret mission lasting less than forty-eight hours. We can guess the subject of their meetings was the layout of the consulate, the whereabouts of its staff, and the planning for an operation to entrap the Saudi journalist there the following Tuesday.

Two more Saudi officials boarded another flight from Istanbul at 5.15 p.m. They were members of a Security Screening Team who had swept the consulate for bugs and other surveillance equipment just the day before Khashoggi's first visit. It was a routine mission to stop Turkish intelligence from spying on the Saudi diplomatic mission in the city.

At the moment their plane took off, Khashoggi was at the BBC's headquarters at New Broadcasting House, where he was a guest on the World Service's *Newshour* radio programme.

'He seemed very relaxed, in no way agitated,' the interviewer, Julian Marshall, told me later. 'He was very much at ease. He came across as very affable.'

Khashoggi was there to talk about the Palestinians but the

microphones were on before Marshall's interview formally began. The BBC later took the unusual step of releasing the unbroadcast portion of the recording. It included this personal attack on the grandiose economic ambitions of the Saudi crown prince, plans which Khashoggi himself had once defended: 'The prince supplies us, every couple of weeks or couple of months, with a huge multi-billion-dollar project that wasn't discussed in parliament or newspapers. The people will clap and say, "Hey, great, let's have more of those?" It doesn't work that way.'

'I don't think I will be able to go home again,' Khashoggi told Marshall during the pre-interview small talk. 'When I hear of an arrest of a friend who did nothing worth to be arrested, make [sic] me feel I shouldn't go.'

Khashoggi was thinking of Essam al-Zamil, the economist who was charged with joining a 'terrorist organisation' and communicating with 'an element of the Qatari regime', in unapproved meetings with foreign diplomats.

'A Saudi economist who was close to the royal court got arrested,' Khashoggi explained. 'That scared many people, because here we are talking about someone who was close to the government. I don't want to use the word "dissident". The people who are being arrested are not even dissidents. They just have an independent mind.'

'I don't call myself an opponent,' he continued. 'I always say I am a writer. I want a free environment to speak my mind. That's what I do at the *Washington Post*. They give me a platform to speak freely and I wish I had that platform in my home.'

The following week – in fact the day after Khashoggi disappeared – the Saudi crown prince admitted in an interview with Bloomberg that some 1,500 people had been detained over the past three years. 'Most of their cases have nothing to do with freedom of speech and most of them will return to their homes when the process is finished,' MbS claimed.

Over dinner in a Turkish restaurant that Saturday night in London, Khashoggi showed his host, Daud Abdullah, tweets posted by his Saudi critics, accusing him of attending a pro-Qatari, Muslim Brotherhood event in the UK. There was no doubt that many of the journalist's friends were indeed pro-Qatari and pro-Brotherhood. There was an Islamist pattern in the journalist's associations overseas that dated back decades, but seemed to intensify both during and after the Arab Spring. This public appearance, like others before it, was seen in Riyadh as just the latest act of betrayal.

By now, that was hardly surprising. In what would turn out to be one of his last *Washington Post* columns, he'd embarked on his most outspoken defence of Brotherhood and other Islamic political parties as an essential part of the Arab world, on the grounds that significant numbers of Muslims would always vote for them.

'There can be no political reform and democracy in any Arab country without accepting that political Islam is a part of it,' he had written the previous month, warning that the group's eradication would result in more revolution, extremism and refugees.[2]

The next day, Sunday, he told a friend he was suffering from the flu and wanted to rest in his hotel. On the Monday morning, he met another friend, the Algerian lawyer Saad Djebbar, for coffee and croissants in a café near the lawyer's home in the diplomatic district of Belgravia.

'There are so many beautiful women around here,' Khashoggi told him. 'Why didn't you bring me here before?'

'You need to lose weight first,' Djebbar joked with him. Khashoggi did not tell Djebbar he had a fiancée waiting for him in Turkey.

The conversation quickly moved on to the crackdown in Saudi Arabia.

'These rulers are unbelievable,' Khashoggi said. 'They are living in another world.'

Uppermost in his mind was the official ban on his eldest son, Salah, from leaving the kingdom, so that it was impossible to see him; and once again the fate of his economist friend, Essam al-Zamil. Khashoggi had tweeted earlier that day that Zamil 'does not deserve such treatment', after he was charged with joining a 'terrorist organisation'.[3]

Earlier that month, he had cried down the phone to Hatice Cengiz after hearing that Salman al-Awdah, a Saudi cleric with 13 million followers on Twitter, was facing the death penalty on terrorism-related charges. Awdah had tweeted in favour of reconciliation with Qatar when, according to his family, the Saudi authorities had ordered him to tweet in favour of the Saudi blockade instead.

'Sometimes I don't know what to do, and I am just stunned,' he told her. After the call finished, she had also burst into tears.[4]

However, Khashoggi was happy at the prospect of returning from London to Istanbul later that day. He told Djebbar that he had many friends there, that he even knew its president, Recep Tayyip Erdoğan.

'Turkey is a perfect balance between the Orient and the West,' he said admiringly. 'They even make their own fridges.'

At lunchtime, Khashoggi took a taxi to the Park Royal industrial estate in Acton, west London. Stopping opposite a parcel depot, the journalist stepped into the headquarters of Al-Hiwar, an Arabic satellite television channel, largely unnoticed amid the estate's drab warehouses and offices.

Al-Hiwar was the kind of controversial, upstart Arab journalism network Khashoggi loved, and he was a regular guest on its programmes. Funded by rich Arab businessmen, it broadcast across the Arab world from three satellites as well as online, and considered itself second only to Al Jazeera in reaching what its editor called the 'Islamic elite'.

The station was accused by the Saudis and their closest Arab allies, as well as Western diplomats, of being a front for Muslim Brotherhood operations in Europe. Its founder was Azzam Tamimi, a Palestinian and long-time Brotherhood member and Khashoggi's friend for over twenty-five years. Tamimi has not denied his links with Hamas, the Brotherhood's offshoot in the Gaza Strip, which is on a terrorism blacklist in both America and the European Union.

The two had met in London in 1992, just after the military-controlled government in Algeria had cancelled elections an Islamist party had been set to win, and together they'd set up the 'Friends of Democracy in Algeria' (later 'Liberty for the Muslim World'). None of their campaigning, however, could stop an estimated 200,000 Algerians being killed in the subsequent civil war. The organisation lasted for six years but eventually folded due to lack of financial support.

Khashoggi had long disagreed with his friend about Saudi Arabia – the Saudi defending its monarchy, while Tamimi lambasted it as a form of dictatorship. The Palestinian's strong association with the Muslim Brotherhood, which was banned in Saudi Arabia from 2014, meant it had long been safer for the Saudi journalist to keep his communications with Tamimi to a minimum. Now they were both living in exile, much of that caution had disappeared.

'I grew up to recognise Saudi Arabia as a major source of evil,' Tamimi now says. 'Jamal believed we shouldn't threaten the status quo, but improve upon it. He started losing that conviction after his friends were arrested.'

Around the corner from Al-Hiwar was a branch of the Nando's chicken restaurant chain, where the Palestinian took Khashoggi to lunch. They discussed the Saudi's next appearance on Tamimi's weekly discussion programme, which was due to take place that coming Thursday in the station's other studio – in Istanbul. The subject of the interview was set to be Khashoggi's new campaigning group, Democracy for the Arab World Now, or DAWN. In the event, the broadcast went ahead with the Saudi's photograph placed upon an empty chair.

Tamimi was one of a small group of friends whom Khashoggi would consult about his articles for the *Washington Post*, either helping the Saudi improve his English, or translating his work for publication into Arabic.

'Personally, I believe he was killed because of those articles,' Tamimi told me in his office at Al-Hiwar, a few months later. 'It never occurred to him that he would be killed the way he was. Never.'

In a conversation earlier in the summer, Khashoggi had told Tamimi of his feelings of despair, that he felt some of his closest friends had abandoned him, that his 'brand' had become so toxic in Saudi Arabia that he felt alone. The journalist was '100 per cent convinced that had he gone back, he would have ended up behind bars, together with his friends,' Tamimi said.

The version of Khashoggi the Palestinian met on that final Monday was far sunnier.

'He was happy,' Tamimi recalled of their lunch together. 'He was really excited, he was getting married.'

Khashoggi told him about the flat he'd bought in Istanbul and about his engagement to Hatice Cengiz. Then they discussed Khashoggi's forthcoming visit to the Saudi consulate for a document confirming his divorce.

'I was surprised,' Tamimi said. 'I was concerned. I said,

"How can you go to the consulate, considering what you've written?" He said: "I was there on Friday." He convinced me it was okay.'

Khashoggi told his friend that the consulate staff had 'initially panicked' when he'd arrived unexpectedly; but that they turned out to be very friendly. He said they were just ordinary Saudis, 'good people', who had joked with him about his marrying a Turkish woman.

After lunch, Tamimi's driver took Khashoggi to his hotel to collect his luggage, before heading on to Heathrow airport.

At 4.30 p.m., the first three of the Rapid Intervention Group arrived in Istanbul on a commercial flight and checked into the Wyndham Grand hotel. Twelve men, the main body of the team, had yet to arrive and would also need somewhere to stay. So, at 7.20 p.m., one of the consulate staff telephoned the Turkish Tourist Centre to ask about the availability of hotel rooms with views of the sea. A booking was made for three suites and seven rooms at the Mövenpick hotel, close to the consulate, for three days. None of the guests were tourists, none of them would be staying more than twenty-four hours, and none required a sea view.

Later that night, at 9.48 p.m., the arrangements were still not complete. More staff at the consulate needed to be informed that a team was flying in from Riyadh:

A VOICE: A commission is coming from Saudi Arabia tomorrow; they have something to do in the consulate. They will have something to do on my floor in the office.
A VOICE: Okay, so on the first floor?
A VOICE: No, next to my office . . . their work inside will take two or three days.
A VOICE: All right, I will be at the consulate at 8 a.m.

A VOICE: The name of the man who will come is Mr Maher, and the commission is a Saudi commission. They will enter with the head of the commission's pass.

In the meantime, Jamal Khashoggi caught the last Turkish Airlines flight of the day back to the woman he was about to marry – blissfully unaware of how his life was about to collide with nine other Saudis who were also in the air and also bound for Istanbul.

9

THE KILLING IN THE CONSULATE

The Saudi consulate is down a slight slope from a busy main highway. Though office blocks tower over it, it sits in a relatively quiet residential back street with security cameras mounted along its walls. Khashoggi gives his fiancée his two mobile phones for safekeeping before he leaves her.

'See you soon, wait for me here,' he says. At 1.14 p.m. he is admitted to the building's visa section and asked if he would like a cup of tea.

He agrees: any suspicion he might have about the Saudis' intentions has been allayed by the hospitality he'd been shown the previous Friday, when he stayed happily talking to his fellow countrymen for over an hour. However, one Western intelligence official later noted drily that this time there is an 'edge' detectable in his voice.[1]

If Friday's visit had left him nostalgic for the company of home, this one brings Saudi Arabia's terror into startling focus. Only three minutes after entering, he is taken upstairs by force to the consul general's office.

'Let go of my arm – what do you think you are doing?' Khashoggi asks.

What frightens him most? The sheer numbers, surely. Up to ten Saudi intelligence and security men are in the building.

The leader of the Rapid Intervention Group, Brigadier General Maher Abdulaziz Mutreb, has been chosen for the task in an attempt to put the journalist at ease. They had worked together at the Saudi embassy in London well over a decade earlier, when Mutreb was deputy chief of station for Saudi intelligence. But there's no indication that this familiarity is having the desired effect, by making the journalist any more compliant or any less afraid.

The dominant voice is Mutreb's, followed by Dr Salah al-Tubaigy, the forensic pathologist. They are heard most often in the next seven and a half minutes. Mutreb tells the journalist to sit down and explains that the team has come to take him back to Riyadh:

> MUTREB: We will have to take you back. There is an order from Interpol. Interpol requested you to be sent back. We are coming to get you. Why don't you go back?
> KHASHOGGI: Why wouldn't I want to go back to my own country? *Inshallah* I will eventually go back.

(*scuffling noises*)

> MUTREB: Interpol is coming, so we have to hold you until they come.
> KHASHOGGI: This is against all kinds of laws. I am being kidnapped!

Khashoggi knows there is no Interpol arrest warrant for him. He knows about secret rendition squads ferrying critics home to Saudi Arabia: this, he must assume, is now his most likely fate, the price he must pay for his catastrophic mistake.

A friend in Washington had warned him that he could be kidnapped when he visited the Saudi embassy there a year earlier. Back then, he had told her she was being ridiculous. Yet he had told others that his greatest fear was waking up in detention in Riyadh, after being bundled onto a private jet. Now that fear has turned to sheer terror in Istanbul; though the journalist maintains sufficient composure to tell them his disappearance will be noticed:

KHASHOGGI: There isn't a case against me. I notified some people outside. They are waiting for me. A driver is waiting for me.
A VOICE (*repeatedly*): Let's make it short.

Next, Mutreb asks him whether he has mobile phones.

Time: 1.22 p.m.

KHASHOGGI: Two phones.
MUTREB: Which brands?
KHASHOGGI: Apple phones.

The journalist explains that he has left them outside with his fiancée.[2] She is sitting on the pavement near the police barriers, only a few metres away, oblivious to his distress. Mutreb gives Khashoggi a mobile phone and orders him to use it:

MUTREB: Send a message to your son.
KHASHOGGI: Which son? What should I say to my son?

(*silence*)

MUTREB: You will type a message. Let's rehearse. Show us!

KHASHOGGI: What should I say? 'See you soon?' I can't say 'kidnapping'!

A VOICE: Cut it short.

A VOICE: Take off your jacket.

KHASHOGGI: How could this happen in an embassy? I will not write anything.

A VOICE: Cut it short.

KHASHOGGI: I will not write anything.

(*scuffling noises*)

MUTREB: Type it, Mr Jamal. Hurry up. Help us so that we can help you, because in the end we will take you back to Saudi Arabia. And if you don't help us, you know what will happen in the end. Let this issue have a good ending.

Then Mutreb orders his men to set out their tools on the table. They are carrying syringes, scissors and a taser stun gun. The sight of the syringes seems to confirm his fate.

Time: 1.33 p.m.

KHASHOGGI: Am I going to be assaulted? I am being kidnapped!

A VOICE: If you don't help us, you know what will happen.

KHASHOGGI: There is a towel here. Are you going to drug me?

A VOICE: We will anaesthetise you.

A group of Saudi agents is ordered by Mutreb to jump on Khashoggi. One of the hit squad tries to cover the journalist's mouth, but Khashoggi resists. The sixty-year-old Saudi is sub-dued with overwhelming force and he doesn't stand a chance:

A VOICE: Did he sleep?
A VOICE: He raises his head.
A VOICE: Keep pushing . . . push here. Don't remove your hand. Push it!

The journalist has apparently been injected with a sedative and then suffocated with a plastic bag:

A VOICE: Let him cut!
A VOICE: It is over, it is over, it is over! Okay, it is over.
A VOICE: Take it off, take it off.
A VOICE: Put this on his head. Wrap it. Wrap it.

Khashoggi's clothes are removed and there is the sound of strenuous human panting – and plastic sheeting being moved about. Then, at 1.39 p.m., what is believed to be the sound of a saw cutting the naked body of the late Jamal Khashoggi up. He is cut into so many parts that even his fingers are reportedly removed; presumably as punishment for the articles he had typed with them for the *Washington Post*.

It takes around half an hour to dismember him. Some of the team begin to feel nauseous and shocked, as if their own brutality has not left them entirely unmoved. At one point, Dr Tubaigy is heard shouting at them, 'Why are you standing there like that?' while he works on the corpse.[3]

According to a CIA assessment, he has been killed in the consul general's office.[4] The briefing room next door is believed to have been used as well. The portraits of three Saudi rulers hang above the diplomat's desk and are silent witnesses to the killing in the consulate. In the centre, Ibn Saud, Saudi Arabia's first king; on the right, his son, King Salman; and on the left, his grandson, Crown Prince Mohammed bin Salman. Their photographs are housed in gold-coloured frames. In the first of its many versions of events, the House of Saud will claim that the killing never took place; but what they cannot deny is that the sovereign diplomatic territory these portraits survey is theirs.

~

Sitting on the pavement outside, Hatice Cengiz can still hear nothing. She believes her fiancé is socialising with Saudi diplomats inside, savouring the memory of home. She reads a newspaper and scrolls idly through her mobile phone. Then she visits the small supermarket across the road for two bottles of water – one for her, and one for Khashoggi, in case he's thirsty once the paperwork is complete. She goes back to the shop for chocolate, knowing how much he loves it.

In the consulate, they are busy packing parts of Khashoggi into suitcases and black refuse bags. Mutreb makes at least three phone calls to Riyadh following the killing.

'Tell yours – the thing is done. It's done,' he says in one of them.

Around 3 p.m., the next phase of the operation begins: the disposal of Khashoggi's dismembered remains. Six vehicles leave the consulate that afternoon, heading variously to the Mövenpick hotel (where some of the squad had been staying), the airport and the consul's residence. Among them is a black Mercedes Vito van with tinted windows – and the diplomatic number plate, 34 CC 1865.

At 3.02 p.m., the van arrives at Consul al-Otaibi's home in Meselik street, 500 metres away. It stays there for four hours, having sped downhill, past a children's playground and a restaurant next door to the residence, then into the residence's garage.

A few minutes later, three men wearing T-shirts are seen taking four black bin bags and at least one rolling suitcase into the consul general's home. Police believe parts of the body are being transferred inside.

~

The Saudi Rapid Intervention Group knows the Turks will trawl through security camera footage from across Istanbul in their search for Jamal Khashoggi, so it hatches a plan to deceive them: one of the hit squad will pretend to be the journalist, walking around one of the city's best-known tourist sights.

Just after eleven that morning, the lookalike had arrived at the Saudi consulate. Brigadier General Mustafa al-Madani was casually dressed in a blue checked shirt, jeans and black trainers with distinctive white heels. He must now put on the dead man's clothes if he is to be a convincing body double.

At 2.53 p.m., Madani and his accomplice, Saif Saad al-Qahtani, emerge from the consulate's back door. Madani is wearing Khashoggi's trousers, jacket and shirt. Even the black T-shirt the journalist had worn as an underlayer looks identical. He's roughly the same height and age as Khashoggi and he's suddenly acquired the disguise of a grey beard which wasn't there in the morning.

He is also wearing the journalist's glasses, though they are perched towards the end of his nose, as if he cannot see where he is going unless he looks over the top of them.

The Khashoggi impersonator and his companion take a taxi to the Sultanahmet tourist district, where they are seen strolling in the grounds of one of Istanbul's most famous sites, the Blue Mosque. The second man, Qahtani, is carrying a white plastic carrier bag and he's wearing a black hooded top. The time is 4.13 p.m.

The square beyond them is protected by an armoured car and Turkish soldiers, on guard against any terrorist attack on tourists; but the soldiers don't know that an undercover Saudi hit squad has murdered a journalist and that two of them are now in the area pretending to be tourists themselves.

At 3.11 that afternoon a second Gulfstream jet marked HZSK-1 arrives at Istanbul's Atatürk airport, empty. It is the 'getaway plane', here to take some of the Saudi operatives home. Like the first plane which arrived before dawn, it is operated by Sky Prime Aviation, a charter service based in Riyadh, which boasts on its website of 'creating unforgettable memories for our esteemed passengers'. Today those memories are not just unforgettable, but also unconscionable and depraved.

Just after 4 p.m., while a Saudi pretending to be her fiancé is walking around Istanbul, Hatice Cengiz decides she can wait for the real Jamal no longer. She calls her youngest sister, Zeynep, asking her to check on the internet what time the consulate closes. The answer comes back – 3.30 p.m., half an hour earlier. She waits another ten minutes or so, then messages her best friend, Arzu, telling her to come as soon as possible.

Cengiz runs towards the iron barricades of the consulate. A Turkish security guard agrees to look inside. 'There's no one there,' he says.

'That's impossible,' she replies. 'He went in. I have his phones. I have been waiting here and he didn't come out.'

Then she telephones the consulate. A man tells her it is now outside working hours, and they don't know of anyone, Jamal Khashoggi or anyone else, who is still inside. She is told that he left without her having noticed.

While she is left reeling in horror at the possibility that the man she is about to marry has been kidnapped, the Khashoggi body double has almost finished his performance. Brigadier General Madani enters a public bathroom near the Blue Mosque to change clothes. When he emerges, he is no longer in the jacket and glasses but back in his original blue checked shirt. His accomplice's mission is almost over too. He's removed his black hooded top and is walking across a patch of grass with the white plastic bag, now presumed to contain Khashoggi's clothes, slung over his shoulder.

The two Saudis then head to the Arasta bazaar around the corner, a long gallery of giftshops selling rugs, jewellery, towels and soap. They stop for a drink in a traditional-looking Turkish teahouse – small wooden chairs set around circular tables. Madani enters the public toilet opposite and then emerges without his false beard.

The pair catch a taxi at 4.29 p.m. The white plastic bag is thrown into a wheeled rubbish skip near a metro station. The men laugh as they walk through an underpass, back towards the lobby of the Mövenpick hotel. They know their mission is almost over and they believe they have produced enough surveillance footage of a living, breathing Jamal Khashoggi touring Istanbul to deceive the Turks.

Hatice Cengiz's memory of what happens next becomes blurred by panic and terror, but she makes a frantic series of phone calls. Yasin Aktay, an adviser to President Erdoğan in Ankara, is top of her list of Turkish officials to contact. Less than a fortnight earlier, Khashoggi had been admitted to a private hospital in Istanbul with bronchitis. When he was discharged, she had asked him whom she should call in any future emergency. Yasin Aktay, he had told her.[5]

Aktay is one of the leading intellectual ideologues in President Erdoğan's ruling Justice and Development Party – Khashoggi would try to see him whenever he was in Turkey. They'd met through their contributions to television discussion programmes, bonding over their shared enthusiasm for the Arab Spring. Their last encounter was in Istanbul six weeks earlier. Oddly enough, the Saudi journalist talked to him about the way Saudi dissidents abroad were kidnapped.

'He said that the Saudi government does not normally carry out assassinations, just kidnappings,' Aktay recalls later, still in disbelief at Khashoggi's disappearance and how prescient their last conversation was.

On this Tuesday afternoon, Aktay is sitting at his desk at party headquarters in Ankara and he's puzzled as to why a woman with a phone number he doesn't recognise is calling him. The time is 4.41 p.m. She reminds him of her work as a doctorate student on Gulf politics, that they'd met in Ankara a year earlier when she'd given him her research papers, but he is still struggling to remember. Then she tells him she is also Jamal Khashoggi's fiancée.

'We have a problem,' she tells him.

'Where are you?' he asks.

'Outside the Saudi consulate,' she says.

'Stay there. I will call you back.'

Aktay then calls a Saudi dissident he knows in Istanbul and tells him Khashoggi has disappeared.

'Why did he go there?' the Saudi asks angrily. 'How many times did we tell him it was too dangerous to go to the consulate? I hope we are not too late.'

While Khashoggi's fiancée and friends have begun raising the alarm, the squad's commander, Brigadier General Mutreb, is inside the consul general's residence. He's understood to be making arrangements to dispose of the body which police believe was driven there.

At 4.53 that afternoon, Mutreb, along with Dr Tubaigy and one other member of the team, takes a consular car back to the Mövenpick hotel. Crucially, they do not appear to be carrying any luggage when they leave the residence. Mutreb checks out half an hour later with a large suitcase and returns to the airport, with only twenty minutes to spare before his flight.

The 'getaway plane' is here to take Mutreb and five others home.

~

On the pavement outside the consulate, Hatice is now calling Turan Kişlakçi, the Turkish journalist friend of Khashoggi who had helped negotiate with her father the terms of her marriage. Kişlakçi's phone is on silent mode and so he misses six calls from her, made over a two-minute period.

'Why didn't you call me before?' he asks her, when he finally hears what has happened.

Kişlakçi then calls everyone he knows in Turkey's political hierarchy: Yasin Aktay, the presidential adviser, who is already on the case; Emrullah Isler, a Saudi-educated former deputy prime minister; and the governor of Istanbul, Vasip Şahin.

'I thought that the only way to get Jamal out of there is pressure from Ankara,' is how Kişlakçi describes his strategy.

When Kişlakçi approaches the consulate door that evening, a Saudi guard tells him Khashoggi has left the building. 'Don't ask me again,' the guard warns him.

'But he didn't come out from this door,' Kişlakçi replies.

'Go away,' the guard says.

Meanwhile, Yasin Aktay has called his friend Waleed al-Khereiji, the Saudi ambassador in Ankara, who tells him he knows nothing. The ambassador says he will call back ten minutes later with information; but despite Aktay messaging him on WhatsApp several times, he doesn't call again for the next two months. Turkish intelligence later analyses a voice recording which allegedly reveals that the consul general was in contact with his ambassador in the days before the murder.

Aktay telephones another friend: Hakan Fidan, the head of Turkish intelligence, as well as Fidan's deputy, and an official in the private office of President Erdoğan. Turkish police say it is Aktay's call to them at around 5 p.m. which first alerts them to Khashoggi's disappearance.

Between 5.30 and 6 p.m., by Aktay's reckoning, the Turkish president has ordered police and intelligence officials to be on high alert. For Erdoğan, this is personal – an apparent kidnapping on Turkish soil of a prominent journalist he has met at least twice before.

At 5.50 p.m., Khashoggi's distraught fiancée is giving her first witness statement at a police station near the consulate. She has been told that a formal investigation can only begin after she files a missing person's report.

But all this is apparently too late. At 6.30 p.m. Brigadier General Mutreb's plane takes off. It hasn't been searched, even though X-ray images of luggage passed through an airport scanner include two syringes, two tasers, ten telephones, five walkie-talkies, a signal jammer, staplers and cutting tools; [6] there is no sign of an electric bone saw – but there is what was later described as 'a sharp object that looked like a scalpel'.[7]

It is the end of a very long day trip to Istanbul for the six passengers on board; a day which had begun before dawn and culminated in the dismemberment and decapitation of a fellow Saudi citizen.[8]

The Gulfstream jet stops in Cairo for twenty-five hours

before returning to Riyadh. Beyond diverting attention from the mission's original destination, we don't know why.

That evening, a reporter from the *New York Times* gets through to the Saudi consulate by telephone. An employee is asked if Khashoggi has been detained.

'We heard the same thing,' he's told, 'but we don't know.'[9]

Another Turkish friend of Khashoggi's, Fatih Oke, alerts the Istanbul press corps to come to the scene as soon as possible. 'A famous *Washington Post* writer went into the Saudi consulate and he hasn't shown up for four and a half hours,' Oke tells them.

'Is he a staff writer, or what?' one of the journalists asks him, unsure whether this is a story he should cancel his evening plans for.

'It doesn't matter,' Oke says. 'Come.'

By sunset, reporters from the Turkish state Anatolian news agency, Al Jazeera television and the *Washington Post* are stationed outside. The Anatolian agency has reporters at both the consulate's exits, front and back, in case the Saudis try to remove Jamal Khashoggi by stealth.

If we continue to wait outside, they will release him, just like they released the prime minister of Lebanon, Fatih Oke thinks to himself. Nobody is contemplating the possibility of murder. In fact, the release of the Lebanese leader Saad Hariri, held against his will in Riyadh the previous November, offers a glimmer of hope.

In Washington, the editors of the *Washington Post* have also concluded that their freelance columnist has been kidnapped. Khashoggi's fiancée has contacted Karen Attiah, the journalist who supervised his work.

When she informs the editorial page editor, Fred Hiatt, he tells her to keep him informed. In his mind, it isn't a life-and-death situation until the following morning, when there is still no sign. However, the *Post*'s chief executive, Fred Ryan, knows he must quickly raise the alarm if a state-sponsored rendition is to be stopped.

Ryan still has in mind the ordeal of Jason Rezaian and his family. Rezaian was the *Post*'s correspondent in Tehran until he was convicted of espionage in a sham trial in Iran and held for 544 days. But this is different: Saudi Arabia is an ally of the United States. The *Post*'s CEO believes that if enough pressure is brought to bear early, the Saudis could claim Khashoggi's detention as 'an administrative oversight', to avoid loss of face – in other words, a screw-up at the local level – and then let him go.

A letter is drafted to the Saudi crown prince asking him to look into the situation. The following day it is sent out. The paper contacts the Saudi foreign ministry but does not receive a reply.

'We have been unable to reach Jamal today and are very concerned about where he may be,' Eli Lopez, the paper's international opinions editor, says in a statement. 'It would be unfair and outrageous if he has been detained for his work as a journalist and commentator . . . we hope that he is safe and that we can hear from him soon.'[10]

Back in Istanbul, a second Gulfstream jet, HZ-SK2, is being searched, after Turkish police claim they have been alerted to a possible kidnapping. But nothing suspicious is found and they allow it to take off at 10.54 p.m. with Dr Tubaigy among seven passengers on board.

An online flight-tracking service shows that the plane flies 170 miles east to Nallihan, in Turkey's Anatolian heartland. It is then possibly forced into a holding pattern by air traffic control, which could suggest that high-level discussions in Ankara are still taking place on whether to force it to land. Though a senior Turkish police officer tells me later he has 'no official information' on that.

The jet eventually reaches Dubai in the United Arab Emirates – Saudi Arabia's closest ally – arriving at 2.30 a.m. It then flies on home to Riyadh later that day.

Only two of the fifteen Saudis who have flown in for this operation have diplomatic passports, but Turkey's president has weighed up the possible diplomatic fallout from stopping them from leaving. It has been decided to let the men go.[11]

The remaining two members of the Rapid Intervention Group are Brigadier General al-Madani, the 'body double', along with Saif Saad al-Qahtani, his accomplice. At about the time they board a Turkish Airlines flight to Riyadh, Hatice Cengiz is giving up her desperate vigil outside the consulate. It is one-thirty in the morning. A day which was supposed to herald the beginning of her married life has turned into a nightmare. There has been no celebratory meal with friends as planned; no agreement on a wedding date; and, above all, no sign of Jamal, who only entered the building to collect a piece of paper so that he could marry her.

I O

AFTERMATH

'There is no such thing as a perfect murder. This was a textbook example of how not to do it. You always leave a clue.'

— Senior Turkish diplomat

At 9 a.m. on the day after Khashoggi disappeared inside the consulate, Hatice Cengiz returned to the crime scene, accompanied by her sister, Zeynep, and friends. She would maintain her vigil till past midnight for a second time. She was still holding the two mobile phones he had entrusted to her. 'We were going to marry this week,' she told a reporter from the *Washington Post*.[1] 'He did not say it, but he was worried,' she told the *New York Times*.[2] Otherwise, she said little to the Turkish and international press now gathering outside. The first morning there were some twenty-five journalists, but by the afternoon that number had doubled.

'I was thinking, *He is still inside*,' she told me later. 'I didn't want to turn it into a circus and complicate the politics of it — by talking about it.'

For her protection, Cengiz would initially be accompanied by two plainclothes police officers. The Saudi hit squad had fled the country, though the consul general, Mohammed al-Otaibi, remained in post, protected from questioning by his diplomatic immunity.

Turkish officials feared retaliation against their diplomats in Riyadh if police entered the consulate by force, so they began to negotiate access to the building on Akasyali street instead.

The 1963 Vienna Convention on Consular Relations, signed by both Turkey and Saudi Arabia, makes a consulate a protected space under international law; though it also says consular premises 'shall not be used in any manner incompatible with the exercise of consular functions'.

First, the Saudis had violated the Convention; they then used the building's diplomatic immunity under the same Convention to delay access to Turkish police for as long as they could.

'According to the information we have, this person who is a Saudi citizen is still at the Saudi consulate in Istanbul,' İbrahim Kalın, President Erdoğan's national security adviser, said on the first full day of the investigation. 'We don't have information to the contrary.'

Twenty-four hours on from Khashoggi's disappearance, the Saudi government put out the first of many statements which were either misleading or blatantly false. 'Mr Khashoggi visited the consulate to request paperwork related to his marital status and exited shortly thereafter,' a Saudi official said.[3]

~

At the Washington DC headquarters of the *Washington Post*, its chief executive, Fred Ryan, telephoned Jared Kushner, who was known to have developed a strong relationship with the crown prince; he also called Mike Pompeo, the US secretary of state, asking them both to seek answers from Riyadh.

The *Post*'s letter to the crown prince, drafted the night before, was delivered first to the Saudi ambassador in

Washington – Prince Khalid bin Salman, the crown prince's brother. Jared Kushner's office sent another copy to Riyadh. The letter never received a reply.

The US State Department did not disclose what Pompeo told the crown prince in a subsequent phone call. The official read-out did not even mention Khashoggi, but said that 'expanding US–Saudi collaboration' was on an agenda which included Iran and the war in Yemen.

That same day, the Saudi ambassador to Ankara, Walid al Khereiji, was summoned to the Turkish foreign ministry. He told Turkish diplomats he had no new information and the case was still being investigated. A statement from the consulate itself said Khashoggi had 'left the building' and it was 'following up on the media reports' of his disappearance. In the meantime, a Saudi official was seen tossing sheets of paper one by one into a brazier in the consulate's outdoor courtyard, while his colleague used a stick to prod the flames. Instructions from Riyadh, perhaps? Or confirmation of passenger names and flight schedules? A security camera filmed the fire from a nearby building but the distance made it impossible to decipher what was being burned.

A diplomat from the Turkish foreign ministry called Khashoggi's fiancée: Secretary of State Pompeo was waiting to be patched through. 'He first checked how I was,' she said, 'and he said we hope for a good outcome, *inshallah*. Maybe he knew the truth, but he came across as if he didn't know it.'

Also waiting for news was Hanan el-Atr, the Egyptian woman Khashoggi had married in America four months earlier. He had joked with her that there was no need to bolt the front door of his apartment in Virginia. Now her frantic calls to the journalist's mobile phone were among dozens which would never be answered.

'I feel bad about her,' Hanan said later of the Turkish woman Khashoggi had been about to marry. 'We were in the same situation; she didn't know about me – and I didn't know about her. If it wasn't for her, we wouldn't know that Jamal had disappeared.'

Later that week, Bloomberg broadcast an interview with the crown prince, recorded just over twenty-four hours after Khashoggi had entered the consulate:

BLOOMBERG: What's the Jamal Khashoggi story?
CROWN PRINCE: We hear the rumours about what happened. He's a Saudi citizen and we are keen to know what happened to him . . .
BLOOMBERG: He went into the Saudi consulate.
CROWN PRINCE: My understanding is he entered and he got out after a few minutes or one hour. I'm not sure. We are investigating . . .
BLOOMBERG: So he's not inside the consulate?
CROWN PRINCE: Yes, he's not inside.
BLOOMBERG: Turkish officials have said he's still inside.
CROWN PRINCE: We are ready to welcome the Turkish government to go and search our premises. The premises are sovereign territory, but we will allow them to enter and search and do whatever they want to do. If they ask for that, of course, we will allow them. We have nothing to hide.[4]

It would take another twelve days before terms could be agreed for Turkish police to enter. The same day the interview was broadcast, the black Mercedes van which police believed had been used to transport the dismembered body was taken to a car wash in Istanbul. The Saudi driver would claim later that he had no knowledge that he was transporting a body.

US senators were by now joining calls by the *Washington Post* and human rights organisations for Khashoggi, a US resident, to be released from Saudi custody. That Friday morning, the paper published a photograph of him on its editorial page. Beneath it was his byline and then a blank space where his words should have been. The headline? 'A missing voice'.

'We categorically reject any insinuations of holding @jkhashoggi,' Saud Kabli, the Washington embassy spokesman, wrote on Twitter, adding later that the two had been friends for over a decade.

While the Saudis could not control speculation in the foreign press, they did what they could to manage the reaction on social media inside the kingdom itself. Some 13 million Saudis are on Facebook and the country claims it has the world's highest percentage of people on Twitter and YouTube, relative to the number of internet users. The public prosecutor put out a statement, reiterating that 'sharing or spreading rumours or fake news that might affect public order and security is considered a cyber crime punishable by 5-year imprisonment', as well as an $800,000 fine.[5]

At the Saudi consulate, the man in charge was sufficiently relaxed to open his doors to the Reuters news agency in a ludicrous display of 'transparency' just four days after the murder. Mohammed al-Otaibi gave a cameraman and reporter a guided tour. Behind the consul general's desk in the room where the CIA would conclude Khashoggi had been killed stood the green Saudi flag with its horizontal sword motif, along with the '*shahada*' or Islamic creed – 'There is no god but God. Muhammad is the messenger of God.'

In the Reuters footage, the diplomat was seen walking

around all six floors of his offices, opening cupboards, filing cabinets and even wooden panels covering air-conditioning units, apparently at random, to show there was nothing there. He avoided eye contact and had one hand thrust nonchalantly in his pocket – a gesture presumably intended to denote that he had nothing to hide and that his conscience was clear.

'I would like to confirm', al-Otaibi said, 'that the citizen Jamal is not at the consulate nor in the kingdom of Saudi Arabia, and the consulate and the embassy are working to search for him and we are worried about his case.'[6]

Some of that was true: Khashoggi was indeed not in the consulate by then; he was possibly still in Turkey, but he was no longer breathing. Diplomats were indeed 'worried' about his case. So worried, that ten members of the Saudi secret police, the 'Mabahith', had flown to Istanbul that morning.

Al-Otaibi claimed the consulate's security cameras only showed live footage and recorded nothing, so no images of Khashoggi entering or leaving could be found.

Later that same day, the Turkish government announced it was beginning a criminal investigation. The *Washington Post* reported the conclusion of Turkish investigators that he had been killed in a 'pre-planned murder' by a team of fifteen Saudis sent from Saudi Arabia and that the body had subsequently left the consulate. The accusation was still not on the record, or backed by any published evidence, but President Erdoğan had been briefed on the conclusions drawn from secret audio recordings, which Turkish intelligence had by now listened through.

Fred Hiatt, head of the *Post*'s editorial page, was visiting his daughter in New York when a call came through from a colleague: 'We are hearing from Turkish sources that Jamal is dead.'

It was Hiatt's task to dictate the paper's response as he walked across Central Park: 'If the reports of Jamal's murder are true,' he said, 'it is a monstrous and unfathomable act. Jamal was – or, as we hope, is – a committed, courageous journalist.'

There were tears in his eyes as he spoke. 'I was crying, and what I remember is that I kept trying to fix the tenses,' he told me. 'I kept it in the present tense, because I felt like we shouldn't accept that he was dead until we absolutely knew.'

Turan Kişlakçi, the head of the Turkish Arab Media Association and the man who had helped broker the terms of Khashoggi's forthcoming marriage, was among the first to be told by Turkish officials that his friend had been murdered.

'Now you understand the Arabs,' a senior politician in Ankara told him. 'They are the worst people. They killed Jamal.'

'Are you sure they killed him?' he replied.

'Yes, we are sure. And they cut up his body too.'

Kişlakçi began to cry. He asked another friend of Khashoggi's to join him in an Istanbul café and they stayed there until three or four in the morning, nursing their shock and grief. The next day, he called every journalist he knew to tell them that 'not even ISIS' had committed a crime like this, that the Saudis had 'torn a man apart like dogs' and then fled the country.

On Sunday 7 October, Turkey was still saying nothing on the record about the killing, citing the diplomatic sensitivity of the case. The Saudis were claiming to the Americans that they were co-operating with the Turks. In fact, the Saudi ambassador to Ankara had been summoned a second time, with the Turks growing increasingly vocal in their request for information. The Saudi press reported that a 'security delegation of Saudi investigators' had flown in the previous day, allegedly to help find the journalist.

Security camera footage and airport records were still being studied, President Erdoğan said, adding that the situation was 'very, very upsetting'.

'I am following it, chasing it and, whatever conclusions come from here, we will inform the world about it,' Erdoğan told a news conference. 'Jamal is a journalist, a friend whom I have in fact known for a long time . . . My expectations are still positive. God willing, we will not be faced with a situation that we do not desire. His fiancée's expectations are the same.'

In fact, Turkish officials were drip-feeding to the media claims that Khashoggi had been tortured and killed, with his body then smuggled out of the building.

~

In the meantime, Hatice Cengiz was clinging to the possibility that the lack of any official confirmation offered hope that he was still breathing.

'I don't know how I can keep living if he was abducted or killed,' she wrote a week after the man she loved had disappeared. 'I remain confident that Jamal is still alive. Perhaps I'm simply trying to hide from the thought that I have lost a great man whose love I had earned.'[7]

In Washington, there was mounting anger that a country which purported to be an ally was allegedly involved in the disappearance of a US resident on Saudi diplomatic territory. The image of fifteen Saudis on two jets had begun to stir memories of 9/11 (fifteen of the nineteen hijackers in 2001 were Saudis) and US senators were beginning to voice their thoughts on possible consequences.

'If this is true – that the Saudis lured a US resident into their consulate and murdered him,' Senator Chris Murphy, a

Connecticut Democrat, wrote on Twitter, 'it should represent a fundamental break in our relationship with Saudi Arabia.'

Fred Ryan, chief executive of the *Washington Post*, had been asking to see the Saudi ambassador for days and was on the point of giving up: 'But then we thought, if there is a one per cent chance that he's still alive, why would we not pursue this as far as we possibly could?'

Ryan finally persuaded Prince Khalid bin Salman to meet him that Sunday at his home in Georgetown. Ryan demanded an explanation. The prince told him Khashoggi had perhaps left through the consulate's back door after about half an hour – even though the journalist had entered through the front door – and that the building's camera security system had failed to store any video pictures that day.

'I cannot believe a consulate in Istanbul doesn't save any video,' Ryan told him. 'You can buy a video system for $150 on Amazon.'

Ryan asked him about Turkey's claims that two Saudi planes had flown in and out of the city on the day of Khashoggi's visit to the consulate. 'There were no jets,' Ryan says Khalid told him. 'The only jets are the ones which come in once a month to inspect the security system, to make sure it's working.'

After an hour and twenty minutes the meeting broke up, with Ryan telling the ambassador that the *Post* would be relentless in pursuing the truth and that if the Saudi state was involved, 'it would be the most depraved and oppressive act against a journalist in modern history'.

~

The following day Prince Khalid was still in full denial mode, claiming that reports the kingdom had detained or killed Khashoggi were 'absolutely false and baseless . . . I don't know who is behind these claims, or their intentions,' he said, 'nor do I care, frankly.'

It was 'outrageous', he said in a statement, to claim Khashoggi had been murdered 'in the consulate, during business hours, and with dozens of staff and visitors in the building'.

'What we do care about is Jamal's well-being and revealing the truth about what occurred,' the ambassador said. 'Jamal has many friends in the kingdom, including myself, and despite our differences, and his choice to go into his so-called "self-exile", we still maintained regular contact when he was in Washington.'

In fact, the *Washington Post* later published the explosive allegation that it was Khalid who had told Khashoggi to go to the Saudi consulate in Istanbul. The paper quoted unnamed sources with knowledge of a CIA assessment which said that American spies had monitored a phone call between the ambassador and Khashoggi, in which Khalid had assured him he would be safe at the consulate in Turkey. The Saudi embassy vehemently denied any conversation about Turkey had taken place.[8]

A few days after saying he cared about revealing the truth, Khalid returned home to Riyadh, amid calls from some senators that he should be formally expelled if his brother, the crown prince, was involved in the killing. The thirty-year-old did not return to Washington until December and in February 2019 it was announced that he was being replaced.

Meanwhile, outside the consulate in Istanbul, a small group of Khashoggi's friends and supporters gathered to demand either his release or confirmation from Riyadh of press reports that fifteen Saudis had been involved in a plot to kill him. The mournful tone of the gathering, however, suggested its mind was made up, that it was obvious Khashoggi was dead.

'What's happening is part of the state terror committed

by the Saudi kingdom against its citizens, inside and outside,' said Tawakkol Karman, a Yemeni journalist and winner of the 2011 Nobel Peace Prize. 'I am here to tell the world to act, to help my friend, the very well-known famous journalist, Jamal Khashoggi. Where is he, where is he now?'

'Consulate officials cannot save themselves by simply saying "he left",' President Erdoğan told a press conference during an official visit to Hungary. 'If he left, you must prove it, you will prove it with video footage . . . is it possible that camera systems didn't exist at the Saudi Consulate, where the incident took place?' Riyadh had been given another warning to co-operate. The Saudis, he said, could 'catch a bird or a mosquito with the advanced systems they have'.

The same day, the Saudi-owned Al Arabiya described the hit squad as tourists, having earlier dismissed Khashoggi's disappearance as 'fake news'. His fiancée, the channel said, had connections with Qatar, while Khashoggi's friend Turan Kişlakçi was associated with an anti-Saudi organisation.

Later that day, President Trump gave his first brief comments on the case, suggesting this was unwelcome news he hoped would go away.

'I am concerned about it,' he said outside the White House, offering no criticism of Saudi Arabia's stonewalling. 'I don't like hearing about it. Hopefully that will sort itself out. Right now, nobody knows anything about it, but there's some pretty bad stories going around. I do not like it.'

By now, Turkey's patience had run out. A week on from his disappearance, the now notorious last images of Khashoggi were released by the Turkish government – the surveillance footage of a grey-bearded, balding Saudi stepping towards the doors of the consulate, with the time of day stamped in the top right-hand corner as 1.14 p.m.

A global audience of untold millions has watched the pictures, such is our morbid fascination with the final moments of a man who has no idea he is a matter of minutes away from death.

That Tuesday evening, a Turkish delegation met the Saudi 'investigators' in another attempt to agree terms on a search of the consulate. The meeting ended in failure at midnight, after the Saudis said that only a visual rather than forensic examination was possible and allegedly demanded possession of Jamal Khashoggi's laptop and phones.

In the meantime, the Turkish press published sensational front-page pictures of one of the Gulfstream jets arriving, of the hit squad booking into the Mövenpick and Wyndham Grand hotels, and of a fleet of black vehicles leaving the consulate, with one – a Mercedes van – arriving at the consul's residence. Adding the most monstrous detail yet to the story of the vanishing journalist, a Turkish official briefed that the Saudi had been dismembered with a bone saw.

'It is like *Pulp Fiction*,' the official told the *New York Times*.[9]

11

INVESTIGATION

'The Turks clearly bugged diplomatic facilities, as
many countries do, but that makes it difficult for us
as journalists to be confident about the information
because we can't interrogate that information in the
way we normally would.'

— Interview with David Ignatius, associate editor,
Washington Post

Turkey's presidential palace sits in a vast compound, atop a
remote and windswept hillside on the outskirts of Ankara. Its
high metal fences are guarded by men in beige-coloured combat
fatigues. Armoured cars are semi-hidden under camouflaged
tarpaulins.

The palace has 1,150 rooms, making it bigger than the
Kremlin or the palace at Versailles. Many of these rooms are
decked out in Italian marble and they are maintained by over
2,000 staff.

Since it opened in 2015, President Recep Tayyip Erdoğan has
been accused of spending over $600 million on a monument to
his own ambition — though he has said that the building only
projects Turkey's newly found status as a regional power; and
that it needed to be constructed because the bathrooms of his

previous office were infested with cockroaches. It can take fifteen minutes to walk to the president's office; and despite the soldiers and the functionaries, the place has the feel of an out-of-town shopping mall or an eerily empty luxury hotel.

Erdoğan is said to be obsessed with electronic eavesdropping against him – hardly surprising, given that a recording of an alleged conversation between him and his son about how to hide millions of euros was published in 2014, prompting furious denials from him. One of the rooms in his palace is said to contain no electric sockets, for the president's extra security.

Perhaps it follows that a leader so worried about surveillance presides over an intelligence service which is so proficient at it. The Saudi consulate in Istanbul was routinely bugged by Turkey's National Intelligence Organisation, known by its Turkish acronym as MIT. Although what the bugs planted by the MIT would pick up on 2 October was anything but routine.

All this begs an obvious question – why did the Saudis think they could get away with the crime undetected?

After all, Istanbul's reputation as a centre for espionage long precedes the events of October 2018. It is not just confined to the fiction of Eric Ambler and Ian Fleming; real-life spies took advantage of Turkey's neutral status to congregate there and spy on one another during the Second World War. In the Cold War, it was a convenient listening post on the Russians from within NATO's far-eastern border.

Istanbul's consulates are not the sleepy diplomatic outposts in Turkey's second city that they might appear. They've long been soft targets for recruiting foreign government employees and tapping into the communications networks of potentially hostile states.

These days, prominent Turks often assume their conversations are wiretapped, with Turkey's national security apparatus expanding under President Erdoğan's increasingly authoritarian rule. For Saudi intelligence officers not to anticipate audio surveillance of their consulate is therefore a great deal more than an injudicious mistake.

Turkish security sources say Saudi intelligence officers visited the consulate on one of their regular missions to 'debug' it only five days before the crime; and so the men who flew in from Riyadh on 1 and 2 October thought it was a safe place in which to operate without being heard.

This was their first substantial error. The Saudis later told the Turks they found ten bugging devices, once they realised that the electronic eavesdropping had taken place.

Many diplomatic missions have 'safe speech' rooms which are vetted for extra security, though the Saudis appear not to have bothered using theirs. Perhaps the number of men involved in this operation made the use of such an area impossible.

The conversations inside the consulate were not listened to in real time – few surveillance operations are, given there are so many of them – but Turkish intelligence personnel listened incredulously on headphones as they transcribed the conversations in the following days; phone conversations before the killing were also recorded in what listeners said was surprisingly good sound quality. It meant that Jamal Khashoggi did not suffer in silence after all.

The initial assessment was that he had been injected with an unknown liquid, and then passed out before being transported alive from the consulate in a container or box. In fact, Turkey's intelligence chief, Hakan Fidan, recalled that he had telephoned the 'head of the kingdom of Saudi Arabia' (understood to be a reference to the crown prince) and asked for the body to be returned. Not long after this call, a day or two after the murder, Fidan finalised his assessment that Khashoggi had been killed.

There's no evidence at the time of writing to suggest that the Turks had prior knowledge that Khashoggi would be captured or murdered; they only found out what had happened after he disappeared, when they scrubbed through what they'd recorded.

Subsequent analysis of the voice patterns and the dialogue identified Brigadier General Maher Abdulaziz Mutreb and the forensic expert Dr Salah al-Tubaigy as playing leading roles. Some of the excerpts read like a lurid and suspiciously badly written spy novel. The difficulty is knowing how much of the dialogue to trust, because Turkish and American officials have dispensed significantly different versions of it to the press. For example, in one version Brigadier General Mutreb is quoted as saying, 'If he doesn't come, we will kill him here and get rid of the body.' The intention to assassinate Jamal Khashoggi could not be clearer here, yet this part of the dialogue was not given to every visiting foreign official.

Similarly, one version of the transcript quotes Khashoggi as asking, 'Are you going to kill me?', while others granted access to the recording did not hear that phrase. Instead, they heard the journalist saying, 'Are you going to drug me?' Either this is an error of omission (the excerpt simply wasn't played) or the verb in the first version has been deliberately changed to reinforce the case for premeditated murder.

Most of the conversations in the consulate I have quoted from in this book come from notes which were taken as the recordings were being played inside MIT headquarters. An investigation led by Agnes Callamard, the UN special rapporteur on extrajudicial executions, was allowed to hear forty-five minutes of tape but was told by Turkish intelligence that they had access to at least seven hours. Callamard was not given an English transcript and Turkey's spy chiefs asked her not to take notes.

In addition, errors in translation are easy to make, given the conversion from Arabic to Turkish and then English. There are also gaps in the recordings, as only excerpts of conversations were played. This means that, intentionally or not, some passages may have been rendered more intelligible and conclusive than they actually were.

This is not to dispute that Dr Tubaigy said he liked to listen to music with headphones while he was cutting up corpses; or that Khashoggi was described as a 'sacrificial animal'; or that a voice said 'let him cut!', then 'it is over', and then 'wrap it' during and after the killing. It is just to point out that investigators and Western intelligence officials do not know what they *haven't* heard.

Some of what has been reported stretches credulity, when the story is incredible enough as it is. Three weeks after the murder, the Reuters news agency reported that Saud al-Qahtani, the crown prince's media adviser, was beamed into the consulate live via Skype from Saudi Arabia that day, so that he could confront Khashoggi himself.

Reuters quoted Arab and Turkish intelligence sources claiming that al-Qahtani hurled insults at Khashoggi over the Skype call and that the journalist did the same back. At one point, Qahtani was allegedly heard instructing his men, 'Bring me the head of the dog.'[1]

A senior Turkish police officer could not confirm these details to me. He told me it was his belief that at least one Saudi official had watched the attack online, but that he did not believe the Saudis would have taken the risk of recording it. A team of investigative journalists from Turkey's *Daily Sabah* newspaper could not confirm this account either. Reuters reported that the audio of the Skype call was in President Erdoğan's possession and that he had refused to release it to the US government.

Turkish police have disputed another account, quoted by the *New York Times*, that the consul general, Mohammed al-Otaibi, objected to the use of his office.

'Do this outside! You will get me into trouble,' al-Otaibi was quoted as saying.

'If you want to live when you come back to Saudi Arabia, shut up,' one of his fellow Saudis allegedly replied.[2] The diplomat flew home on 16 October and has not been seen or heard of since.

In one version of the transcript, there are several gaps in the dialogue between Khashoggi and his killers – when only the garbled sounds of screaming and cutting can be heard. The transcript reverts to single-word descriptions: 'scream' and 'gasping', especially when Khashoggi has been jumped upon and is fighting for his life.[3] Then the word 'saw', followed by 'cutting' – a 'sssssssh' sound, according to an official who has heard the tape.

However, no electric saw was identified in the X-ray images of the luggage leaving Istanbul's Atatürk airport; and one source with access to the tape told me no screaming could be identified either.

'To some listeners you can't really hear a saw,' said Baroness Helena Kennedy QC, who heard the tape in January 2019 as an adviser to the UN's rapporteur's inquiry. 'For me it was a kind of hum. It could have been the hum of a central heating or air-conditioning system. But the Turkish intelligence officer said, "That's the saw."'

'There was absolutely no bone saw,' a Saudi official said,

claiming Dr Tubaigy was there solely to remove evidence from the crime scene, not to carry out the crime himself.[4]

Perhaps an unpowered surgical cutter was used on the body. Why bring an autopsy expert, who can be heard bragging about cutting up bodies, if assassination wasn't always the plan, or an option at the very least? 'Will the body and hips fit into a bag this way?' Brigadier General Mutreb had asked, even before Khashoggi arrived.

For all the caveats outlined above, for all the possible Turkish mistranslations or even exaggerations, the Saudis have failed to provide a plausible alternative to Turkey's central claim of murder. In fact, they have done all they can to frustrate Turkey's investigation, and one cannot escape the conclusion that the Turks have produced chilling and compelling evidence of a dying man's final moments.

The time codes on Turkish intelligence's recordings reveal the journalist was drugged eighteen minutes after he arrived in the consulate and that the sound of a saw was heard six minutes after that, when he was barely dead. 'I don't think there was much of an attempt to negotiate,' a senior Turkish diplomat told me. 'It takes a sick mind to organise something like this – and sick people are dangerous.'

The transcripts of the killing in the consulate were shared with the White House, the CIA and 'friendly' intelligence agencies around the world. The Americans were eventually given copies of the recordings to keep, as were the Saudi authorities, but not every organisation was accorded the same degree of access; and we don't know if the Turks provided clones – exact duplicates – rather than copies, which would allow voice pattern experts to establish whether the tape was authentic or had been interfered with.

'We gave it to Saudi Arabia,' President Erdoğan said on

10 November. 'We gave it to America. To the Germans, French, British, all of them. They have listened to all the conversations. They know. There is no need to distort the issue. They know for certain that the killer – or killers – is among these fifteen people.'

At first, the Turks refused to allow the recordings to leave the country, forcing the CIA director, Gina Haspel, to fly secretly to Turkey. A Turkish intelligence source claimed Haspel became emotional when she heard Khashoggi's last moments. In her world of espionage, it was also something of a professional scoop for the Turks. She had been the CIA's deputy station chief in Ankara earlier in her career and so knew her Turkish counterpart, Hakan Fidan, well. His officials briefed that she congratulated him on an intelligence coup which she said had only been achieved 'once or twice' before.[5]

It may have been flattery for a purpose: what else did the Turks record, and did it incriminate the crown prince?

President Trump refused to hear the audio himself. 'I don't want to hear the tape, no reason for me to hear the tape,' he said. It was a sentiment shared by his national security adviser, John Bolton. 'I don't speak Arabic,' Bolton told reporters at a White House briefing. 'I haven't listened to it, and I guess I should ask you, why do you think I should?'

It sounded like an attempt to insulate themselves from the horror of what had happened; that would certainly make it easier to make emotionless and arguably more pragmatic judgements about where America's national interest really lay.

However, the Turks also manipulated the release of gruesome details about the murder for their own purposes, in what one of the Turkish president's advisers described to me as a 'perception campaign'. Key figures in that campaign were

Fahrettin Altun, Erdoğan's chief of communications; and İbrahim Kalın, his spokesman and national security adviser — rivals for the president's ear and part of his inner circle.

A senior Turkish diplomat told me that the primary goal had been to force the Saudi government to admit that Jamal Khashoggi had not left the consulate; and once that goal was achieved, then to admit that he was killed in a premeditated attack.

'Turkey wanted this thing to come out, but it did not want to be the one accusing Saudi Arabia,' one of Erdoğan's advisers told me. 'It wanted the press to do the job.'

The Turkish president would use the audio tape as leverage to secure Saudi co-operation in the investigation and, he hoped, action from President Trump. Although as we shall see later, this strategy hardly proved successful.

Leaking the details of the murder wasn't difficult. Most domestic newspapers and broadcasters are either government-controlled or run by business figures on friendly terms with President Erdoğan. Not that Turkish journalists needed much encouragement from officials in Ankara to reprint the edited extracts of conversations. It was an astonishing story.

Major international news organisations, especially the *New York Times* and *Washington Post*, were briefed by Turkish officials too, to the fury of their Turkish rivals, who naturally wanted to break the news first. Editors no doubt loved the scoops, but many of the allegations were unverifiable. Journalists were being used to help shape the case against Riyadh.

The Saudis' second major mistake, after failing to stop themselves being bugged for sound, was failing to stop themselves being filmed as well.

At least six closed-circuit cameras stand near the consulate's front entrance, with another seven at the back. The Turkish

Jamal Khashoggi as a young man visiting Egypt. He later called the Arab Spring's failure there the 'loss of a great opportunity to reform the entire Arab world.'

In the offices of the *Al Hayat* newspaper, Jeddah. 'Everyone thinks journalists cannot be independent, but I represent myself, which is the right thing to do,' he wrote.

On the conference circuit. Khashoggi was an unofficial interpreter of Saudi government policy but in 2016 an aide to the crown prince told him that he could no longer write or broadcast.

With Hanan el-Atr on their wedding day in Virginia, 2 June 2018. The ceremony was kept secret and the union not legally registered.

With his future fiancée Hatice Cengiz in Turkey, July 2018. To her, Khashoggi's defining characteristics seemed to be his open-heartedness and warmth.

© Reuters

Dr Salah al-Tubaigy in medical scrubs, dressed as a lieutenant colonel and leaving Istanbul airport. 'Give me my headphones so I can forget myself while cutting,' he was heard saying.

Brigadier General Maher Mutreb photographed in the Saudi crown prince's delegation visiting Downing Street in March 2018; entering the Saudi consulate in Istanbul on the day of the murder; with Crown Prince Mohammed in Houston, Texas, 7 April 2018.

© Wenn

'See you soon, wait for me here.' CCTV screenshot of Jamal Khashoggi saying goodbye to Hatice Cengiz for the last time, 2 October 2018.

Screenshot of Khashoggi walking towards the Saudi consulate. Saudi officials mistakenly thought they had removed all the CCTV footage.

The last known image of Khashoggi before his death, approaching the consulate doors. The time code is stamped 1.14 p.m.

Khashoggi impersonator Mustafa al-Madani with a false beard and wearing the journalist's glasses and clothes. Turkish police notice he hasn't changed his shoes.

Al-Madani and accomplice Saif al-Qahtani pretending to be tourists near Istanbul's Blue Mosque. The impersonator is now back in his own clothes.

Al-Madani smiling as he returns to the Mövenpick hotel. He flies back to Riyadh the day after the murder.

Aerial view of the Saudi consulate. The CIA believes Jamal Khashoggi was killed in the consul general's office upstairs.

The consul general Mohammed al-Otaibi giving journalists a tour of the consulate just four days after the murder, 6 October 2018.

Mohammed al-Otaibi in his office, flanked by pictures of Saudi crown prince Mohammed, Ibn Saud and King Salman, 6 October 2018.

Saudi officials believed to include a chemist, a toxicologist and secret police arriving at the doors of the consulate, 15 October 2018.

Turkish police entering the consul general's residence on 17 October, more than two weeks after the murder. 'We had to push and push to be allowed in,' the chief prosecutor said.

© Reuters

'We face our challenges together': Saudi crown prince Mohammed greeting US Secretary of State Mike Pompeo. Riyadh, 16 October 2018.

© Reuters

King Salman and the crown prince receiving Salah Khashoggi, the journalist's eldest son. A foreign travel ban on him was lifted afterwards. Riyadh, 23 October 2018.

© Shutterstock

President Erdoğan speaking to the Turkish parliament. 'This savage murder did not happen instantly but was planned,' he said. Ankara, 23 October 2018.

© Shutterstock

President Trump boasting of $12.5 billion arms sales to Saudi Arabia. 'That's peanuts for you,' he told the crown prince. Washington DC, 20 March 2018.

© Reuters

'The cover-up was one of the worst in the history of cover-ups': President Trump talking to White House reporters about the killing in the consulate, 23 October 2018.

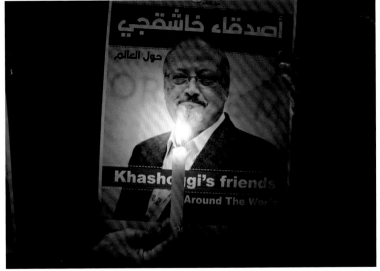

© Reuters

A picture of Jamal Khashoggi held by a demonstrator during a candle-lit vigil outside the Saudi consulate. Istanbul, 25 October 2018.

© Reuters

Agnes Callamard, the
UN special rapporteur on
extrajudicial executions.
'The people directly
implicated in the murder
reported to him,' she
said of the crown prince.
Geneva, 7 March 2019.

© Reuters

Hatice Cengiz testifying
on Capitol Hill. 'It
wasn't just Jamal that
was killed . . . it was the
values that the United
States represents,' 16
May 2019.

© Shutterstock

President Trump offers his hand to the Saudi crown prince during the G20 summit group
photo in Japan. President Erdoğan is to Trump's right. Osaka, 28 June 2019.

police repeatedly asked the Saudis for the footage and were told there wasn't any.

'When we demanded the footage, they wouldn't even give us the recording units,' a high-ranking Turkish police officer told me. 'They said they had no visual evidence.'

The cameras sent live feeds of pictures over the internet onto a storage server inside the consulate. Police in Istanbul believe the killers took this server with them in their luggage back to Saudi Arabia – and safely assumed that now there would be no visual evidence of their comings and goings on 2 October.

However, the Turks say the Saudis forgot that at least one camera was also feeding images into a security booth outside the consulate's main entrance. By the time Saudi consular staff realised their mistake, the day after Khashoggi's disappearance, it was too late.

'They went into the booth to block the pictures, but we had already taken them away,' a Turkish police source told me.

Just over a week after Khashoggi's disappearance, the Turkish newspaper *Sabah* published video pictures of fifteen members of the Saudi Rapid Intervention Group, along with their names and years of birth. The Turkish authorities, who had leaked the pictures, identified the hit squad by cross-referencing images of them arriving at the consulate with footage of them at airport passport control and in the lobby of their hotel.

In response, a Saudi news channel, Al Arabiya, put out a report claiming the men were in fact just on holiday.

'Unlike what reports said about them arriving in a private jet, the tourists are shown to be in a terminal gate waiting area, in an airport crowded with travellers,' the channel said.[6] 'Those travellers were in Turkey as regular tourists,' Al Arabiya concluded.

It later emerged from more security camera footage that two members of the group had indeed strolled around one of Istanbul's most famous tourist sites, the Blue Mosque. One of them, 57-year-old Mustafa al-Madani, wore Khashoggi's clothes in an attempt to resurrect him from the dead that was so crude and amateurish that it fooled no one.

'Khashoggi's clothes were probably still warm when al-Madani put them on,' a Turkish official told CNN.[7]

'The Saudis knew we were going to chase the CCTV footage,' a Turkish police officer told me. 'They faked it so we would have evidence to show he was alive, if they got caught.'

Istanbul's police chief, Mustafa Çalışkan, was the first to spot the most obvious clue that the man on camera was not Jamal Khashoggi. When Madani left the consulate through the back door after the killing, he was not wearing the journalist's size 42 black shoes; instead, the same trainers with distinctive white heels that he'd been wearing when he arrived that morning.

Turkish police then visited Istanbul's municipal recycling site at Kemerburgaz and paid the boys who scavenge there to hunt for Khashoggi's clothes among the rubbish. The boys found nothing.

Madani's accomplice, 45-year-old Saif Saad al-Qahtani, could be identified because his details, along with several other team members, were stored in the contacts of users of the 'MenoM3ay' caller ID phone app, which is popular in Saudi Arabia. Seven users of the app identified Qahtani as working in the 'Crown Prince's office'.[8]

Both men would leave Turkey the day after Khashoggi's disappearance, on a Turkish Airlines flight, routed via Cairo to Riyadh.

The body double's visit to the Blue Mosque with his accomplice echoed the circumstances surrounding the attempted assassination of a former double agent, Sergei Skripal, by Russian intelligence officers in the English city of Salisbury earlier that year. Although the Russian plot did not succeed and left an innocent English woman dead, could this state-sponsored attack, with more than an element of twisted sensationalism, have inspired the Saudi operation seven months later?

The two Russians who were identified as having smeared a toxic nerve agent on Mr Skripal's front door in March 2018 later made the ludicrous claim on Russian television that they were tourists visiting Salisbury cathedral. In other words, they had used the same counter-story. Vladimir Putin, Russia's president, certainly compared the Salisbury and Istanbul incidents, albeit to make the claim that there was no evidence to call either of them state-sponsored murder attempts. Yet in Madani's case, his use of a false beard right after the crime showed he had come to Turkey prepared to 'replace' Khashoggi. It again suggested the murder was planned.

Why was the consulate used as the location, aside from the obvious point that Khashoggi had an appointment there? A Western intelligence official told me that those in charge of this operation wanted to make a statement, in the same way that the Russians deliberately used a nerve agent in Salisbury. In other words, it was meant to be clear who the culprits were, in what amounted to a conspicuous display of Saudi impunity which exposed the security failings of Turkey, a rival state.

Not that the Saudis expected the killing to be overheard; but they did expect the journalist's disappearance to send a chilling message that critics of Crown Prince Mohammed bin Salman could not consider themselves safe, especially not in Turkey.

The Saudis could have killed Jamal Khashoggi in the street; they could have followed him from the consulate back to his flat in Istanbul and killed him there or nearby. Either they wanted to 'own' the operation by killing the journalist inside Saudi sovereign territory, or the opposite – they stupidly thought they could make him disappear without trace.

The biggest mystery of all was this: what did they do with the body? The Saudi operatives explored various options for its disposal in the hours leading up to the murder. Istanbul police discovered that the night before Khashoggi's visit to the consulate, Saudi officials had driven around Istanbul, looking for suitable parks and open areas. Police did not conclude the Saudis were looking for a 'safe house' in which to interrogate Khashoggi; instead they believed this was a hunt for somewhere to hide his remains.[9] Along with the audio recordings, this scouting mission was another pointer towards premeditated killing.

Evidence came from security video footage at the entrance to the Belgrad Forest national park, 10 miles north of the city. A grey BMW with green Saudi diplomatic plates was recorded entering the forest gates at 6.28 p.m. on 1 October. The car's occupant was named to me by police as Abdulaziz Soliman Algumizi, an intelligence attaché from the consulate. He would leave Turkey with his family on the day of the murder, but return two days later.

Farmland in Yalova, 60 miles south of Istanbul, was also searched, after investigators established that one of the fifteen Saudis, Mansour Othman Abahussain, had telephoned the Saudi owner of a villa there the day before the killing, wanting to know how far it was from Istanbul.

Abahussain was a foreign intelligence officer, previously stationed at the Saudi embassies in Syria and Jordan. The state Anatolian news agency reported that the villa's owner, known as 'Ghozan', was abroad at the time.[10] Turkish intelligence later transcribed their phone call:

GHOZAN: The bridge has been opened. It takes an hour and fifteen minutes to get there via the highway. It takes forty-five minutes from the airport.
ABAHUSSAIN: Is there anyone there?
GHOZAN: No, there is nobody. Just a caretaker.
ABAHUSSAIN: Very nice.

Turkey's chief prosecutor claimed the phone conversation 'was regarding what would be done to destroy/hide the body of Jamal Khashoggi, who was killed and dismembered'.[11] A source told me the call lasted 160 seconds.

Drones and sniffer dogs were deployed to comb the area; and a well was searched for human remains, although it was a frustrating theme of this investigation that phone intercepts and intelligence work did not lead to what police really wanted – material evidence of Khashoggi's bodily remains.

'Nothing came out of Yalova,' a senior Turkish police officer told me. 'Maybe they were planning to bury the body there.'

At the crime scene itself, police put a remarkable lack of evidence down to repeated attempts by the Saudis to destroy it. Seventeen Saudis were involved over a two-week period. The first 'investigation' team of ten arrived on the same day as an official delegation to negotiate with President Erdoğan. Khaled Yahya al-Zahrani, a toxicologist, and Ahmad Abdulaziz al-Junabi, a chemist, were among those sent to Istanbul. But the Turks quickly concluded they were 'wipers' – sent with the sole purpose of cleaning up the consulate. Turkish intelligence claimed the 'wipers' spent all day and all night in the building on 12 October, before returning on the evening of the 13th. At 11 p.m. on the 14th, they were back again, apparently destroying any potential evidence until 4 a.m.

'They tried to sterilise the place,' a senior Turkish diplomat told me. 'Imagine the frustration of [Khashoggi's] family and fiancée. Imagine our frustration as well.'

The Saudi interior minister, Prince Abdulaziz bin Saud bin Nayef bin Abdulaziz, stressed in a statement that 'supposed orders to kill Jamal are outright lies and baseless allegations against the Kingdom's government',[12] though at the time he said this, police access to the consulate with the required forensic equipment was still being denied.

'They say: "You can't make a proper investigation here, you just come here for a cup of tea and we will show you around,"' a Turkish official complained in the *Washington Post*.[13]

On 15 October, thirteen days after Jamal Khashoggi had disappeared inside the consulate, Turkish investigators were finally allowed inside. However, a team of commercial cleaners armed with buckets and mops had beaten them to it, arriving at half past seven that morning.

Television crews, camped behind a police barricade, filmed the cleaning crew filing into the consulate's front door with a whole crate of bottles of what looked like cleaning solution or bleach. It was strange behaviour for a government that claimed its conscience was clear and that it had nothing to hide.

Turkish police experts were not allowed in until after eight o'clock in the evening – and even then Saudi officials accompanied all four Turkish forensic teams. The Turks complained that they could smell chemicals because the clean-up had been so comprehensive.[14]

'They are trying to make fun of us and our willingness to co-operate,' a Turkish official told the *Washington Post*.[15]

President Erdoğan said that investigators would look into possible 'toxic materials and those materials being removed by painting them over'. However, every police action inside the consulate had to be agreed with the Saudi authorities, with two samples taken of everything: one for the Turks, one for the Saudis. Access to the crime scene was restricted to some six hours, and although police say they managed to stay two hours longer, it was still a race against time.

There was not a trace of blood or DNA in the consul general's office. Though on the carpet of the briefing room next door, investigators found what they called 'a path in which drops follow each other within certain distances and generate an irregular curved line'. Several areas of the briefing room had reacted to ultra-violet light and luminol liquid tests. Nothing, though, from which they could draw any firm conclusions.

'We collected luminol reactions,' an investigator recalled. 'What was strange, in our opinion, was that the reactions of the luminol were not very clear. Do you understand what I mean? Even in a normal room, we would expect more reactions.'

The 'wipers' from Saudi Arabia had done their job well.

'Turkish teams did some work in the consulate, but they could find nothing,' the defence minister, Hulusi Akar, said later.

While the Saudi government has continued to deny authorising the murder of Jamal Khashoggi, the obstruction of justice afterwards was so deliberate and so extensive that it adds up to as great, if not a greater case for state culpability. If the state did not order the operation, then why cover it up?

It wasn't until late afternoon on Wednesday 17 October, more than two weeks after Khashoggi disappeared, that police access to the consul's residence was finally granted.

'We had to push and push to be allowed in,' the chief prosecutor recalled later. 'There was a lot of anger management on our part.'

Forensic specialists entered the residence in white overalls, shoe covers and gloves. They filmed the location from above with a small drone. Inside, a sniffer dog named Melo reacted with interest to a fridge in a storage area, though again nothing conclusive could be established.

Once again, the Saudis claimed the CCTV cameras around this building were also out of order on 2 October, although the Turks obtained footage. Some fifteen Saudi consular vehicles had to be searched at the same time as the visit to the residence, which the Saudis restricted to thirteen hours. Police had held off from applying for a search warrant for the cars for more than a week, believing they were covered by diplomatic immunity; although the Vienna Convention states that, unlike diplomatic vehicles, consular cars are not protected.

'We were struggling with them as we collected the samples,' the chief prosecutor said. 'It started raining and we asked them to move the cars to protect them. But they refused to move the vehicles, so that we had to work under a sheet that we brought and under the rain.'

Of more immediate interest was a well in the property, where Khashoggi's remains might have been hidden. A request to allow the fire brigade to investigate was turned down. The well was 21 metres deep, though filled to a level of only 9 metres of water.

Saudi officials denied a Turkish request to empty it, only permitting the extraction of a water sample. The sample produced no evidence of matching DNA, which was not entirely surprising, given that a sufficiently well-wrapped-up body, or body parts, would not necessarily contaminate water.

Another possibility police considered was that the body had been dissolved in acid – although that could take days to complete. Several months later, a Turkish police report claimed that the body may have been destroyed in a tandoori oven alongside genuine cooking meat in the consul's garden. The report said the oven could reach temperatures of up to 1,000 degrees Celsius to 'destroy all DNA evidence without a trace', and that the oven had been lit after the Saudi hit squad had killed Khashoggi.

'They ordered thirty-two portions of meat from a famous restaurant in Istanbul, half of them uncooked. Was cooking meat in the tandoori a part of their plan from the beginning? These questions will be answered,' the police report concluded with all the gusto of a second-rate detective drama.

The sensational reporting of Khashoggi's body being cremated or dissolved was beginning to smack of police desperation, as if the Turks were casting around for an explanation as to why they had failed to find anything.

However, the consul general's residence still seemed the most likely destination for the corpse. This was because security camera footage revealed that on the afternoon of the killing, the Saudis had transferred luggage from a van into the consul's residence. The Turkish TV channel which obtained the pictures, A Haber, claimed the luggage contained Khashoggi's dismembered remains.[16]

The journalist's head might have fitted inside one of the suitcases or bags; but the torso of a tall, overweight man weighing perhaps 20 stone in all might prove a tougher challenge, even if, as the Turks claimed, the limbs had been removed with a saw. The Rapid Intervention Group had themselves been heard discussing the possibility that the straps on their luggage would not be able to take the strain of the dead man's weight.

'We are certain the van was carrying the body,' a senior Turkish police officer assured me. It was a conclusion he'd reached because every other line of inquiry had been exhausted with no positive results. He said that 400 to 500 police and intelligence officials had been involved in the investigation, viewing the equivalent of around 150 days of camera footage from Istanbul and beyond.

It was also possible that Khashoggi's body was no longer in the country, that the hit squad had smuggled it on board one of the two private jets that took off on 2 October. If so, the question remains as to why the police did not find it in their search of the second plane, given that it didn't take off until after 10 p.m., more than four hours after Hatice Cengiz had filed a missing person report with police.

A senior Turkish police officer confirmed to me that thirteen of the fifteen suspects who had flown in for the operation were not flying on diplomatic passports, so could not claim diplomatic immunity. However, Turkish officials insisted to me that the privileges accorded to government officials meant they had little choice but to let them go.

'They were about to leave,' a senior adviser to President Erdoğan said. 'We couldn't do anything without the Saudi government's permission.'

The Istanbul police chief, Mustafa Çalışkan, was similarly defensive: 'If we had continued searching, there would have been a diplomatic crisis,' he told me.

Turkey's defence minister, Hulusi Akar, a former chief of the defence staff, came as close as anyone to admitting that not only may the Turks have let the suspects escape the country, but those suspects may have taken the body as well.

'Because of the diplomatic immunity they left very easily, without having any problem with the luggage. Possibly in the luggage they carried the dismembered body of Khashoggi,' Mr Akar said.[17]

It was an awkward admission, because it ran counter to the

entire thrust of the official Turkish narrative, which was that the body was probably disposed of inside the consul's residence; and that Saudi obstruction was to blame for not finding it.

'I think there is every likelihood that it [the body] was flown out of the country,' Baroness Helena Kennedy, the adviser to the UN rapporteur's investigation, told me.

Perhaps parcels of human cargo were loaded on board one of the Gulfstream jets in Istanbul. Perhaps Khashoggi's body was driven from the consulate to another airport outside the city and then flown out from there. 'We cannot find the body, which means we cannot make much progress,' a senior Turkish diplomat said.

The consul general, Mohammed al-Otaibi, was also allowed to fly back to Saudi Arabia the day before Turkish police finally entered his home. The Vienna Convention permits the arrest or detention of a consular officer for a 'grave crime', but the Turkish government clearly decided not to escalate the crisis by stopping him and interviewing him. Even though the audio recordings apparently revealed he had been involved in planning the operation, discussing hotel rooms with sea views for his Saudi visitors. At the very least, he was a vital witness.

President Erdoğan later penned a newspaper article in which he vented his anger at al-Otaibi in particular. 'It is deeply concerning that no action has been taken against the Saudi consul general,' he wrote, adding that he had 'lied through his teeth to the media and fled Turkey shortly afterwards'.[18]

The greatest progress in the Khashoggi investigation came as a result of reviewing surveillance camera footage, and of course the audio recordings by Turkish intelligence – and not from forensics on the ground. In that sense, traditional police work did not play a substantial role in the case.

It is astonishing, to the point of stretching credulity, that the killing appeared to leave no physical trace at all. If this was really the case, and not the result of poor police work, the Saudi clean-up had proved to be the most effective part of the operation so far. It was also possible the Turks were withholding vital information, perhaps for use against the Saudis at a later date, though as time passed that seemed unlikely.

Could the Turks have entered the residence where the body was allegedly first taken earlier? The Vienna Convention states that 'neither the consul's residence nor property has any inviolability'. The Turkish government did not require Saudi consent to search it, unlike the consulate itself. In theory, police could have entered the residence without waiting over two weeks for the privilege.

Even if that was the case, Ankara feared Saudi retaliation against its own diplomats in Riyadh. The Turkish response to this crisis was also evolving in real time, goading the Saudis to co-operate without wishing to sever ties completely, the Turks perhaps holding out for some bigger if undefined diplomatic or financial payback from Riyadh over the course of time.

For Turkish police, the biggest unanswered question was what happened to Khashoggi's body. For Turkish intelligence, it was who gave the order to kill him – and did the chain of command stretch all the way up to the crown prince himself?

The Turkish audio transcript claims that Mutreb, the hit squad's commander, made at least three phone calls to Riyadh after the killing. A Saudi official has denied that, claiming that a review of the intelligence in his government's possession showed that 'nowhere in them is there any reference or indication of a call being made'.[19]

That may have been true – the Turks did not give the Saudis all the evidence they had – but it was also disingenuous, as the existence of these phone calls was widely reported. The pro-government Turkish newspaper *Yeni Safak* reported that Mutreb used his mobile phone to call the head of the crown prince's private office four times.[20]

However, most of the leaks of phone calls and messages on the afternoon of 2 October have appeared in the more reliable American press.

Crown Prince Mohammed is not mentioned by name in any of these recordings, but a CIA assessment, leaked to the *Wall Street Journal* and *New York Times*, stated that the crown prince sent at least eleven messages to his media adviser, Saud al-Qahtani, on WhatsApp in the hours before and after the killing. American intelligence officials indicated that they hadn't read the actual contents of the messages, while the Saudis claim the messages had nothing to do with harming Khashoggi.

The public prosecutor in Riyadh hired the private investigation firm, Kroll, to examine Qahtani's mobile phone. Kroll's supposedly confidential findings were leaked to the *Wall Street Journal*.[21] Their report concluded that the aide also sent the crown prince fifteen messages on 2 October; but Kroll concluded that none of them 'contained clear or identifiable references to Jamal Khashoggi'. Qahtani had deleted one message, but this was because of a typographical error he had made. Other messages concerned the translation of a speech by a foreign leader and a forthcoming press release about solar energy.

The Kroll report said the prince's messages back to his aide around the time of the killing covered routine issues and orders while both men were in Saudi Arabia. 'How many times did I say this news shouldn't be broadcast before receiving my permission?' MbS texted Qahtani about a Saudi Press Agency report.

The texts reportedly reveal no evidence of the prince commenting on the killing just after it happened. However, the

CIA concluded that on the same day the crown prince was in contact with Qahtani, the aide was in direct communication with Mutreb, the hit squad's commander, on the ground in Istanbul.

Both Turkish and American officials claim that Mutreb told a superior by telephone to 'tell your boss' shortly after Khashoggi was killed.[22] The Americans believed he was telling Qahtani back in Riyadh that the mission had been accomplished, but they couldn't be definitive.

'A phone call like that is about as close to a smoking gun as you are going to get,' Bruce Riedel, a former CIA official, told the *New York Times*.[23] Though John Bolton, President Trump's national security adviser, insisted that the audio tape of the murder itself 'does not, in any way, link the crown prince to the killing'.[24]

However, US intelligence had important evidence of a phone conversation between the crown prince and another aide, Turki Aldakhil, over a year earlier, in which MbS had talked of having Khashoggi returned to Saudi Arabia by force. If that failed, then 'with a bullet', the crown prince allegedly said.

The call was made in September 2017, after the journalist had fled into exile but just before he started writing for the *Washington Post*. The crown prince's use of the word 'bullet' was picked up in the US intelligence agencies' retrospective trawl through key 'trigger' words in a database of his intercepted communications.[25] Had those agencies assessed the call earlier – and we do not know why they did not – they could have warned Khashoggi, but it was too late.

Aldakhil, on the other end of the call, was general manager of the Al Arabiya television network and, according to US intelligence, had suggested dangling the carrot of a job in order to entice Khashoggi back to the kingdom. The crown prince reportedly doubted the tactic would work. Aldakhil has denied the whole story and any involvement in Khashoggi's murder. In February 2019, he was appointed Saudi ambassador to the kingdom's closest ally, the United Arab Emirates. The *Wall Street Journal* also reported that MbS had told associates back in August 2017, not long after Khashoggi had fled to Washington, that 'we could possibly lure him outside Saudi Arabia and make arrangements'.[26]

It wasn't the only evidence of the crown prince harbouring a longstanding grievance against Khashoggi. Days before his conversation with Aldakhil, the crown prince had reportedly complained to Saud al-Qahtani that the journalist had switched from at first supporting his agenda, to using Twitter to attack the kingdom and becoming too influential in the process.

When Qahtani warned that reining in Khashoggi would be too risky, MbS reportedly told him international reaction to the handling of a Saudi citizen should not matter, that he 'did not like half-measures – he never liked them and did not believe in them', according to an American official, quoted by the *New York Times,* who had read the US intelligence report.

MbS may have also inadvertently revealed his own grievance against Khashoggi. In a phone call to the White House on 9 October, a week after the murder, with Jared Kushner and John Bolton on the line, the crown prince had allegedly disparaged the journalist as a dangerous Islamist and a member of the Muslim Brotherhood.

Saudi officials denied the claims about the call made by senior US administration officials, but Brotherhood membership was an easy enough accusation to make, given the journalist's youth in Saudi Arabia, his many friendships with Brotherhood figures, his support for the Arab Spring uprising in Egypt as well as the fact that Khashoggi was no longer alive to defend himself.

'Jamal Khashoggi was not a member of the Muslim Brotherhood,' countered his family in a statement to the *Washington Post*, adding that he had himself denied it and 'was not a dangerous person in any way possible'.

It read like a rare rebuke of MbS from a family that would not countenance the journalist's character assassination on top of the shock of having to deal with his murder.

Friends claimed that towards the end of his life, Khashoggi had adopted a 'plague on all your houses' approach to Arab politics, keeping a critical distance from Islamist politicians and more secular-minded liberals alike.

'The Islamic circle felt he was not Islamic or conservative enough to fit with them,' said his friend Nihad Awad. 'And the secularists did not see him as progressive enough to be like them.'

Fred Ryan, the CEO of the *Washington Post*, described MbS's reported accusation that the journalist was a dangerous Islamist as 'presented almost like a justifiable homicide'. The crown prince of course wasn't saying he had wanted him dead; but his vilification of Khashoggi certainly suggested that he wasn't sorry to see him gone.[27]

Beyond the findings of US intelligence outlined so far, the composition of the Rapid Intervention Group also strongly points to the crown prince's involvement. So who were they?

The CIA concluded that the fifteen men were assembled from a mixture of the crown prince's top Royal Guard units along with five members of the royal court's media department – the so-called Centre for Studies and Media Affairs, run by Saud al-Qahtani. According to the CIA's leaked assessment, the department had a history of involvement in kidnapping and detaining Saudis for harsh interrogation, causing physical harm. These covert operations had allegedly been under way since 2015, when the crown prince reportedly gave the order 'to target his opponents domestically and abroad, sometimes violently'.[28]

'They were in the closest circle of the crown prince', was how Yasin Aktay, an adviser to President Erdoğan, described the fifteen men. 'They could not even go to the toilet without his permission or his knowledge.'

David Ignatius of the *Washington Post* reported that some of the Rapid Intervention Group received special-operations training in the United States, under State Department licence. Ignatius wrote that the CIA had cautioned other government agencies that some of this special-operations training might have been conducted by Tier 1 Group, based in Arkansas. The training occurred before the killing of Khashoggi, and Tier 1's parent company would neither confirm nor deny whether any of the operatives had been trained in America.[29]

What we do know is that the hit squad was scrambled together, over the space of a weekend, and that its members' past experience was derived from different branches of the Saudi security apparatus.

The commander, Brigadier General Maher Abdulaziz Mutreb, was a fluent English speaker and had served under diplomatic cover as 'first secretary' at the Saudi embassy in London from 2002 to 2007. The 47-year-old was now reported to be 'assistant secretary general for security' in the media centre run by al-Qahtani, although, as we have seen, he'd also appeared in the crown prince's immediate entourage during his tours of Europe and America earlier in the year.

A European surveillance expert identified him as having attended a course on how to spy on phones and computers in 2011. The two-week course in a military compound in a suburb of Riyadh provided instruction on how to infect a computer and gain data on a phone user's GPS position. One of the trainers told the BBC that Mutreb's temper had earned him the nickname 'dark face'.[30] If anyone in the team should have been aware of the threat of phone-tapping in the consulate in Istanbul, surely it should have been 'dark face' himself.

It is not clear what Waleed Abdullah al-Sehri's qualifications were, though it emerged the 37-year-old had once competed in a spoken poetry competition on television. He had recently been promoted to major in the Saudi air force; as an incentive, Saudi websites said, to 'give more in the performance of his duty to serve the religion and the homeland'.

Mohammed Saad al-Zahrani, aged thirty, of the Royal Guard, was filmed, dressed in black military uniform and beret, standing next to the Saudi crown prince in a television news report from the previous year. Another of the team, Thaar Ghaleb al-Harbi, aged thirty-eight, was also standing next to him at the time.

A week after the killing, the *Washington Post* got through to al-Harbi by telephone. He denied having visited Turkey, declined to say if he worked for the crown prince, and then claimed his profession was 'personal information' before he hung up.[31]

Mishal Saad al-Bostani, thirty-one, failed to delete his Facebook page in time to stop the press discovering that he was an air force lieutenant who had studied at Louisville University in Kentucky.

Naif Hassan al-Arifi, thirty-two, made the same mistake. At any rate, a man with the same name was listed on Facebook as an officer in the Saudi special forces and even photographed holding weapons, including a silver-coloured revolver and a Kalashnikov.

The biography of Dr Salah al-Tubaigy has already appeared in Chapter 1. A week after the murder, a man claiming to be the forensic scientist's uncle tweeted that neither his nephew nor any other Saudi had been involved in the killing. 'He grew up in a house of faith and knowledge,' wrote @tobagi1. 'It is not my country that would do such criminal acts. Search for who would benefit from this dirty plot.'

In a sign of continuing Saudi nonchalance, if not carelessness, Tubaigy's own Twitter profile – @VELWYErtYVTc9cn – had still not been taken down in early 2019.

The flaws in the hit squad's tradecraft and its ability to cover its tracks were staggeringly obvious. They included the ludicrous and now notorious impersonator with a false beard; and the group's failure to ensure that all the consulate's surveillance footage was removed and destroyed. It all suggested that these men were used to operating freely inside Saudi Arabia and doing what they wanted without being questioned there. The *New York Times* reported the US intelligence conclusion that at least some of the men had been involved in clandestine missions to silence dissidents before; and that in the summer of 2018, months before Khashoggi's murder, they had even asked for a holiday bonus to mark the end of the Eid al-Fitr Ramadan holiday, because they had been so busy.[32]

If there was one exception to their incompetence, it was surely the disposal of the journalist's body.

'I know for a fact, they have not found anything,' his fiancée, Hatice Cengiz, said seven months after the killing.

While the Turkish police regarded this as a failure, it was, in her mind, some grounds for hope that the man she loved was not dead and one day might come back to her.

'If someone came up to me and said he was alive, I would believe it,' she said.[33]

1 2

TRUMP AND THE HOUSE OF SAUD

'He may be an SOB but he's our SOB.'

— Attributed to President Roosevelt

After a week of furious Saudi denials, contradicted by Turkish intelligence leaks, pressure was mounting not just on Saudi Arabia to come up with an explanation for what had happened, but on a White House which had been lying low for days. It had taken six days for a usually loquacious Donald Trump to say anything.

The president had his reasons — commercial and political, even his own business interests — for biding his time. Notoriously transactional in his outlook and inclined to establish potential profit and loss before deciding on his response, Trump proceeded on the assumption that a damage-limitation exercise was required to preserve the relationship with Saudi Arabia, despite the death of a journalist who lived just 14 miles from the president's home.

Complicating that task was Khashoggi's fiancée, Hatice Cengiz, who had taken to the pages of the *Washington Post* to implore the president and his wife Melania to help resolve the mystery of the journalist's disappearance. She also urged King Salman of Saudi Arabia and his son the crown prince to release the closed-circuit television footage from the consulate, which could shed light on Saudi claims that Khashoggi had left the building.

The following day, President Trump told reporters he wanted to 'bring her to the White House', describing Cengiz as Khashoggi's 'wife', after she had written him and the First Lady a 'beautiful letter'.

Cengiz, however, would not be placated easily. Two weeks later, in an interview with a Turkish television channel, she turned down Donald Trump's invitation.

'The statements Trump made in the first days around his invitation and the statements he made afterwards opposed each other,' she told a Turkish channel, Haberturk. 'I do not think of going to the United States. Whether I will go or not will depend on the formation of conscience.'

Trump was also facing a rebellion in the US Senate. A bipartisan group of senators had invoked the Global Magnitsky Act, designed to punish those involved in human rights abuses worldwide. The act had evolved from a Russian cover-up of the death in prison custody of Sergei Magnitsky, a lawyer working for a US firm; now, remarkably, it was being invoked against Saudi Arabia, a key ally. The senators asked President Trump to report back in 120 days on whether sanctions on the Saudis should be imposed, if 'a foreign person is responsible for an extrajudicial killing, torture, or other gross violation of internationally recognised human rights'.

On 10 October, President Trump was asked by Fox News whether it was likely the Saudis had killed Khashoggi. 'I guess you would have to say so far it's looking a little bit like that and we're going to have to see,' he said.

The president was being dragged towards a conclusion of culpability he didn't want to reach.

'Maybe we'll be pleasantly surprised, but somehow I tend to doubt it,' he told reporters earlier that day. 'I have to find out who did it. People saw him go in, but they didn't see him come out, as they understand it, and we're going to be taking a very serious look at it.'

However serious that look would be, the president repeatedly distanced himself from the crime by pointing out that Khashoggi, although a US resident, was not an American.

'It's not our country, it's in Turkey. And it's not a citizen,' he said the following day.

'This took place in Turkey, and, to the best of our knowledge, Khashoggi is not a United States citizen,' he said. 'Is that right?' The more 'foreign' the Saudi journalist was in the eyes of the president and his fellow Americans, the less he was America's responsibility too.

By contrast, it was Trump's duty to do all he could to boost trade and jobs – which meant the notion of Washington blocking further arms sales did not warrant serious consideration. 'Frankly I think that would be a very, very tough pill to swallow for our country,' he told Fox News, adding that relations with the kingdom were 'excellent'.[1]

Trump would note repeatedly how much the Saudis were spending on American weaponry. Between 2013 and 2017, Riyadh accounted for 18 per cent of total US arms sales, worth about $9 billion, according to a report by the Stockholm International Peace Research Institute.

'Saudi Arabia is a very wealthy nation, and they're going to give the United States some of that wealth,' he had said ahead of a meeting with the crown prince that March.

The president claimed repeatedly that $110 billion in arms sales was at stake – and that if the Americans didn't close the deals, then Russian and Chinese weapons manufacturers would.

'Everybody in the world wanted that order. Russia wanted it, China wanted it, we wanted it, we got it,' he told CBS.[2]

Trump had first signed letters of intent for arms deals worth $110 billion in Riyadh in May 2017, during his first foreign trip as president. The choice of Saudi Arabia as his very first destination was a bold declaration of the president's priorities. It drew a line under the Obama era of foreign policy, and with it all the bad feeling generated between Riyadh and Washington over Obama's decision to lift sanctions against Iran. Instead, Trump was siding wholeheartedly with Saudi Arabia, Iran's closest historical and regional rival. The president addressed leaders of some fifty mostly Muslim nations, gathered in the Saudi capital, urging them to fight terrorism, condemn extremist ideology and stand up to Iran.

In pictures which went viral on social media, Trump, King Salman and President al-Sisi of Egypt had placed their hands on a glowing translucent globe inside the new 'Global Center for Combating Extremism' in Riyadh. The globe illuminated the leaders' faces, with the photographs of them standing around it inadvertently evoking comparisons with a coven of evil male witches; but in Trump's mind, this triumvirate represented a new world order taking the lead in battling Islamic extremism.

Not only had President Sisi launched the toughest crackdown on the Muslim Brotherhood in Egypt's modern history; he also flattered Trump in Riyadh by telling him that he was 'a unique personality that is capable of doing the impossible'. In the president's mind, new relationships with Middle Eastern strongmen were bearing fruit fast.

While Jared Kushner was keen for the president to visit Riyadh first, the idea was opposed by Rex Tillerson, his short-lived secretary of state, who didn't want the administration too beholden or too close to Saudi Arabia. By the time of

Khashoggi's disappearance, much of that critical distance Tillerson had advocated was lost, replaced by apparently mutual admiration.

By contrast, President Obama had temporarily restricted arms sales to Saudi Arabia and Egypt, citing human rights concerns, an issue which Trump did not mention in Riyadh. 'We are not here to lecture,' he said, in what sounded like a characteristic admonition to his predecessor. 'We are not here to tell other people how to live, what to do, who to be, or how to worship. Instead, we are here to offer partnership, based on shared interests and values.'

It wasn't clear what those shared values were. Instead, it sounded as if the new president was giving away any diplomatic leverage he might have wished to keep in reserve by removing the issue of Saudi Arabia's human rights abuses on day one.

As for arms sales, the president appeared to forget, or not to want to know, that President Obama had also struck over $110 billion in arms deals with the Saudis, though only about half of these resulted in sales.

'A lot of times the Saudis will express interest in buying something, but then it never happens,' Gerald Feierstein, the former senior State Department official, told me. 'There's no follow-through.'

The new arms deals Trump had actually approved by 2018 were closer to a much lower figure than $110 billion, nearer $20 billion.[3] Additionally, he couldn't stop himself from inflating how many American jobs from Saudi weapons contracts were at stake. Some analysts limited it to tens of thousands, with the majority of employment created in Saudi Arabia itself. Over the space of less than a week that October, the figure of American jobs the president gave journalists rose from 450,000 to 500,000 to 600,000 – then, a few minutes later, to over a million.[4]

'I don't want to lose a million jobs,' he concluded. 'I don't want to lose $110 billion in terms of investment. But it's really $450 billion if you include other than military.'

He also apparently believed he could compel the Saudis to buy more weapons by threatening to withhold American military support. The president had spoken by phone to King Salman during what would turn out to be Jamal Khashoggi's last weekend in London. Then, at a rally in Mississippi on the day of the journalist's disappearance, he revealed that he had effectively told the king to spend more.

'We protect Saudi Arabia. Would you say they're rich?' he asked the rally. 'And I love the king, King Salman. But I said: "King, we're protecting you. You might not be there for two weeks without us. You have to pay for your military, you have to pay."'

However, amid the subsequent furore over Khashoggi's murder, Trump switched to warning that the Saudis might abandon America's arms industry and not pay billions for weapons after all. Indeed, in June 2018 the crown prince visited Moscow and talked to the Russians about buying a new S-400 air defence system. Switching to other, often less technically advanced arms providers would not be easy. It would take many years for Saudi Arabia's armed forces to rearm and retrain on Russian or Chinese weaponry. They had long been reliant on American Apache helicopters, F-15 fighters and British Tornado aircraft; but, in theory at least, not holding the Saudis close could lead to trade losses worth untold amounts of money.

It wasn't just arms sales and jobs that President Trump felt he was fighting for. His own business interests unsurprisingly shaped his thinking, although he denied having any, calling it 'fake news' in a presidential tweet.

In 1991 his yacht *Trump Princess* had been sold to the Saudi billionaire Prince Alwaleed bin Talal, by coincidence Jamal Khashoggi's future mentor. The future president had bought the floating palace from another Khashoggi, Adnan, who happened to be the journalist's second cousin. Ten years later, the forty-fifth floor of the Trump World Tower in New York was purchased by the Saudi government. The Saudis had deep pockets and Trump had loved them for it for years.

In June 2015, Trump made a speech from inside the same tower, announcing his run for president. 'Saudi Arabia, they make $1 billion a day – $1 billion a day. I love the Saudis,' he said. 'Many are in this building. They make a billion dollars a day.'

Then two months later, at a campaign rally in Alabama, Trump sang their praises again. 'Saudi Arabia, I get along with all of them,' he said. 'They buy apartments from me. They spend $40 million, $50 million. Am I supposed to dislike them? I like them very much.'[6]

Since the first half of 2016, as the presidential election campaign intensified, Saudi bookings at the Trump hotel in Chicago had increased by 169 per cent. The general manager of another Trump hotel, in Manhattan, put a badly needed increase in its revenue down in part to 'a last-minute visit to New York by the crown prince of Saudi Arabia' – though 'accompanying travellers' had stayed there rather than the prince himself. No wonder the president liked the Saudis very much.

The *Washington Post* reported that Trump dissolved eight shell companies in Saudi Arabia a month after his election in 2016, as he was forced to abandon hopes of building a hotel there.[7] Still, in his administration's earliest days, Saudi money continued to flow in: lobbyists working for the Saudi government paid for $270,000 worth of rooms and food at his Trump International hotel in Washington during the three months following the president's inauguration.[8]

So it was that the investigation Trump authorised into Jamal Khashoggi's disappearance came from a president who claimed to want answers, but in reality was fearful of where those answers might lead. Trump's national security adviser, John Bolton, his secretary of state, Mike Pompeo, and his son-in-law, Jared Kushner, had all spoken to MbS about the case. The White House said they all asked for details and a transparent investigation; but the real pressure appeared to be coming from Congress rather than from within the administration itself.

The fate of a Saudi journalist proved a tipping point for lawmakers, unleashing as it did a host of concerns that had been mounting for the past three years about the behaviour of a capricious and belligerent crown prince. The roll call of MbS's alleged misdeeds was a long one, including the apparent kidnapping of the Lebanese prime minister, the 'shakedown' of businessmen at the Riyadh Ritz-Carlton, the arrests of women who'd been campaigning for the right to drive, and the war in Yemen, by now described by the United Nations as the world's worst humanitarian crisis. It did not help that the image of a fifteen-man hit squad of Saudis arriving on planes conjured up memories of the 11 September attacks, seventeen years earlier.

'I've never been more disturbed than I am right now,' said Lindsey Graham, a Republican on the Senate Armed Services Committee and close confidant of President Trump. In fact, the two had played golf during the weekend following Khashoggi's disappearance, at one of the president's courses in Virginia, the state where Khashoggi lived.

In Graham's mind, despotic regimes around the world, from Iran to North Korea, would be emboldened unless the president took action.

'If this man was murdered in the Saudi consulate in Istanbul . . . if it did happen there would be hell to pay,' the senator said. 'If they're this brazen, it shows contempt. Contempt for everything we stand for, contempt for the relationship.'

It wasn't just Turkey claiming to have audio recordings of Saudis interrogating and then murdering Khashoggi. US intelligence had scrubbed through their surveillance records for the past year at least. As we saw in the previous chapter, they found evidence of Saudi officials, including the crown prince, discussing a plan to lure Khashoggi back from the United States and then detain him. The contents of some of these intercepts was shared with senators with clearance to access such sensitive information. Of course, the White House knew about the intercepts too. Some senators complained that the flow of intelligence they were given access to then began to dry up, as the administration became increasingly reluctant to reveal what it knew.

'I can only surmise that probably the intel is not painting a pretty picture as it relates to Saudi Arabia,' said Bob Corker, the Republican chairman of the Senate Foreign Relations Committee.[9] 'Everything points not to just Saudi Arabia, but to MbS.'

There was no firm conclusion agreed by all US intelligence agencies that the crown prince had ordered the killing, though the CIA was increasingly convinced of his culpability. It seemed inconceivable that a hands-on leader like Mohammed bin Salman, the de facto head of an autocratic regime, would not know about it beforehand.

The White House responded with the opposite of a rush to judgement and, perhaps unusually for Trump, a surfeit of caution. The administration was debating whether the crown prince qualified for a 'free pass' because his involvement could at a stretch be described as circumstantial and not proven beyond reasonable doubt. That would give Donald Trump the wiggle room to absolve his ally of personal responsibility.

～

On 15 October, the day the Saudis finally allowed Turkish police into the consulate, King Salman called Donald Trump for about twenty minutes to issue what the president called a 'flat denial' of any knowledge of or involvement in the disappearance.

The Saudis had become worried by an unusual degree of criticism in Trump's latest comments. The president had told CBS 'we're going to get to the bottom of it', threatening 'severe punishment' if it was true that Saudi agents had killed Khashoggi. 'It's being looked at very, very strongly, and we would be very upset and angry if that were the case,' he said. 'As of this moment, they deny it, and deny it vehemently. Could it be them? Yes.'[10]

It marked a brief change in tone. It even suggested that this was a crime so terrible that the White House was not prepared to whitewash it, even on behalf of a valuable ally. Though Trump repeated his caveat that he didn't want to halt arms sales.

In an angry statement from their foreign ministry, the Saudis threatened to 'respond with greater action' to any talk of economic sanctions or political pressure or 'repeating false accusations'. It was a reminder that the world's biggest oil exporter would not be bullied – it could refuse to do what Trump wanted, which was to increase oil production to lower the price.

The timing of Khashoggi's disappearance coincided with an attempt by the Trump White House to persuade Saudi Arabia to do just that. This was because the president's decision to renew US sanctions against Iran would remove most Iranian oil from the market, driving the global price higher. The administration had set itself a deadline for those Iran sanctions to begin by 4 November. In addition, political chaos in Venezuela and a lack of investment in production there meant that increasing Saudi output was even more critical to lowering the price of oil.

Although America was, by 2018, the world's biggest oil producer, with a daily output of over 10 million barrels of crude, it was still importing around 800,000 barrels a day from Saudi Arabia. That was 600,000 barrels fewer than a decade earlier, thanks to the boom in US domestic shale production. A unilateral cut in Saudi oil supplies could therefore be made up from America's own fields, but that wasn't really the point: the intertwined economies of the world would feel the effects of any significant removal of Saudi oil from the market. It was one more reason to tread carefully with Riyadh.

It was also the case that confronting Iran was rising to the top of Trump's foreign policy agenda; and no ally was more supportive than Saudi Arabia in achieving this goal, apart from Israel.

However, Khashoggi's disappearance had members of Congress thinking less about confronting Iran than challenging Saudi Arabia's behaviour instead.

Mike Pompeo was dispatched by the president to Riyadh on 16 October. The Saudis had been given two weeks to provide their closest ally with a credible version of events but still had not done so. Instead, a key witness, the Saudi consul general, Mohammed al-Otaibi, had flown to Riyadh on the same day Pompeo was flying there.

Although the US State Department characterised Pompeo's talks with the king and his son as 'direct and frank', there was no trace of tension in the American's appearance in the obligatory 'greeting shots' for the television cameras. In fact, Pompeo looked and sounded surprisingly affable, given the seriousness of events.

'How was your trip? I hope you don't have jet lag,' the crown prince asked him as they sat down in palace chairs. Pompeo claimed he would feel the effects of the change in time zone later. 'Thank you for hosting me,' he said.

'We are strong and old allies,' the crown prince reminded his guest. 'We face our challenges together.'

'Absolutely,' Pompeo replied, the tone of both men friendly and relaxed. President Trump was then dialled in to their meeting behind closed doors.

Trump said afterwards that the crown prince had 'totally denied any knowledge of what took place' and had 'already started, and will rapidly expand, a full and complete investigation'.

'Here we go again with, you know, you're guilty until proven innocent, I don't like that,' the president complained to the Associated Press, anxious to give King Salman more time to explain.[11] The king had told him, Trump said, that Turkey and Saudi Arabia were working 'hand in hand, very closely' to get to the bottom of the affair. In reality, Turkish police were still being kept out of the consul general's residence.

'I just spoke with the king of Saudi Arabia,' he said, 'who denies any knowledge of what took place with regard to, as he said, his Saudi Arabian citizen. I don't want to get into his mind, but it sounded to me like maybe these could have been rogue killers. Who knows? . . . And it sounded like he, and also the crown prince, had no knowledge.

The 'rogue killers' theory would lie at the heart of Saudi Arabia's new line of defence, thereby absolving the state of any responsibility. The president was trying the theory out for size, giving it its first public outing before the Saudis announced it themselves.

One Democratic senator tweeted his disgust. 'Been hearing the ridiculous "rogue killers" theory was where the Saudis would go with this,' Chris Murphy, from Connecticut, wrote. 'Absolutely extraordinary they were able to enlist the President of the United States as their PR agent to float it.'

At the age of eighty-two, and believed to be suffering from Alzheimer's disease, it was indeed possible that the king knew nothing, as he had told the US president. It was also clear that the Saudis were preparing to shift their storyline for the first time.

Trump sounded inclined to believe whatever the Saudis announced. 'I think the investigation will lead to an answer,' he said. 'And they're going to do a very thorough investigation. I believe they're working with Turkey.'

The Saudis had just opened their consulate in Istanbul to Turkish police, but only after a comprehensive cleaning operation and almost a fortnight of stonewalling. The president's faith in a thorough Saudi investigation prompted comparisons with foxes patrolling henhouses. The administration was not calling for an international investigation. Although the US secretary of state said he'd been assured the Saudi public prosecutor would produce 'a full and complete conclusion with full transparency for the world to see', the White House, with so much at stake in the Saudi relationship, was as interested in damage limitation as its Saudi hosts.

Pompeo was asked whether Saudi accountability would extend to members of the royal family. The Saudis 'made no exceptions to who they would hold accountable', he replied, with senior officials included, though given that this pledge to him had come from the crown prince personally – and that many of the men visiting the consulate had worked for the prince – how much was that pledge worth?

On the day of Pompeo's visit to Riyadh, the *New York Times* confirmed that at least nine of the fifteen suspects identified from Turkish surveillance pictures worked for the Saudi security services. Further newspaper investigations would reveal that all of them, including the forensic scientist Dr al-Tubaigy, were government employees with military or intelligence backgrounds.

As awkward as the emerging facts were, Pompeo did not want to discuss them. 'I don't want to talk about any of the facts,' he told a travelling pool of journalists. 'They didn't want to, either.'

The Saudis had however realised that they could no longer brazen this crisis out by maintaining that Khashoggi had left the consulate alive. Security cameras, which they thought they had disabled, not only revealed to Turkish police the identities of those who had entered the building, but also that the journalist had never been seen leaving it.

The version of events the Saudis were preparing to unveil would absolve the crown prince of any knowledge – but for that plan to work, it depended upon the Turks, and the CIA, not releasing any intelligence that might incriminate MbS further.

However, several leading senators had already made up their minds. 'I'm going to sanction the hell out of Saudi Arabia,' Senator Lindsey Graham, a close ally of the president, said in an extraordinary outburst on *Fox & Friends*, calling upon the kingdom to choose a new leader.

'This guy is a wrecking ball,' he said of the crown prince, describing him as 'toxic' and a man who 'has got to go' and who 'can never be a leader on the world stage'.

'He had this guy murdered in a consulate in Turkey, and to expect me to ignore it? I feel used and abused,' he said. 'I'm not going back to Saudi Arabia as long as this guy's in charge.'

Graham could be as damning in his conclusion as he was because of Senate access to intelligence assessments, the existence of which the president himself had not yet acknowledged.

The same day, a Saudi donation of $100 million, pledged back in August, arrived in a US government bank account to help pay for 'stabilisation' in north-eastern Syria. US officials briefed the press that the timing was a coincidence and that the money had been long expected, but it certainly reminded the Americans that their strategic partnership with Saudi Arabia was wide-ranging and included financial benefits.

Pompeo's next destination, Ankara, gave him the chance to hear Turkey's version of events, though his meeting with President Erdoğan was restricted to forty minutes at the city's Esenboga airport. A Turkish newspaper had just made the sensational claim that it had details of a secret audio recording of Khashoggi's final moments. The leak was part of a Turkish government campaign to apply pressure on the Americans, who might in turn apply pressure on the Saudis to co-operate and tell the truth. Khashoggi had been killed within minutes of his arrival, then dismembered, beheaded, his fingers allegedly cut off. Regardless of Turkey's recordings, Pompeo, a former CIA director himself, surely knew by now that intercepts obtained by the National Security Agency provided enough evidence of a plot to bring Khashoggi home by force, although the Trump administration preferred giving the appearance that it was responding to Turkish intelligence first.

Within the space of two days, Pompeo had shuttled between two significant American allies with vastly different agendas and irreconcilable versions of the truth. However, as we shall see in the next chapter, relations with Turkey, a NATO member, were already at their lowest level in decades.

The Saudis, by contrast, were plunged into this diplomatic crisis after almost two years of being welcomed and pampered by Washington. Jared Kushner's friendship with MbS was at the heart of this relationship. It could even be argued that the Trump administration had emboldened the crown prince by making no public stand against his previous transgressions. In the case of his Ritz-Carlton round-up, Trump had even endorsed it on Twitter.

The Saudis would, Secretary of State Pompeo said, be given 'a handful of days more' to complete their investigation 'so they get it right'.

That week, the *Washington Post* published Khashoggi's posthumous final column, submitted by his translator and assistant to the paper the day after he'd disappeared. 'What the Arab world needs most is free expression', ran the headline.

From beyond the grave, the journalist returned to what he regarded as what should have been the greatest event of his lifetime: the Arab Spring of 2011. 'The Arab world was ripe with hope,' he wrote. 'These expectations were quickly shattered; these societies either fell back to the old status quo or faced even harsher conditions than before.'

He wrote about his friend, the prominent Saudi writer Saleh al-Shehi, who was serving a five-year prison sentence for 'insulting the royal court'. Al-Shehi's apparent crime was one Khashoggi could easily have committed himself. He had appeared on Saudi television and talked about corruption within royal court circles over the purchase of land.

The journalist thanked the *Post* for publishing many of his articles in Arabic and advocated yet another of his many schemes for the Arab world – the creation of a new media platform publishing Arab voices.

Too often, he argued, the international community was staying silent in the face of Arab government clampdowns on freedom of the press. 'These actions may trigger condemnation quickly followed by silence,' Khashoggi wrote. *Condemnation followed by silence*; it read like a grim foretelling of the global reaction to his own murder.

Khashoggi's editor, Karen Attiah, who had hoped to edit the article with him, added her own comment: 'This column perfectly captures his commitment and passion for freedom in the Arab world. A freedom he apparently gave his life for.'[12]

On 18 October, almost two and a half weeks after Khashoggi's disappearance, President Trump faced up to the reality of the situation – that there would have to be consequences for Saudi Arabia, his closest Arab ally, because the journalist had been killed.

'This one has caught the imagination of the world, unfortunately,' he told the *New York Times*.[13] 'Unless the miracle of all miracles happens, I would acknowledge that he's dead.'

In an interview which the paper described as 'uncharacteristically guarded', Trump said it was still 'a little bit early' in the process to draw definitive conclusions about who ordered the killing. The CIA, however, was reported to be increasingly convinced of the crown prince's culpability.

'They've been a very good ally, and they've bought massive amounts of various things and [made] investments in this country, which I appreciate,' Trump said of the Saudis. It sounded as if he still wanted to make excuses for them, even as the evidence was stacking up.

'This is bad, bad stuff,' he admitted later, as he boarded a flight to Montana for a political rally, 'and the consequences should be severe.'

The *New York Times* reported that the president was now telling allies he barely knew the crown prince and that he was playing down his son-in-law's relationship with him too.

'They're two young guys, Jared doesn't know him well or anything,' Trump later told the *Washington Post*. 'They are just two young people. They are the same age. They like each other, I believe.'[14]

Kushner was said to be urging the president to stand by the prince in the hope that the crisis would blow over. However, at least three lobbying firms in Washington DC cancelled their contracts with the Saudis, who had spent $27 million on lobbying in 2017. It came as no surprise that the Saudi embassy cancelled its annual national day reception, apparently out of fear that its usual supporters might not show up.

In a show of defiance, the crown prince had refused to postpone his investment conference known as 'Davos in the Desert'. He was reported to be surprised by the international backlash and to have formed a 'crisis committee' of advisers to keep him informed of the latest developments.

Still, if he was to be absolved of responsibility for the murder, somebody else would have to take the blame. The Americans were told that the Saudis were preparing to assign fault to a Major General, Ahmed al-Asiri, the deputy head of intelligence and a close adviser to the crown prince. Asiri spoke good English and French and up to the summer of 2017 had spent two years as a public spokesman for the Saudi military campaign in Yemen.[15]

Asiri had past form in covering up for Saudi mistakes. 'Why would we acknowledge something that doesn't exist?' he asked a reporter in 2015, denying that air strikes in Yemen had killed non-combatants.[16]

~

On Saturday 20 October, the Saudi government finally changed its story; from seventeen days of outright denial of any knowledge, what their interior minister called 'lies and baseless allegations' that Khashoggi had been killed, to admitting that he was indeed dead.

The Saudis had no choice and realised they could no longer brazen this out. President Trump had as good as said that the journalist was no longer alive.

It was a dramatic change of course, and it came in the form of a tweet from the Saudi foreign ministry released in the early hours of Saturday morning. The tweet said that a prosecutor's preliminary investigation had shown that 'suspects' had travelled to Istanbul to meet the journalist 'after indications appeared of the possibility of returning Jamal Khashoggi to the country'.

'Discussions' with him had taken place, the statement said, as if there was a real possibility of a mutually agreed return home. These 'discussions' had not gone as required, the foreign ministry said – in fact, they 'escalated negatively', which 'led to a fight and then a quarrel between some of them and the citizen'.

'The brawl aggravated to lead to his death and their attempt to conceal and cover up what happened.'

The new version of events was that a rendition attempt had gone so badly that it ended with a fight, in which Khashoggi died. In other words, this was no premeditated murder but an accident. Although nothing on the audio tape of the killing suggested anyone had tried to resuscitate the journalist; and nobody on the recording could be heard expressing surprise at the outcome.

'The Kingdom expresses its deep regret at the painful developments that have taken place and stresses the commitment of the authorities in the Kingdom to bring the facts to the public,' the statement said.

The Saudis said eighteen unnamed people had been detained. It was later claimed that fifteen of them were members of the Rapid Intervention Group listed by the Turks as having flown into Istanbul, as well as three intelligence officers from the consulate itself. There was no information as to where the body was, though Saudi officials told journalists it had been handed over to a 'local collaborator' for disposal.

An additional five officials were listed by the Saudi news agency as having been fired by royal decree. Even though the Saudis were saying Khashoggi had died in a brawl, senior officials were being hung out to dry. Four of them were intelligence officers of major-general rank and above. The most senior being General Rashad bin Hamed al Mohammed, director of the General Directorate of Security and Protection.

As the Americans anticipated, the group included Major General Ahmed al-Asiri, the deputy head of his country's spy agency, the General Intelligence Directorate.

The fifth to be sacked was described as a 'senior adviser of the royal court', understood to be Saud al-Qahtani: the crown prince's aide who had banned and blacklisted Khashoggi and was believed to have been in touch with the leader of the hit squad in Istanbul on the day of the murder. A Saudi official, quoted by the New York Times, said he had been fired because he knew about the operation; but although Qahtani altered his Twitter biography some twenty-four hours later, he still listed himself as head of the 'Saudi Federation for Cybersecurity'.[17]

How serious the Saudis were about sanctioning Qahtani, who as we shall see did not face trial, would become a contentious issue between Washington and Riyadh. Reuters had it confirmed from four sources the following month that MbS's right-hand man was still at liberty, although operating discreetly.[18]

In a farewell tweet after the announcement of his sacking, Qahtani said he was indebted to what he called his 'masters'.

'I will forever be a loyal servant to this country and this nation shall always stand tall,' he wrote to his 1.3 million Twitter followers.[19]

It was certainly not a confession, let alone an apology; more like confirmation that he was bowing out in the belief that he had acted in the Saudi national interest. It recalled an earlier tweet Qahtani had written in August 2017, boasting that his authority came from the top: 'I am an employee and trustworthy executor of the orders of the king and the crown prince.'

The official Saudi statement did nothing to reduce the clamour for answers. The governments of the UK, France and Germany issued a joint statement the following day.

'There remains an urgent need for clarification of exactly what happened on 2 October – beyond the hypotheses that have been raised so far in the Saudi investigation, which need to be backed by facts to be considered credible,' the statement said.

It continued: 'We thus stress that more efforts are needed and expected towards establishing the truth in a comprehensive, transparent and credible manner. We will ultimately make our judgement based on the credibility of the further explanation we receive about what happened and our confidence that such a shameful event cannot and will not ever be repeated.'

Scuffles could be heard in the audio recording of Khashoggi's final moments, but the notion that he had been accidentally killed in a brawl was backed up by no evidence.

'If Khashoggi was fighting inside the Saudi consulate in Istanbul, he was fighting for his life with people sent to capture or kill him,' said Congressman Adam Schiff, the ranking Democrat on the House Intelligence Committee, who'd received a classified briefing on what America's spy agencies already knew.

If Khashoggi's death really was an accident, why had Brigadier General Mutreb asked if it was possible 'to put the body and hips into a bag' before the journalist had even arrived? And why did Dr Tubaigy respond in the negative, complaining that his fellow Saudi had 'buttocks like a horse'?

'They would have been better off saying that Colonel Mustard did it in the library with the candlestick,' Steven Cook of the US Council on Foreign Relations told the *New York Times*. 'Who would want to be associated with this story?'[20]

CIA officials had by now listened to the audio recordings from inside the consulate: they did not corroborate the claim of a fight. The sixty-year-old man had been physically overwhelmed and one of the men involved could be heard saying 'let him cut!' If Khashoggi was dead less than half an hour after his arrival, how much persuasion or even intention can there really have been to bring him home?

And hadn't the crown prince lied on 3 October, when he told Bloomberg News his understanding was that Khashoggi had 'got out after a few minutes or one hour'? Given that two of those supposedly sacked – the media adviser and deputy head of intelligence – were known to be close to the crown prince, what were the chances that the prince knew nothing about the crime?

'They now expect the world to believe that Jamal died in a fight following a discussion,' commented Fred Ryan, chief executive of the *Washington Post*. 'This is not an explanation – it is a cover-up.'

President Trump told the *Post* in an interview that Saudi Arabia was 'an incredible ally' and that although 'there's been deception and there's been lies' and 'their stories are all over the place', he was keeping an open mind on the crown prince's involvement.

'Nobody has told me he's responsible. Nobody has told me he's not responsible,' Trump said. 'I would love if he wasn't responsible.'

'There is a possibility he [the crown prince] found out about it afterward,' he explained. 'It could be something in the building went badly awry . . . he could have known they were bringing him back to Saudi Arabia.'

He once again praised Riyadh for buying American weapons and said 'we've got nobody else over there' to protect Israel. 'Iran is as evil as it gets,' he added, his mind apparently more focused on Tehran than Riyadh.

The president was touring an air force base in Arizona when he announced that although he wasn't satisfied with the Saudi answers given so far, the Saudi statement and arrests were 'a big first step':

TRUMP: It's only a first step, but it's a big first step.

REPORTER: Do you consider it credible, their explanation?

TRUMP: I do, I do. I mean it's, again, it's early. We haven't finished our review or investigation. But it's a very important first step, and it happened sooner than people thought it would happen.

King Salman and his son the crown prince called Salah Khashoggi, the journalist's eldest son, to express their condolences. The king ordered that a new commission should review Saudi intelligence operations and report back within a month. Three new government departments would be created, including one for legal affairs, meant to ensure that all intelligence operations complied with human rights treaties and international law.[21] Adding to Saudi Arabia's credibility problem, the commission was chaired by the crown prince himself.

In the meantime, a vast network of Saudi twitter handles provided the Saudi government with the chorus of support it craved. By the time Riyadh admitted in the middle of the night that Khashoggi was dead, the Arabic hashtag 'We all trust in Mohammed bin Salman' was trending as among the most popular in the world, appearing more than 1.1 million times.

Within Saudi Arabia's 11 million Twitter users was a network of loyalists, some of them real, some of them apparently government-backed automated accounts. And once Khashoggi was pronounced dead, the trolling of him intensified.[22]

'Hope you're killed, God willing,' one supporter of the crown prince wrote on Twitter.

A column in the *Saudi Gazette* on 18 October had called the Khashoggi incident 'a comedy act . . . orchestrated by haters and ill-wishers in Qatar who were working day and night to come up with this skit'.

'As for [Saudi] opponents,' it continued, 'they are nothing more than small parasites with a very short life cycle.' The column was headlined: 'The drama will be over soon and Saudis will have the last laugh.'

There was also support from Saudi Arabia's Arab allies, the United Arab Emirates, Bahrain and Egypt, with the foreign ministry in Cairo praising the 'kingdom's keenness and commitment to finding the truth'. Saudi Arabia's closest regional partners were already united in their opposition to the Muslim

Brotherhood, with which Khashoggi was accused of associating. They were also part of the Saudi-led coalition at war in Yemen and they had all severed relations with Qatar at the same time.

'This was an operation that was a rogue operation,' the Saudi foreign minister, Adel al-Jubeir, told Fox News, disassociating the kingdom from the men who had killed the journalist in this alleged accident. 'They told us that he left the consulate. They came back to Saudi Arabia. They filed a report to that effect. They made a mistake when they killed Jamal Khashoggi and they tried to cover up for it. Even the senior leadership of our intelligence service was not aware of this.'

Several senior intelligence officers of major-general rank and above had in fact been sacked, which suggested the opposite. And what about the deliberate destruction of evidence for several days afterwards? The foreign minister sent his nation's condolences to the journalist's relatives. 'We feel their pain,' he said.

It was nothing like the pain of Jamal Khashoggi's family; the sorrow of Hanan el-Atr, the Egyptian he had married that summer, or of his Turkish fiancée, Hatice Cengiz. On the day the Saudis produced their first official explanation, Cengiz posted on Twitter a video of one of the journalist's final television interviews. Suddenly a tortoiseshell cat could be seen jumping into his lap, halting the interview and reducing him to fits of laughter. 'They took your bodily presence from my world,' Cengiz wrote, 'but your beautiful laugh will remain in my soul for ever.'

Another Saudi official expanded on the official statement by telling the *Washington Post* that Saudi intelligence had given a general order to 'negotiate with people outside to come back home'. In Khashoggi's case, those talks had gone wrong, but 'there was no order for a kidnapping. There was no order for a killing.'[23]

It was possibly the same senior Saudi official who was quoted telling Reuters there was a 'standing order to negotiate the return of dissidents peacefully', to prevent them from being recruited by enemies of the state, a standing order which did not require 'going back to the leadership'.

Once again, credulity was stretched beyond breaking point: why send fifteen men equipped with tasers and syringes to negotiate? Surely something as major as soldiers, intelligence officers and a forensic scientist flying on privately chartered jets with diplomatic clearance in a covert swoop on an unsuspecting Saudi abroad required authorisation at the highest level?

The same Saudi official claimed that Ahmed al-Asiri had assembled the fifteen-member team to go to Istanbul to try to convince Khashoggi. Asiri had asked Saud al-Qahtani if he could borrow one of his employees to conduct the negotiations – Brigadier General Mutreb. Mutreb was deliberately picked because he had known the journalist in London and so was in the best position to persuade him.

The alleged plan was to hold Khashoggi in a safe house outside Istanbul for a 'period of time' but to release him if he refused to go home. This new Saudi version of events was allegedly based upon testimony from the detained suspects.

After all, Khashoggi had exclaimed 'I am being kidnapped' in the audio recording, followed by a voice saying 'we will anaesthetise you'.

Then when Khashoggi raised his voice, the team panicked and resorted to violence, covering his mouth and placing him in a chokehold from which he did not recover.

'They tried to prevent him from shouting, but he died,' the anonymous Saudi official told Reuters. 'The intention was not to kill him.'

In this account, it was claimed that it was the job of Dr Salah al-Tubaigy, the autopsy expert, to clean up the crime scene, not to dismember the body. Yet Tubaigy's qualifications suggested otherwise and the Turks were sharing audio recordings with friendly intelligence agencies containing evidence of Tubaigy discussing the practicalities of cutting up a corpse.

The Saudi official said the journalist's body was not beheaded, but rolled up in a rug, then taken to a consular vehicle and given to a 'local collaborator', an Istanbul resident, for disposal.[24]

The Turks repeatedly asked the Saudis to reveal the identity of this individual. They also claim that his existence was subsequently denied by the Saudi prosecutor, Saud al-Mujeb, during a visit to Istanbul.[25]

As for the 'body double', the official in Riyadh admitted that one of the Saudis had left through the consulate's back door, wearing Khashoggi's clothes, glasses and even his Apple watch before heading to the Blue Mosque. However, this was meant to fool the Saudi government more than anyone else.

There was no mention of a fight in this official's account to Reuters, even though the foreign ministry explanation a day earlier had referred to this as the cause of death; no knowledge of where the body was either. At the very least, the Saudis were admitting to having sent fifteen agents to persuade a dissident to return home voluntarily, when previous cases of kidnapping and rendition pointed to there being nothing voluntary about it. The CIA was far from convinced that this was anything other than premeditated murder. In Turkey, President Erdoğan was still waiting for the Saudis to confess to an assassination plot sanctioned at the highest level, even though hundreds of years of bad blood between Saudis and Turks told him they never would.

13

ERDOĞAN AND
THE HOUSE OF SAUD

In Ankara, Turkey's president immediately rejected the official Saudi explanation for Jamal Khashoggi's death. Riyadh still couldn't explain where his body was, beyond claiming that a 'local collaborator' had taken it.

'First they said he walked out and that he wasn't dead. Then they said he happened to die during a fight,' one of President Erdoğan's advisers told me. 'Then they couldn't even come up with a body. Lie after lie after lie! Nobody believes anything that they say.'

The first Saudi delegation, sent to Ankara ten days after the killing, was led by Prince Khalid al-Faisal, aged seventy-eight and the governor of Mecca. It was an astute choice of envoy, given that Khalid was the half-brother of Prince Turki al-Faisal, Khashoggi's former employer and friend. The Saudis believed one of the al-Faisal clan would be best placed to sound out Ankara on a deal that would make this diplomatic crisis go away.

Turkey, after all, was in financial trouble. The country had run up foreign debts of more than $200 billion and was beginning to slide into recession; the lira had lost nearly 40 per cent of its value since the beginning of the year, weakened by President Trump's doubling of tariffs on steel and aluminium imports in a dispute over Pastor Andrew Brunson, an American evangelical Christian jailed in Turkey, accused of being in league with terrorists and trying to overthrow the government but held for over a year without charge.

Qatar, Saudi Arabia's regional rival, had pledged to invest $15 billion in the Turkish economy that summer. Could Saudi Arabia now outspend its rival, possibly in the form of low-interest loans, to make Khashoggi's disappearance disappear?

A 'political ally' of President Erdoğan was quoted by the *New York Times* as saying that the Saudi offer even included an end to its embargo on Qatar, if only the Turks would drop their case against Riyadh.[1] However, the meeting with Prince Khalid broke up after a few hours without agreement.

'Erdoğan said to him, "Are you bribing me, are you trying to buy me?"' a source close to the talks said.

'When Erdoğan is angry, that is it with him,' a senior Turkish diplomat told me. 'So when people say he will "do a deal", they don't really know him.'

Prince Khalid al-Faisal returned home empty-handed. 'It is really difficult to get out of this one,' he told relatives, according to the *New York Times*. Saudi Arabia's ability to buy its way out of a crisis, its belief in the power of money, did not apparently include the ability to buy President Erdoğan.[2]

The history of conflict between the Turks and the al-Saud family stretches back hundreds of years. This history matters a great deal more to the Saudis than it does to the Turks, because it forms part of their nation's founding narrative. It not only hovers in the background of the killing of a man of Ottoman descent, but informs how the Saudi crown prince responded to the affair.

In the late eighteenth century, the Ottoman Empire was

challenged by the emergence of a tribal state in the Arabian peninsula. It was led by the al-Saud clan, in alliance with the puritanical Islamic 'Wahhabi' sect – an alliance which still lies at the social and structural heart of modern Saudi Arabia.

The Ottoman sultan used the title of 'caliph' or Supreme Islamic Ruler, governing from Istanbul, as a means of asserting his authority. Sultan Selim I (r. 1512–20) had first won the title when he overthrew the Mamluk rulers of Syria and Egypt, who held sway over the Hejaz and the holy places of Islam – Mecca and Medina.

In the 1800s, Mecca was captured from the Ottomans and Medina was sacked. The culprits were the al-Sauds and Wahhabis, determined to return the holy places to a purer form of Islam.

In 1818, an Ottoman-Egyptian army took revenge on the al-Sauds by capturing and destroying their capital, Diriyyah, in what is now a suburb of Riyadh. Saud family members were executed while Abdullah bin Saud, the emir, was sent to Istanbul and publicly beheaded there.[3]

Turkish diplomats say the event has never been quite forgiven or forgotten. 'The Saudis reminded me of it while I was there,' Yaşar Yakış, a former Turkish ambassador to Saudi Arabia and foreign minister, told me. 'The Saudis regard the Turks as people who beheaded the king's family.'

As the Ottoman Empire collapsed, it lost control of Mecca and Medina in 1916 and 1919 respectively. The 'Arab revolt' against the Ottomans during the First World War would lead to the partition of vast swathes of the Middle East. The last sultan was forced into abdication and exile in 1922 and with the abolition of the caliphate, there was no longer a Supreme Islamic Ruler in Istanbul.

After hundreds of years of using Arabic script, the newly

created country of Turkey abandoned it in favour of a Latin alphabet. From a new capital, Ankara, a western-facing and Turkish national identity was created. The country became a multi-party democracy, so secular that men were banned from wearing turbans and women were forbidden from wearing the veil outside mosques.

In the meantime, Saudi Arabia, created in 1932, headed in a very different direction as the guardian of its strict Wahhabi faith. Saudi kings took on the title of 'Khadim al-Haramayn al-Sharifayn' or 'Custodian of the Two Holy Places' in Mecca and Medina. Their Turkish overlords were gone for good, although the bulldozing of Ottoman structures in the two Saudi cities, often replaced by grandiose Saudi building schemes, frequently prompted Turkish complaints.

Ankara and Riyadh represent two different branches of Sunni Islam but they are bound together by the religious obligation of all Muslims to perform the hajj pilgrimage at least once in their lifetime – 80,000 Turks were expected to make the journey to Mecca and Medina in 2019.

However, for years irritation has been mounting in Saudi Arabia over Erdoğan's alleged 'neo-Ottomanism' and the increasingly visible role he has played in the Arabic and wider Islamic world.

In 2010, Israeli commandos killed ten Turkish activists on a ship carrying aid to the Gaza Strip. Erdoğan was outraged and became one of the loudest spokesmen for the Palestinian cause. Ever since 1967, King Salman had been head of the fund-raising group, the Popular Committee for Aiding Martyrs, Families and Mujahedin in Palestine. Now his leadership of the Arab Peace Initiative, which began in 2002, was overshadowed and arguably even undermined by Erdoğan.

After the initial success of the Egyptian revolution in 2011,

Erdoğan headed to Egypt as an honoured guest. The Muslim Brotherhood, founded in 1928, had gained traction in Egypt as an Islamist welfare organisation and, after being banned by President Nasser for its terrorist attacks, was now poised to form the first democratically elected government there. Erdoğan's own political career had been inspired by the group and he had entered politics by running the youth wing of an Islamist Welfare Party in Istanbul.

'The freedom message spreading from Tahrir Square has become a light of hope for all the oppressed through Tripoli, Damascus and Sanaa,' Erdoğan said in Cairo, receiving several standing ovations. 'Democracy and freedom is as basic a right as bread and water for you, my brothers.'[4]

Erdoğan's support for the Muslim Brotherhood and for the 'Arab Spring' in general would make him enemies in Riyadh. Ever since the era of Atatürk, modern Turkey's founder, the Turks had tried to avoid involving themselves in intra-Arab disputes, with their diplomats warning that it could only end badly: 'The Arabs eventually forgive each other,' those diplomats said, 'but they will not forgive the former colonial power for whatever it does.'

Erdoğan undoubtedly put this non-interventionist policy into reverse. The same year as his triumphant visit to Egypt, he backed demonstrations against President Assad in Syria. Turkey's southern neighbour descended into a civil war which left hundreds of thousands dead, though Erdoğan's hosting of 3.5 million Syrian refugees also allowed him to claim that his newly assertive country was a sanctuary to Muslims in distress.

Turkey and Saudi Arabia both supported Salafist 'Army of Conquest' rebels, fighting Assad's forces. Though the group splintered after failing to hold its ground in the face of the

Russian bombardment of Aleppo; and Erdoğan became distracted by and fixated with the need to stop Kurds in northern Syria from creating a fledgling state along the Turkish border.

In 2014, the Saudis outlawed the Muslim Brotherhood as a terrorist organisation, thereby confirming that they regarded Turkish support for it as unwelcome interference in Arab affairs. Ankara even allowed a so-called Egyptian parliament-in-exile of Brotherhood politicians to meet in Turkey, after they had fled from Egypt following the coup in 2013. By way of revenge, Saudi Arabia and Egypt reportedly campaigned and successfully blocked Turkey's bid for non-permanent membership of the UN Security Council.

Istanbul had also become a refuge for Arab opposition groups and broadcasting networks, several of them linked to the Muslim Brotherhood. Along the city's main shopping street, Istiklal Caddesi, you were now almost as likely to hear Arabic spoken as Turkish, amid an influx of Syrian and other refugees fleeing the repression and war which followed the failures of the Arab Spring. Turks complained that the increase in sweet pastries on sale reflected the tastes of these new Arab immigrants rather than their own. Catering to this new clientele, one of Istiklal's best-known Turkish restaurants, Haci Baba, was pointedly renamed 'Al Medina' instead, to complaints from Turkish regulars.

'Erdoğan opened up to Arabs and Muslims everywhere,' said Azzam Tamimi, among the last of Khashoggi's friends to see him alive. 'And that is something Arab dictators hate.'

In March 2015, Erdoğan performed the pilgrimage to Mecca himself and met King Salman, Saudi Arabia's new ruler. The two succeeded in developing a personal rapport, though a meeting with his ambitious son, Prince Mohammed bin Salman, did not reportedly go so well.

A Turkish source claimed that the future crown prince, then aged only twenty-nine, would barely let Erdoğan speak and refused to be interrupted by him. It was an inauspicious beginning to a relationship that would reach its lowest point after Jamal Khashoggi's murder.

The following year, the Saudis hired a fleet of some 500 Mercedes Benz vehicles to transport King Salman's vast entourage during his visit to Turkey. Erdoğan took the unusual step of greeting the 'Custodian of the Two Holy Places' at Ankara airport. At the Turkish leader's brand new presidential palace, the king was greeted by an honour guard of Turkish soldiers, as well as sixteen warriors dressed in period costumes, some of them clad in chain mail, representing the various Turkic empires in world history: the display reflected not just Erdoğan's love of the imperial past, but also his desire to project a power, rooted in Islam, which he believed his nation had rediscovered.

In March 2018, six months before Khashoggi's killing, the Saudi crown prince was quoted as describing Erdoğan's ambition as nothing less than an attempt to reinstate the Islamic caliphate, abolished nearly a century before. In a meeting with Egyptian newspaper editors, MbS went even further than that. He was quoted as describing Turkey as part of a 'triangle of evil', with Iran and hard-line Islamist groups forming the other sides of that triangle. It was an extraordinary indication of the hatred he appeared to harbour for the Turkish leader – the most powerful, charismatic and overtly Islamist Turkish leader since Atatürk created the country from the ashes of the Ottoman Empire.[5]

Erdoğan's supporters claimed that Prince Mohammed bin Salman simply could not tolerate the president's championing of Muslim humanitarian causes around the world, from the persecuted Rohingya of Myanmar to the millions Turkey helped feed in Somalia during the 2011 famine there. Six years later, the Turks opened their biggest overseas military base in the Horn of Africa, to train Somali soldiers. Erdoğan's strenuously active foreign policy, combined with his religious piety, was hardly a claim to be Supreme Islamic Ruler – yet the crown prince had come to regard it as a challenge to his own authority.

'All this blather about Erdoğan wanting to become head of the Sunni Muslims is completely false,' an adviser to the Turkish leader told me. 'Arab leaders in general detest Erdoğan because he embarrasses them. Their own people look up to Erdoğan rather than to their own leaders.'

'MbS has this very ambitious vision in the region,' said Hilâl Kaplan, a journalist and friend of the Turkish president. 'He sees himself as the guardian of all the Muslim nations, especially the Sunni bloc. But Erdoğan has a certain sympathy in the Arab street. That's why MbS sees him as a problem.'

The Saudis, and indeed many Arabs, would counter that, as a Turk, Erdoğan commanded very little sympathy at all. Indeed, given the disaster that was Syria, the Turkish leader had dangerously overreached himself there. He stood accused of backing Islamists who threatened the stability of the entire region and of neo-colonial meddling in Arab affairs.

It was Erdoğan's support for the Arab Spring and the Muslim Brotherhood which would draw an enthusiastic Jamal Khashoggi into ever more frequent visits to Turkey. In fact, his personal friendship with the Turkish leader may well have contributed to his misplaced belief that he would be safe there.

Yasin Aktay, the president's adviser, told me that it was the Saudi billionaire Prince Alwaleed Waleed bin Talal who introduced the journalist to the president. Erdoğan had taken the news of his murder personally.

'His death wasn't just an attack on Turkey,' Aktay explained to me. 'It was an attack on the president's friend.'

Khashoggi felt at home in Istanbul. He told friends that the city reminded him of the Medina of his childhood years; and the more 'Arabised' the city became, the more at home he felt. The journalist had long argued that the 'Turkish model' could inspire tolerant, Islamic democracy elsewhere. Even if many Turks would have countered that under Erdoğan, their country was growing increasingly intolerant, locking up more journalists than ever before.

'Jamal said the Saudis could not tolerate any democratic development in the Islamic world,' said Yasin Aktay. 'The Saudis tried to create a phobia about Turkey, because the Turkish model upsets them.'

One of Khashoggi's closest friends in Istanbul was a dissident Egyptian politician, Ayman Nour, who had fled into exile there following the ousting of Egypt's Muslim Brotherhood government in 2013.

Nour had served over three years in jail during the era of President Mubarak, after daring to be the first man to run against him for the Egyptian presidency in 2005. Now Nour was campaigning for democratic reform across the Arab world, beneath a banner reading 'The Defence of Democratic Arab Revolutions', which hung on his office wall in Istanbul.

Nour, like Khashoggi, was friends with Yasin Aktay, and it was inconceivable that such a prominent Egyptian dissident would have been allowed to stay in Turkey without a political decision taken at the highest level.

One of the Egyptian's projects was Al-Sharq TV, an Arabic channel based above a car showroom in a working-class, industrial district of Instanbul. The channel claimed 2 billion views on Facebook in 2018. Though Nour was not himself a member of the

Muslim Brotherhood, state-controlled media in Egypt accused him of links to the outlawed group and accused his television channel of being funded by Qatari businessmen.

In an Arab world bitterly divided over what role Islamist groups should play in the aftermath of the Arab Spring, Nour would endure a lot of the same kind of online abuse that his friend Khashoggi received. The Egyptians were furious with the Turks for sheltering him.

The Egyptian campaign against Nour was so vindictive that in February 2018, the Arabic Twitter feed of Turkey's Anatolian state news agency was hacked for five minutes, during which time a document was posted online accusing the politician of drinking alcohol and hiring prostitutes. The hacker also published potentially compromising photographs of him.

Turkish officials told Nour they believed it was a cyber-attack, launched by Egyptian intelligence. Seven months before Khashoggi's disappearance, it was a clear sign from Saudi Arabia's ally that Arab dissidents could not consider themselves safe in Istanbul.

Ayman Nour claims Khashoggi had agreed to help him set up another television station called 'Middle East TV' before his death. He also provided what he said was the journalist's own account of meeting the crown prince in mid-2016.

MbS had addressed a gathering of prominent writers, Khashoggi included, at an event which lasted around two hours. At the end, the prince pointedly asked the journalist, 'Why do you meet Ayman Nour every time you go to Turkey?'

Khashoggi replied that they were friends. MbS reportedly disliked this answer and their conversation ended there. The journalist certainly carried on visiting the Egyptian dissident – but the very fact that the crown prince asked him about it was surely a sign of how sensitive he was to the presence of Arab dissidents in Istanbul. Why, and how, did the crown prince even know Khashoggi was meeting Nour there?

~

In June 2017, Saudi Arabia led Bahrain and the United Arab Emirates in cutting off diplomatic ties with Qatar. President Erdoğan responded by sending troops to his Gulf ally, fearing it might be invaded. Qatar had once formed part of the Ottoman Empire in the late nineteenth century – now Turkey was establishing its first modern military base there, in what the Saudis regarded as far more than a symbolic Turkish return to Ottoman territory.

Saudi Arabia issued thirteen written demands to end its dispute with Qatar, including the closing down of the Al Jazeera television network and an end to Qatar's support for radical groups; but Erdoğan's Turkey was also the subject of one of Saudi Arabia's demands. Qatar was ordered to 'shut down the Turkish military base that is being established and halt any military co-operation with Turkey in Qatar'. Both Turkey and Qatar refused.

It was into this milieu of mounting tension between Turkey and Saudi Arabia that Jamal Khashoggi, a homesick Arab, stepped during those final weeks of his life in Istanbul.

It is possible that Khashoggi was murdered there purely as a crime of opportunity. After all, the Saudi hit squad had four days' notice that he was coming to collect a document in their consulate, where they could be sure that they would not be interrupted or arrested while they silenced him. Reaching him there would be much easier than in Washington or London.

However, it is not unreasonable to argue that the journalist was also 'collateral damage' in a bigger regional dispute. In fact,

Saudi media initially claimed his killing had been fabricated by Qatar and Turkey. Saudi commentators also blamed a Qatari conspiracy for the international condemnation of Saudi Arabia which followed.[6]

Unsurprisingly, the Saudis fell back on their status as the guardians of Mecca to defend the crown prince's character in the aftermath of Khashoggi's death. On 19 October 2018, the imam of Mecca, Sheikh Abdulrahman al-Sudais, preached a sermon at Friday prayers for God to protect MbS from international conspiracy theories, calling him a 'young, ambitious, divinely inspired reformer'.

'All threats against his modernising reforms are bound not only to fail, but will threaten international security, peace and stability,' the imam said.[7]

Given Erdoğan's acrimonious relationship with the crown prince, it could be argued that he wanted the steady drip of leaks about Khashoggi's killing to force King Salman into choosing a different heir. However, the Turkish leader was acutely sensitive to blatant foreign interference in government. He frequently railed against Fethullah Gülen, a Turkish preacher living in Pennsylvania whom he accused of masterminding a 2016 coup attempt against him; and when his friend Nicolás Maduro, the Venezuelan president, was under American pressure to step down from office, Erdoğan staunchly defended him.

If Erdoğan pushed an international campaign against MbS too far, it could trigger a palace coup in Riyadh and possibly even an assassination attempt against the crown prince. The Turkish leader would therefore never publicly suggest a change of leadership in Saudi Arabia, even though he would prefer not to deal with MbS. It was more likely that Erdoğan wanted to clip the wings of the crown prince, to marginalise him.

Besides, the Turks' own evidence of MbS's involvement had

one major element missing. There was no named reference to him in their audio recordings of the killing, even though the Turks were convinced he'd authorised it.

As a result, Erdoğan often insinuated that MbS was responsible without taking aim at him directly. He wrote in the *Washington Post* that he believed the killing was ordered 'at the highest levels of the Saudi government', although he did 'not believe for a second' that King Salman was aware. 'We must reveal the identities of the puppet masters,' he added darkly.

'The crown prince is fully in control of everything,' one of Erdoğan's advisers told me. 'There is no doubt the man did it. MbS thought he had a licence to do anything. Like James Bond. Like 007.'

'What we are faced with now is not a normal country, not a normal leader,' Erdoğan told Khashoggi's grieving fiancée, Hatice Cengiz.[8] Marginalising that leader would be much easier to achieve if Donald Trump withdrew his support; but Turkish diplomats could see that Trump was not rallying to the Turks' cause. It didn't help that President Erdoğan had managed to lose important friends on the world stage even more successfully than a crown prince now accused of involvement in murder.

14

THE LONELY TURK

If the Saudi crown prince thought he had a licence to kill, maybe it was because of his friendship with the American president, which stood little chance of breaking.

While the UN secretary general, António Guterres, had joined European governments in calling for a thorough and transparent investigation, Trump was still inclined to give the Saudi 'rogue killers' version of events the benefit of the doubt.

In this, he found an ally in Vladimir Putin, who no doubt sensed that while much of the Western world was holding its nose at Khashoggi's murder, here was a potential opening for Russian commercial advantage in Riyadh.

'Those who believe that there was a murder must present evidence,' Putin said in the Russian resort of Sochi, comparing events in Istanbul with allegations that Russian agents had used a nerve agent in Salisbury earlier that year. If Russia found it acceptable to break with the so-called 'rules-based order' and send agents to kill Sergei Skripal, a former double agent, in Salisbury, then it followed that Moscow would be inclined to turn a blind eye to Riyadh's covert operations too.

'There is no reason that would lead anyone not to believe Saudi Arabia's announcements,' Dmitry Peskov, the Kremlin spokesman, said at the end of that month.

However, the German chancellor, Angela Merkel, announced that arms sales to Saudi Arabia 'can't take place in the current circumstances', until the facts of Khashoggi's murder were established. Although this suspension would prove disruptive to defence industry supply chains across Europe, the volume of Germany's sales was insignificant in comparison with those of the US, UK and France. The Skripal case had resulted in the expulsion of Russian diplomats from twenty countries, including the US, Canada and most of the European Union. There was barely any discussion of a similar move against the Saudis.

President Erdoğan felt he needed to apply more pressure, if more international action was to be taken against Riyadh. The same weekend the Saudis revealed their 'rogue killers' explanation, the Turkish leader countered it with a threat to reveal everything Turkey knew.

'Why did these fifteen people come here, why were eighteen people arrested?' he asked. 'These need to be explained in detail.'

'We seek justice and this will be revealed in all its naked truth,' he promised. 'The incident will be revealed entirely.'

He had talked up a forthcoming speech to Turkey's parliament, but in the event the 'naked truth' he revealed did not amount to much. The president confirmed the timing and sequence of events on 2 October even though much of this had already appeared in the Turkish press. Instead, Erdoğan posed a series of questions which were never likely to receive an official answer. 'Why has the consulate general building not been opened to investigation right away but days after?' he asked. 'When the murder was so clear, why have so many inconsistent statements been made? Why has the body of someone, the killing of whom has been officially admitted, not been found yet?'

He also demanded the extradition of the eighteen suspects

the Saudis had arrested and he flatly contradicted the official Saudi claim that Khashoggi's death was an accident. 'This savage murder did not happen instantly but was planned,' he said. 'The conscience of humanity will only be satisfied once everybody is called to account, from those who gave the orders, to those who carried them out.'

With his speech in parliament, the Turkish leader had enjoyed his biggest moment in the international spotlight during the entire crisis and yet had failed to strike a significant blow. He had mentioned neither the audio tapes nor the crown prince. He was begging for Saudi co-operation, asking for the eighteen arrested men to be tried in Istanbul, even though the Saudis were bound to reject that.

It seemed he had decided that neither Turkey's diplomats in Riyadh nor its economic interests would benefit from this diplomatic crisis escalating much further. Yet the view of the president's advisers in Ankara was that the crown prince's name needed to be sufficiently blackened to deter any reckless behaviour in future. It was a question of striking the right balance.

It was also possible that Erdoğan had not entirely thought through what the endgame of his command of the news agenda was, what all this grandstanding was for. He had concluded that King Salman was innocent, and he remained steadfastly deferential towards him.

'I do not believe for a second that King Salman, the Custodian of the Holy Mosques, ordered the hit on Khashoggi,' the Turkish leader wrote in the *Washington Post*.[1] Yet what prospect was there of the king disowning his favourite son?

'The king is physically fit,' a senior Turkish diplomat told me. 'But his brain is not. He would not abandon his son, because with the al-Sauds, family is everything.'

If Erdoğan was not interested in Saudi Arabia's financial assistance, perhaps he could reduce the standing of a regional rival in the aftermath of their disagreements over Qatar, the Muslim Brotherhood and the Arab Spring itself. The problem was, he had so few friends in the west to be able to achieve anything.

Although he invoked Turkey's membership of NATO, writing that 'no one should dare to commit such acts on the soil of a NATO ally again', Turkey's leader had refused to follow the lead of several NATO countries in expelling Russian diplomats after the nerve agent attack on Sergei Skripal in Salisbury.[2]

He had also provoked the fury of NATO commanders and the Americans in particular by agreeing to spend a reported $2.5 billion on a Russian S-400 missile air defence system in 2017. Ironically, the Saudis, keen to demonstrate their own independence from Washington, had been toying with buying the same system.

In Europe, Erdoğan was seen as a useful neighbour, though not one held in high regard. In 2015, more than 900,000 refugees and migrants had arrived in Europe, many by boat, the vast majority from Syria, Iraq or Afghanistan. The European Union then agreed to pay the Turkish government €6 billion in what was in effect a colossal bribe to Erdoğan to keep Muslim migrants at bay. Turkey's own talks on joining the EU had ground to a halt, primarily on human rights grounds, though Erdoğan's insults hadn't helped: in 2017, he had compared the Dutch and German governments to Nazis.

The irony in Erdoğan's championing of justice for Jamal Khashoggi was Turkey's own reputation for locking up journalists, whom he often branded as terrorists. Six members of the Turkish media were jailed for life in 2018 for alleged links to the coup attempt against him two years earlier. Amnesty

International said 180 news organisations had been closed in the previous two years, with 120 journalists detained.

One of those who stood trial was Can Dundar, the editor of one of Turkey's oldest newspapers, *Cumhuriyet*. Dundar was imprisoned after publishing an article alleging that Turkish intelligence had illegally delivered weapons to Islamist groups in Syria. The journalist then fled to Germany, where an attempt to extradite him back to Istanbul failed.

'Whenever I hear Erdoğan vow to follow the case of Khashoggi's murder to the very end, I can only laugh,' Dundar wrote, accusing the Turkish leader of no genuine concern for freedom of the press.[3] By the end of 2018, Turkey had earned the shameful reputation of being the world's biggest jailer of journalists.

It also had more than its fair share of people who had vanished. For years, dozens of relatives had gathered in Istanbul every Saturday to remember and demand justice for the hundreds of Turks and Kurds who disappeared during the 1980s and 1990s, often while in state custody during the conflict with Kurdish separatist guerrillas. Just over a month before Khashoggi's own disappearance, the protestors, known as the 'Saturday Mothers', were dispersed by riot police with tear gas.

Turkish officials have also effectively admitted to their own abduction and arrest programme, claiming to have brought home 100 suspects from eighteen countries, including Kosovo, Mongolia, Azerbaijan, Pakistan, Gabon and Ukraine. All of them were accused of involvement in the 2016 coup attempt: according to a German investigation, at least two private planes used for the prisoner returns had owner addresses linked to Turkish intelligence.[4]

If Europe considered Erdoğan something of a lost cause, America's relations with the Turkish government were at their lowest point in several decades. In a self-inflicted PR disaster for the Turkish president, fifteen of his palace bodyguards were criminally indicted for attacking demonstrators during his visit to Washington in 2017. US prosecutors said the guards 'had assaulted and kicked protesters' outside the Turkish embassy, but charges against eleven of them were quietly dropped.

Erdoğan had repeatedly criticised the United States for failing to extradite Fethullah Gülen, the preacher he accused of orchestrating the coup against him. In what looked like a reciprocal move, the Turks then detained Andrew Brunson, an American pastor, on what looked like ridiculous and politically motivated charges of links to the coup plotters, as well as to Kurdish terrorists. Trump retaliated by imposing sanctions on Turkey's interior and justice ministers and doubling import tariffs on Turkish aluminium and steel. Turkey then responded with its own sanctions and tariffs.

'Those who think that they can make Turkey take a step back with ridiculous sanctions have never known this country or this nation,' Erdoğan said defiantly. 'We have never bowed our heads to such pressure and will never do so.'

It wasn't until ten days after Jamal Khashoggi's death that Pastor Brunson was released and the sanctions were mutually lifted, in what many analysts believed was an attempt by Erdoğan to find a way back into Washington's favour. However, it didn't work. Erdoğan was so unpopular in the West that when it came to the disappearance of a journalist, Turkey – the world's biggest jailer of them – was largely on its own.

15

DAVOS IN THE DESERT

'The man thought he had carte blanche to do what he
wanted. He thought his big brother in the White House
was behind him, so that anything he did would not be
questioned.'

— Adviser to President Erdoğan, describing the
Saudi crown prince

Three weeks on from the murder, on the same day that President
Erdoğan was fulminating about it in the Turkish parliament,
the Saudi foreign ministry released a video of MbS amid a
crowd of Arabs, posing for a selfie, still the image of the youthful, media-friendly, reform-minded prince. In a vast conference
centre adjoining the Ritz-Carlton hotel in Riyadh — where he'd
ordered leading princes and businessmen to be interrogated
under house arrest a year earlier — MbS was presiding over his
so-called 'Davos in the Desert' summit. Unsurprisingly, an
event intended to showcase the Saudi economy and its willingness to diversify away from oil was overshadowed by the global
controversy surrounding Khashoggi's killing.

Some leading Western sponsors and chief executives had
pulled out of the event, though the US treasury secretary,
Steve Mnuchin, only did so after weeks of indecision and after

leading American and European business executives had made the first move. Uber's chief executive, Dara Khosrowshahi, was among those to cancel, even though the Saudis owned a $3.5 billion stake in his company.

'I'm very troubled by the reports to date about Jamal Khashoggi,' the Uber CEO said in a statement to CNBC. 'We are following the situation closely, and unless a substantially different set of facts emerges, I won't be attending.'

Richard Branson, the British chairman of the Virgin Group, put it rather more bluntly. 'I think that people cannot go around killing and cutting up journalists in this day and age, and I think if they do, everybody in the world has to make a stance against that,' he said.

Those who did not cancel had their eyes on the bigger picture: continuing trade and investment. The Pakistani prime minister, Imran Khan, claimed his country was 'desperate' for debt relief. When he returned home from Riyadh with a $6 billion package of aid, it was mission accomplished.

Saudi Aramco, the state-owned oil company, signed memoranda of understanding on deals worth $34 billion – six of the fifteen deals were with US companies – but for an economy that was supposed to be diversifying away from oil, it wasn't the kind of forward-looking project the crown prince liked to talk about.

The moderator of the first discussion panel, a prominent businesswoman named Lubna Olayan, began by telling the audience that she had known Khashoggi. 'May he rest in peace,' she said. 'I want to tell all our foreign guests, for whose presence this morning we are very grateful, that the terrible acts reported in recent weeks are alien to our culture and our DNA.'

There was, however, no hint of criticism of the Saudi

authorities, with Ms Olayan concluding that under the current leadership, she was confident the 'truth would emerge' and that her country would emerge from the crisis stronger.[1]

The same day witnessed the first brief meeting between Khashoggi's eldest son and the crown prince in a palace in Riyadh. As MbS shook his hand for the camera, Salah Khashoggi looked understandably pale and shaken. His father had been killed by men who worked for the man standing in front of him.

The crown prince's unruffled, unapologetic appearance was presumably intended to show a lack of guilt and a total absence of remorse. What choice did the journalist's son have but to take part in this reconciliation? Just a few, sound-less seconds of it were released by Saudi state television to foreign broadcasters.

Prior to this meeting, Salah, a 35-year-old dual Saudi-US national, had been prevented from leaving Saudi Arabia. Shortly after extending his hand to the man widely accused of ordering his father's murder, he was allowed to fly to the US to join his mother, sisters and brother. It looked like a reward for participating in this photo opportunity and keeping rela-tively quiet.[2]

'Jamal used to tell me that what bothered him most was how the Saudi authorities used his children,' Karen Attiah, Khashoggi's editor, said afterwards. 'I think that photo-graph spoke a thousand words and seemed intended for a domestic audience.'[3]

In Salah's first interview alongside his brother on CNN, he said the encounter was widely misinterpreted. 'I mean there was nothing, they were just over-analysing the whole situation', he said. 'The king has stressed everybody involved will be brought to justice,' he continued. 'And I have faith in that.' A wise response, if he wanted to return to his job with the National Commercial Bank in Jeddah and to his wife and daughter.

The Saudi foreign ministry tweeted that the leaders passed 'their deepest condolences and sympathy to the family of Jamal Khashoggi, may God rest his soul'.

The next day MbS gave a speech to 3,000 business delegates at the Davos summit, where he called the killing a 'heinous crime that cannot be justified'.

'The crime that happened is very painful for all Saudis and I believe it is painful to every human in the world,' he said. 'Today, Saudi Arabia is carrying out all legal measures to finalise the investigation, to co-operate with the Turkish government and to present the perpetrators to court.'

The speech, his first since the death had been confirmed, was frequently interrupted by rapturous applause from a mostly Saudi audience. Sitting on stage and also clapping was Saad Hariri, the Lebanese prime minister. Ironic, given that Hariri was himself detained against his will in Riyadh the previous year, allegedly on the crown prince's orders.

Now, three weeks after Khashoggi's murder, MbS even joked about Hariri's fate. 'Prime Minister Hariri will be in town for two more days,' he said. 'So don't anyone say he's been kidnapped.'

It was a bravura performance, and above all an appeal for foreign investment so that Saudi Arabia and the region could become a global economic powerhouse.

'All of our projects are proceeding, reform is proceeding, our war on extremism is proceeding, our war on terrorism is proceeding, developing the kingdom of Saudi Arabia is proceeding,' he said. 'I don't want to leave this life without seeing the Middle East at the forefront of the world.'[4] There was a standing ovation after that. However, the 'amazing deal' he'd promised would be announced during the conference was never revealed, apparently having fallen through.[5]

Among those rushing to the crown prince's defence were Khashoggi's former patrons and friends, Prince Alwaleed bin Talal and Prince Turki al-Faisal. 'I believe the Saudi crown prince will be 100 per cent vindicated and exonerated,' Prince Alwaleed told Fox News.

Prince Turki had been Khashoggi's employer when he was ambassador in London and Washington; but no emotion he may have privately felt would be allowed to interfere with his loyalty to the king's son and presumed heir.

'The more criticism there is of the crown prince, the more popular he is in the kingdom,' Turki explained. 'That's because Saudis feel that their leader is being unfairly attacked in the foreign media. That's true of the royal family as well. They feel this is an attack on Saudi Arabia and the royal family, not just Mohammed bin Salman.'[6]

More significantly, King Salman's last surviving full brother – on paper, at least, a potential threat to the crown prince in the line of succession – flew home from his retirement in London, in what looked like a 'circling of the wagons' of senior Saudi royals.

Prince Ahmed bin Abdulaziz, in his seventies, had reportedly been frightened to return to the kingdom until now, in case the crown prince placed him under house arrest, as other princes had been. That September, Prince Ahmed had been confronted on a London street by protesters chanting against the royal family and the Yemen war. 'Those responsible are the king and his crown prince,' Ahmed had replied.

The video of this exchange was posted on the internet, stirring interest because it suggested a rare display of divisions within the ruling family. Jamal Khashoggi had dismissed the incident at the time.

'Ahmed is as useless as everyone else!' he had told the Palestinian journalist Wadah Khanfar. 'Even if he goes home, he will not radically change anything.'

Khashoggi was posthumously proved correct. When Prince Ahmed returned to Saudi Arabia after two and a half months away, the crown prince greeted his uncle at the airport, suggesting that any family rift had been healed, or put aside at least.[7]

Steven Mnuchin, Trump's treasury secretary, had stayed away from the Davos summit, but he did agree to meet the crown prince; a treasury spokesman said the two discussed the killing, but the focus was clearly on America's regional strategic objectives which Saudi Arabia shared; chiefly isolating Iran, with renewed economic sanctions against the Iranians due to begin the following month.

Mnuchin was the first senior American official to meet MbS since the Saudis confirmed Khashoggi was dead, but the US Treasury notably refrained from posting the usual photograph or statement afterwards.[8] Jared Kushner talked to the prince several times by phone. He told CNN he'd advised MbS 'to be fully transparent' and that the Trump administration's fact-finding was continuing so it could 'determine what we want to believe and what we think is credible and what we think is not credible'.

Kushner's phrase 'what we want to believe' was an interesting indication of the administration's thinking.

MbS strongly denied his involvement to President Trump himself. 'This was at a lower level,' the president said he was told. Although Trump was continuing to reserve judgement on the crown prince's involvement, on 23 October he revoked the visas for and blacklisted twenty-one Saudis the US identified as involved in the operation.

'They had a very bad original concept,' he said, as if he was judging the business skills of a contestant on his hit television show, *The Apprentice*. 'It was carried out poorly, and the cover-up was one of the worst in the history of cover-ups. Very simple. Bad deal. Should have never been thought of. Somebody really messed up. And they had the worst cover-up ever.'

Although his secretary of state talked about this not being the administration's last word on the subject, wider economic sanctions called for by US senators were not on Trump's agenda; still less so, the suspension of arms sales or ending support for the war in Yemen.

Other leaders had begun to take a more confrontational stance. Theresa May called King Salman, Prince Mohammed's father. A Downing Street spokesman said May had told the king that 'the current explanation lacks credibility' and that 'all individuals' responsible for the killing 'must be properly held to account'. Suspects would be prevented from entering the UK and any visas already issued would be revoked.

'This issue has become fairly hysterical,' said the Saudi foreign minister, Adel al-Jubeir. 'I think people have assigned blame on Saudi Arabia with such certainty before the investigation is complete.'

However, it wasn't until 29 October, almost a month after the killing, that the top Saudi prosecutor and head of the official inquiry, Saud al-Mujeb, met his Turkish counterpart in Istanbul, only staying for three days.

'When the crown prince telephoned me, he said, "Can I send my chief prosecutor?" President Erdoğan explained. 'And I said, "Of course, he is welcome to come."'

The prosecutor's visit produced a third Saudi version of

events, following on from outright denial and then the claim that Khashoggi was killed in a fight. In a brief statement, the prosecutor acknowledged that Turkey's evidence indicated the 'suspects in the incident had committed their act with a premeditated intention'.[9]

In other words, there had been a plan to kill the journalist, that it was not a mistake as had been previously claimed. It wasn't the Saudis' final explanation – there would be another a few weeks later – but their latest shift was probably a result of Turkey agreeing to share some of the audio recordings with Saudi intelligence.

'The recording is truly atrocious,' Erdoğan told a Turkish newspaper. 'In fact, when the Saudi intelligence officer listened to the recording he was so shocked that he said, "This one probably took heroin. Only someone who took heroin would do it."'[10]

The Turkish side asked the Saudi prosecutor who had ordered the mission and where the body was and was exasperated when he refused to provide any answers. No statement from any of the eighteen suspects supposedly under arrest was provided either. The Saudi prosecutor had still not identified the alleged 'local collaborator' who was accused of disposing of the body: the Turks concluded this figure was a myth.

'Instead of co-operating with us, he was trying to milk us for information,' an adviser to President Erdoğan told me.

Al-Mujeb wanted access to Khashoggi's mobile phones. Given that they contained his contacts and a record of whom he'd spoken to – and given those people and their relatives could be in danger themselves if the Saudis identified them – the Turks refused to hand them over. Obstruction was met with obstruction.

'They wanted Khashoggi's contacts, his emails, his

pictures – things which were not relevant to the case,' a senior Turkish diplomat told me.

Al-Mujeb invited his Turkish counterpart to Riyadh for joint interrogations of the eighteen suspects, but the Turkish leader called this 'a desperate and deliberate stalling tactic' and dismissed the offer. If Mujeb's team of investigators ever found any evidence of their own (unlikely, given the whole point was to destroy it) then it was never shared with the Turks.

President Erdoğan was additionally frustrated that no action had been taken against the Saudi consul general, who, in the president's words, had 'lied through his teeth' before fleeing to Saudi Arabia.

'You should show us the body,' Erdoğan said. 'If you cannot make them talk . . . then give them to us and we will put them on trial.'

Saudi Arabia does not extradite its citizens, and so Istanbul's chief prosecutor, Irfan Fidan, had begun putting together a criminal case without the prospect of suspects ever appearing in a Turkish dock. Turkish media reports said more than a dozen Turkish members of staff at the consulate, including drivers and telephone operators, were being interviewed.

The prosecutor's task was much harder than the security camera footage and the sensational details leaked to newspapers might suggest. Despite a police review of hundreds of hours of closed-circuit television footage from eighty locations and a forensic examination of the consulate and residence, even of the nearby underground sewers, no human remains had been found. It was the most glaring omission from the prosecutor's findings so far.

The 1963 Vienna Convention on consular relations, signed by both Turkey and Saudi Arabia, makes a consulate a protected space under international law. It was also unclear how admissible recordings illegally obtained by espionage would be in court, assuming Turkey's spies would even release them.

In his first statement, Turkey's chief prosecutor, Iran Fidan, did not refer to any audio recordings but said that Khashoggi had been 'strangled as soon as he entered the consulate' as part of 'premeditated plans'. The body was then 'destroyed by being dismembered, once again confirming the planning of the murder'.

Fidan added that meetings with his Saudi counterpart to establish the truth had not led to a 'concrete outcome'.[11]

Not only had all the suspects fled the country, but laying charges for a trial *in absentia* in Turkey would inevitably result in a spotlight on its domestic human rights record, including widespread allegations of arbitrary detentions and, ironically, the unfair trials of journalists. Nevertheless, the Turks prepared extradition requests for eighteen Saudis.

'Hand them over to us,' Erdoğan said. 'The event took place in Istanbul. We will judge them.'

On 2 November, the Turkish president penned an opinion piece in the *Washington Post* claiming that 'Khashoggi was killed in cold blood by a death squad, and it has been established that his murder was premeditated.'

But Khashoggi's children, all of them now in America, were not about to risk their ties to their homeland by implicating their government in their father's death. The journalist's eldest son, Salah, depended on government permission to leave his home in Jeddah and travel to the United States to sort out his father's affairs.

In their first interview, Salah and his brother Abdullah told CNN they scoured the media for details about their father's killing; but they avoided any criticism of Riyadh. 'It's confusing and difficult,' 33-year-old Abdullah said. 'It's not a normal situation and not a normal death. I really hope that whatever happened wasn't painful for him, or it was quick. Or he had a peaceful death.'[12]

Abdullah described his father as 'like a rock-and-roll star as a journalist', and said that he had joked with him about his alleged membership of the Muslim Brotherhood. 'It's just labels and people not doing their homework properly,' he told the interviewer dismissively.

Above all, the brothers wanted the body returned for burial at the Al-Baqi cemetery in Khashoggi's home city of Medina. Given the body hadn't been found, there was no chance of that.

'Jamal was never a dissident,' added Salah, in a performance of the utmost diplomacy. 'Jamal was a moderate person. He was liked by everybody . . . he believed in the monarchy, that it is the thing that is keeping the country together.'

With the Saudis still refusing, in Erdoğan's words, to 'reveal the puppet masters', more leaks of the Turkish investigation were given to the press. It was revealed that a chemist and toxicologist had helped clean up the crime scene as part of the team of eleven 'investigators' the Saudis had sent to Istanbul.

Although the Saudis were still insisting that prosecutors would bring all the perpetrators to justice, they were still providing no details. At the UN in Geneva, the head of the kingdom's human rights commission, Bandar al-Aiban, declined to answer questions about the status or whereabouts of the eighteen suspects. While Arab states did not even raise the case, more than forty other countries, the US included, had called for a thorough inquiry, though by now several Western delegations were making even more demands: the ending of male guardianship over women, freedom of religion, the ending of the arrest and imprisonment of journalists and activists.

Al-Aiban responded that women could now vote and stand in municipal councils and hold driving licences. Freedom of expression was limited by laws ensuring the 'prerequisites of national security and public order,' he said.[13]

The Saudi royals were hoping that the worst of the crisis was now over. King Salman embarked on a rare domestic tour of the kingdom, a reassuring reminder that the octogenarian was still in charge during a turbulent period for Saudi Arabia on the world stage. His son, MbS, accompanied him, the de facto commander-in-chief also posing for pictures with Saudi soldiers stationed near the border with Yemen.

In the meantime, President Erdoğan was stepping up his war of words with Riyadh, by naming the crown prince for the first time, unsubtly indicating where he believed responsibility ultimately resided.

'The crown prince says, "I am going to clarify the incident and do what is necessary,"' he said. 'The crown prince tells this to my special representatives, and we are waiting patiently . . . we want the person who gave the order to be revealed.'[14]

The drama was about to enter a new phase, with Riyadh issuing the most detailed account of the murder yet. Although, to the fury of Turkish officials, the Saudis were still insisting that the individual who disposed of Khashoggi's body was not a Saudi at all, but an unnamed and unidentifiable Turk.

16

THE SAUDIS VS THE CIA

On 15 November, Saud al-Mujeb, the Saudi prosecutor, produced his final report.[1] It confirmed the findings of 19 October – that the order from the deputy head of intelligence (Major General al-Asiri) had been to bring Khashoggi home alive, not dead, 'by means of persuasion, if not by force', but that 'the head of the negotiation team decided to murder the victim if the negotiations failed'.

Jamal Khashoggi's death was no longer an accident. Instead, the decision to kill him was taken by Brigadier General Mutreb on the ground in Istanbul. In other words, the world was supposed to believe that the hit squad's commander had changed the mission's purpose and defied the orders of his bosses in Riyadh.

No suspects were named, but five individuals were said to have confessed to the murder. The prosecutor made no reference to MbS, although his spokesman said later that 'he did not have any knowledge'.

'Absolutely, his royal highness the crown prince has nothing to do with this issue,' added Adel al-Jubeir, the Saudi foreign minister.

The prosecutor's report said the journalist had been involved in a 'physical altercation' and then drugged so heavily that the overdose killed him.

'It was after a struggle, a fight, and the administering of a high dose of a lethal injection which led to his death,' explained Shaalan al-Shaalan, the prosecutor's deputy. 'May God rest his soul.' In the new Saudi version, the lead negotiator – Mutreb – had decided that transferring Khashoggi out of the building alive by force was impractical, so when the journalist didn't co-operate in his rendition, he was killed in the consulate. His body was then 'dismembered by the individuals who killed him and it was then taken out of the consulate building'.

The prosecutor explained the presence of a forensics expert (presumed to be Dr Salah al-Tubaigy, but again not named) as being 'for the purpose of clearing any evidence from the scene, in case force had to be used to return the victim'. There was no reference to his alleged use of a bone saw, though the Saudis were now admitting for the first time that Khashoggi had been cut into pieces.

The Saudis said that after five men removed his corpse, one of them gave it to a 'collaborator'. There was an artist's impression of this figure, which was not made public.

'The prosecutor said he was Turkish-looking,' a senior Turkish diplomat told me. 'We didn't take it seriously, so we didn't request the picture.'

The Saudi report admitted that the consulate's surveillance cameras had been deliberately disabled and that an unnamed culprit had been identified.

Eleven anonymous suspects in all had been charged with crimes related to the killing – a reduction from the fifteen operatives the Saudis originally said formed the team. A lower number too than the eighteen suspects the Saudis said they had arrested the previous month. It later emerged that the consul general, Mohammed al-Otaibi, a likely accessory to the crime at the very least, was not among those arrested or charged. Of the eleven, the death penalty was being sought for an unnamed five – presumed to include those at the scene of the murder – chiefly Brigadier General Mutreb and Dr Tubaigy.

Major General Ahmed al-Asiri was accused of issuing the order for Khashoggi's return on Saturday 29 September, the day after the journalist's first visit to the consulate, even though Turkey's spies had audio recordings of a plot being hatched on the day itself.

Without naming any of the men but identifying their positions and roles, the prosecutor's statement made it clear that al-Asiri had asked Saud al-Qahtani, the crown prince's media adviser, to lend him Mutreb for the mission, 'because of his previous relationship with the victim'. (Mutreb had worked at the Saudi embassy in London when Khashoggi was a government spokesman there.) Qahtani had agreed and had even met some of the agents before they flew to Turkey, to 'give them some useful information'.

Qahtani had told the agents of his belief that the 'victim had been co-opted by organisations and countries hostile to the kingdom and that the victim's presence outside Saudi Arabia represents a threat to national security' – presumably a reference to unproven allegations that Khashoggi was in league with the Muslim Brotherhood and conspiring with Qatar.[2] Despite this official admission of Qahtani's involvement with the operation, indeed his provision of a motive, the *New York Times* reported that he had not been charged with any crime.[3]

In short, neither Qahtani nor al-Asiri, both advisers to the crown prince, had authorised murder: it was all decided at the local level and officials in Riyadh had been terribly misled. The Saudi team had covered its tracks and lied to the Saudi authorities by claiming Khashoggi had left the consulate safely.

'Why bring a bone saw to a kidnapping, Your Highness?' was

the headline response of an article in the *Washington Post*, which insisted the killing must have been authorised at the highest levels of the Saudi government.[4]

Saudi officials had previously described Khashoggi's death as an accident during a fight. Now it was caused by injecting the journalist with a large dose of tranquilliser after a physical altercation. Why, Turkish officials asked, did so many men with so many tools come prepared to dismember him, if this was not premeditated murder?

'Sometimes mistakes happen,' Adel al-Jubeir told a press conference. 'Sometimes people exceed their authority.'

A representative of Khashoggi's family asked for Saud al-Qahtani to be brought before the court; but six months after the killing, that had still not happened.

The Saudi prosecutor's report on 15 November had made it clear there was no expectation a body would be found, a 'local collaborator' having allegedly spirited it away; so the next day, a Friday, the Khashoggi family began an official period of mourning, now that they knew for sure that there would be no funeral.

The journalist's eldest son, Salah, stood in line with two of his uncles to receive condolences from hundreds of male visitors. Several prominent businessmen attended the event in Jeddah, including Saleh Kamel, the media magnate who had been among those detained in the Ritz-Carlton. British and American diplomats paid their respects, but senior members of the Saudi royal family stayed away.[5] Tens of thousands of worshippers also prayed for the deceased in Mecca and Medina, Khashoggi's home town, though the imams did not name the well-known journalist.

Simultaneously, hundreds gathered for prayers outside the Fatih mosque in a rainswept Istanbul, not far from the apartment Jamal Khashoggi had bought and in an area where many Arab exiles had made their home. The mourners gathered round a slab of marble, where the journalist's body should have been laid out before burial, and said the Salat al-Gha'ib, the prayer for the dead who are missing.[6]

'Just because we have performed his funeral prayers does not mean we will stop asking for his body,' said Yasin Aktay, Khashoggi's friend.

His fiancée, Hatice Cengiz, tweeted a picture of him with the caption: 'Dear Jamal, rest in peace. We will meet in heaven, God willing.'

'As I waited in hope that he would come out of the consulate, every hour, and then every day, felt like a year,' she had written earlier that month in the *Washington Post*.[7]

'The Trump administration has taken a position that is devoid of moral foundation,' she continued. 'Some in Washington are hoping this matter will be forgotten with simple delaying tactics. But we will continue to push the Trump administration to help find justice for Jamal. There will be no cover-up.'

What followed was not the justice Cengiz had in mind. Just hours after charges against eleven unnamed Saudis were announced in Riyadh, the Trump administration said it was imposing financial sanctions on seventeen, most of whom, but not all, were already in Saudi custody – what Trump called 'heavy sanctions, massive sanctions on a large group of people'.[8]

The president's over-emphasis seemed intended to shut the door on a subject he wanted closed. It certainly wasn't the response Cengiz had hoped for.

Most significantly, the US Treasury's list named Saud al-Qahtani as 'a senior official of the Government of Saudi Arabia who was part of the planning and execution of the operation that led to the killing of Mr Khashoggi'.[9]

The 'that led to the killing' might have appeared to absolve the crown prince's adviser of culpability for the murder itself; but the fact remained that America had taken action against a man the Saudis themselves had not charged with any crime.

The operation was 'co-ordinated and executed by his [Qahtani's] subordinate Maher Mutreb', the US Treasury statement said. Fourteen other operatives who had flown with Mutreb to Istanbul were also named individually by Washington, including Dr Tubaigy.

'The Saudi officials we are sanctioning were involved in the abhorrent killing of Jamal Khashoggi,' the US treasury secretary, Steven Mnuchin, said in a written statement. 'These individuals who targeted and brutally killed a journalist who resided and worked in the United States must face consequences for their actions.'

Mnuchin called on Saudi Arabia to end the targeting of dissidents and journalists. America would hold accountable, his statement said, all those it found responsible 'to achieve justice for Khashoggi's fiancée, children, and the family he leaves behind'.[10]

Mohammed al-Otaibi, the consul general who had fled home from Istanbul, was also among those named by Washington as being responsible for or complicit in serious human rights abuses. The Saudis had not charged him with any crime either. Yet America's sanctions list did not include Major General al-Asiri, whom the Saudis indicated had ordered the rendition — and whom the Germans were understood to have included on their list of eighteen Saudi nationals banned from Europe.

The Canadians sanctioned seventeen Saudis; the French eighteen. Any sense of a co-ordinated international response to the killing was strikingly absent. None of those named by the Americans could be said to be members of the Saudi leadership.

Apart from Qahtani and Mutreb, none of the reasoning for inclusion on Washington's list was given.

So why was Major General Asiri not on America's list? The month before the killing, Asiri had met US Secretary of State Mike Pompeo in New York. It later emerged that Asiri was involved in a plan to train and modernise the Saudi intelligence service, involving a US company and former CIA officials.[11] Perhaps the Americans knew from their relationship with Asiri, or from their own communications intercepts, that he wasn't involved, or they wanted to protect him. Either he was guilty as charged, or he was the 'fall guy' for someone higher up the chain of command, possibly the crown prince himself, who may have decided to sacrifice the general in his place.

If the Trump administration hoped its financial sanctions on seventeen individuals would be the end of the affair, it must have known that it wouldn't be so easy.

'We are pretending to do something and doing NOTHING,' tweeted Rand Paul, the Republican senator from Kentucky, in response.

'The administration appears to be following the Saudi playbook of blaming mid-level officials and exonerating its leadership,' said Senator Tim Kaine, a Democrat from Virginia, where Jamal Khashoggi had made his home.[12] Kaine met some of the journalist's children and was advocating a 'fundamental re-evaluation' of US–Saudi relations.

It wasn't just Congress that wouldn't drop the subject quietly. Still to come was the CIA's own inquiry into what happened to the US resident. A leaked version of it appeared the day after US sanctions were imposed on the seventeen individuals.

The CIA's assessment, first reported by the *Washington Post*, concluded that Crown Prince Mohammed had most likely ordered the killing. If the conclusion was hardly surprising, given the intelligence leaks and the speculation that MbS must have been involved, it was nevertheless shocking to read it in black and white: the man set to rule the world's biggest oil exporter for the next fifty years or more was accused of having a journalist murdered.

The CIA's conclusion was reached with 'medium to high confidence'. The crown prince, the agency said, 'person-ally targeted Khashoggi' and 'probably ordered his death',[13] although 'to be clear, we lack direct reporting of the crown prince issuing a kill order'.[14] Although this critical piece of the intelligence jigsaw was missing, all the other pieces provided a compelling picture of the crown prince's involvement.

'We assess it is highly unlikely this team of operators . . . carried out the operation without Mohammed bin Salman's approval,' the report said, adding that MbS had ordered the targeting of opponents at home and abroad, sometimes vio-lently, since 2015.

'The accepted position is that there is no way this happened without him being aware or involved,' a US official was quoted as saying, adding that MbS 'goes from zero to 60, [and] doesn't seem to understand that there are some things you can't do'.[15]

The National Security Agency had gone back through its computerised archive of routine intercepts of senior Saudi royals and found a phone call between the crown prince's brother, Prince Khalid, then ambassador in Washington, and Khashoggi. The ambassador allegedly assured the journalist it would be safe to visit the Saudi consulate in Istanbul to collect the documents he needed for his marriage. The *Post* reported 'people familiar with the call' as saying it wasn't clear whether Khalid knew Khashoggi would be killed; but that Khalid's call to the journalist had been made at the direc-tion of his brother, the crown prince.

Evidence the CIA had reviewed also included the eleven messages MbS reportedly sent Saud al-Qahtani in the hours before and after the journalist's death. There was also a phone call made from inside the consulate from the operation's leader, Maher Abdulaziz Mutreb, to Saud al-Qahtani, advising him the operation had been completed. 'Tell your boss,' was the phrase Mutreb had used. As we've already seen, Qahtari had boasted about his confidential relationship with his boss, none other than the presumptive heir to the Saudi throne.

∼

The Saudi embassy's spokeswoman in Washington responded by claiming its ambassador had never discussed Khashoggi's visit to Turkey. Then the ambassador tweeted his own denial, claiming his last contact with the journalist had been by text message almost a year before the killing, on 26 October 2017.

'I never talked to him by phone and certainly never suggested he go to Turkey for any reason,' Prince Khalid tweeted.

By naming MbS, the leaker of the CIA assessment had no doubt concluded it was the only way to deter him from launching any further attacks on dissidents abroad. In that sense, the publication of the agency's findings could be seen as doing Donald Trump's administration a favour, in that they sought to rein in MbS's allegedly murderous behaviour. On the other hand, the worldwide media interest made it harder to defend the crown prince.

The president instinctively tackled problems by thinking about them in business terms. Here was a moment when he could cut his losses and accept that his bet on MbS had failed to pay dividends. On some level, that would involve a loss of face Trump was apparently not prepared to accept, especially when those dividends were still on course to pay out in the form of completed arms deals. In the absence of evidence of a firm 'kill order' from the crown prince, Trump decided to tough this scandal out.

It wasn't just the arms deals. Severing ties would also mean walking away from a leader President Trump's own son-in-law, Jared Kushner, had befriended and cultivated above and beyond the usual channels of diplomacy. As a White House adviser, Kushner's own credibility was already endangered by constant delays to his enormously ambitious pet project, the delivery of a Middle East peace agreement between Israel and the Palestinians. Any attempt to jettison the crown prince would reflect even more badly on the judgement of Jared Kushner himself.

The CIA's assessment was that MbS was likely to survive the scandal and become king. It was not, the White House concluded, in America's interests to attempt to change the course of Saudi history. For several weeks now, US intelligence had made available to the White House phone intercepts suggesting the crown prince's involvement; and for weeks, the president had pushed back at the evidence, claiming it was not definitive. It was the US's own phone intercepts, rather than Turkey's recording of the killing itself, which had proven more important pointers towards the crown prince's culpability, and for President Trump those pointers still weren't good enough.

'If we abandon MbS, does it guarantee the Saudis will choose someone else we like better?' was the argument put by officials in Washington pressing for continuing engagement with Riyadh. 'If we only worked with the virtuous in the Middle East, we wouldn't work with anyone,' said one retired Western ambassador to Riyadh.

A copy of the Turkish audio recording of the murder had arrived in Washington, and although Trump's CIA director, Gina Haspel, had talked him through it, the president saw no reason to hear it for himself. 'We have the tape. I don't want to hear the tape. No reason for me to hear the tape . . . it's a suffering tape, it's a terrible tape. I've been fully briefed on it,' he said.

Perhaps the president knew he was prone to his emotions getting the better of him. In April 2017, he had been sufficiently moved by video images of a chemical attack in Syria to launch air strikes against Syrian military targets. By contrast, remaining deaf to the audio of Khashoggi's killing – a crime he called 'violent, vicious and terrible' – would presumably make it easier for him *not* to act.

Trump played for time, saying he was awaiting a full government report. 'They haven't assessed anything yet. It's too early,' he said of the CIA findings.[16] Although Gina Haspel had briefed him that operatives employed by the crown prince were directly involved in the killing, he was apparently trying to avoid being cornered by the CIA's conclusions.

'Recent reports indicating that the US government has made a final conclusion are inaccurate,' a State Department statement said.

The president told Fox News that the crown prince had told him 'maybe five times' that he wasn't involved. 'Will anybody really know?' Trump asked.

'He did have, certainly, people that were reasonably close to him and close to him that were probably involved,' he conceded. 'But at the same time, we do have an ally and I want to stick with an ally that in many ways has been very good.'[17]

In the meantime, Turkish officials were still insisting the murder was planned and premeditated and that a rendition of the journalist back to Riyadh had never been seriously contemplated, given that Khashoggi was dead about twenty minutes after his arrival at the consulate.

None of Turkey's pressure, nor pressure from Congress, was moving President Trump to alter his position. He had placed a commercial and strategic bet on the Saudi crown prince. He was not going to lose his money on it.

17

'MAYBE HE DID, MAYBE HE DIDN'T!'

'The world is a very, very vicious place.'
— President Donald Trump, 23 November 2018

On 20 November, Donald Trump released a written statement with his final conclusion on the killing in the consulate, a conclusion in fact so inconclusive that it seemed intended to let the crown prince off the hook: 'It could very well be that the crown prince had knowledge of this tragic event — maybe he did and maybe he didn't!'

The document, dictated by the president himself, was entitled 'America First!' and demonstrated a ruthlessly amoral mind at work.

'The world is a very dangerous place!' it began, proceeding to criticise not Saudi Arabia, but Iran: 'The Iranians have killed many Americans and innocent people throughout the Middle East,' the statement said. Trump was signalling that he had bigger strategic priorities than the murder of a journalist.

The president repeated his outlandish claim that Saudi Arabia had agreed to spend and invest $450 billion in the United States, 'a record amount of money', and that Russia and China would stand to gain if $110 billion of arms contracts were cancelled. Never mind that those figures had been queried for weeks by economists and defence analysts who said they were grossly inflated projections.

In a line which might well have caused gratuitous offence to Khashoggi's grieving relatives and fiancée, Trump referred to Saudi Arabia's claim that Jamal Khashoggi was a member of the Muslim Brotherhood – thereby appearing to endorse it – while claiming disingenuously that he wasn't.

'Representatives of Saudi Arabia say that Jamal Khashoggi was an "enemy of the state" and a member of the Muslim Brotherhood,' the president wrote. 'But my decision is in no way based on that.'

The president concluded that the facts surrounding what he called 'an unacceptable and horrible crime' may never be known, but that the US intended to remain steadfast to its ally in 'our very important fight against Iran', an ally which had also helped the president to stabilise global oil prices. 'America First!', his statement ended, just as it had begun.

His secretary of state, Mike Pompeo, managed to sum up the president's better-the-devil-you-know, lesser-of-two-evils approach in just a few words: 'It's a mean, nasty world out there,' he said.

The death of a journalist would not be allowed to sway America's strategic goals in a turbulent Middle East. The choice had been taken to defend the crown prince, in as much as it ever amounted to a choice at all.

The president was flying to Florida for Thanksgiving, having pardoned not just the seasonal turkeys but the heir to the Saudi throne as well. 'It's just like I said, I think it was "maybe he did, maybe he didn't,"', Trump said before boarding his helicopter. 'The CIA has looked at it, they have studied it a lot, they have nothing definitive.' Intelligence is rarely definitive, but a judgement call based on all the information available. In the president's mind, the CIA's 'medium to high confidence' that the crown prince had ordered the murder was not definitive enough.

Two days later, at his Mar-a-Lago resort in Florida, he suggested the CIA had not made a decision either way. 'They didn't conclude, they did not come to a conclusion,' he said. 'Nobody has concluded. I don't know if anybody is going to conclude that the crown prince did it.'

'Who should be held accountable?' a reporter asked him.

'Maybe the world should be held accountable,' he replied, 'because the world is a very, very vicious place.'

The Turkish government was angered by the US president's prevarication but hardly surprised. 'He tried to defend the crown prince, to make the case forgotten,' Yasin Aktay told me. 'But they can't hide it. Everything is obvious.'

At the *Washington Post*, the CEO Fred Ryan appealed to Congress for justice for his columnist, now it was obvious that the White House would not pursue the case that much further.

'President Trump is correct in saying the world is a very dangerous place,' Ryan said. 'His surrender to this state-ordered murder will only make it more so. An innocent man, brutally slain, deserves better.'[1]

Outraged members of Congress claimed that the president had sent a signal to dictators and despots the world over that they could murder with impunity. Senator Lindsey Graham, a Republican of South Carolina and one of Trump's closest allies, wrote on Twitter that the crown prince was 'beyond toxic'. 'When we lose our moral voice, we lose our strongest asset,' Graham added pointedly.

'I'm pretty sure this statement is Saudi Arabia First, not America First,' tweeted another Republican, Senator Rand Paul.

'I never thought I'd see the day a White House would moon-light as a public relations firm for the crown prince of Saudi Arabia,' tweeted Senator Bob Corker, the Republican chair of the Senate Foreign Relations Committee.

By contrast, President Trump seemed oblivious to this crit-icism on Capitol Hill. The day after his 'Maybe he did, maybe he didn't!' statement, he tweeted his unequivocal thanks to the Saudis for helping reduce the oil price to $54 a barrel.

'Great! Like a big Tax Cut for America and the World,' he wrote. 'Enjoy! $54, was just $82. Thank you to Saudi Arabia, but let's go lower!'

Perhaps it was no coincidence that his tweet came just before Thanksgiving, the busiest time for long-distance car travel and petrol consumption in America's calendar. Attuned to the political effects of the price of fuel, the president had also pushed for an increase in Saudi oil production ahead of the mid-term elections earlier that month. Ironically, it was his own sanctions against Iran which had threatened to drive the price higher, by reducing global supply.

It wasn't that senators didn't agree that the relationship with Riyadh was as important as the president claimed. What irked them was that he had not even attempted to square the circle of maintaining that relationship and sanctioning the crown prince. Not that it was obvious that America could continue to do both at once.

The *Washington Post* tried to argue that it could. In an opin-ion piece by its editorial board, it claimed that the Middle East would be more stable if MbS was weakened and held in check. 'It is entirely possible to sanction and shun the Saudi leader while still doing business with his regime,' the paper concluded.[2]

What this argument failed to take into account was the

extent to which the future of Saudi Arabia and the future of Crown Prince Mohammed bin Salman had become one and the same. In an absolute monarchy with an ageing king, nothing was likely to happen without the permission of the young and dynamic heir who had already assumed unprecedented power. It was the same argument the *Post* and many others had previously used to make the case for his involvement in Jamal Khashoggi's capture and murder.

Although the White House hadn't said it in quite these terms, it followed that if you wanted to do business with Saudi Arabia – to lower the price of oil or co-operate against jihadist terrorism or Iran – there was apparently no getting around MbS. Sidestepping him was arguably not an option, without triggering even greater regional instability.

Representative Adam Schiff of California, the incoming Democrat chair of the House Intelligence Committee, highlighted the need for caution. He agreed that the relationship needed to change in the light of Khashoggi's death; but he resurrected an argument that had been used for decades to moderate criticism of Saudi Arabia: the kingdom might collapse without America's support.

'The danger to the US is if we act too precipitously and the House of Saud should fall,' he said. 'That would be completely destabilising [to] the region, and we don't know what would follow.'[3]

Besides, why make the death of a single journalist the tipping point for jeopardising America's oldest alliance in the Middle East?

'We recognise killing journalists is absolutely evil and despicable, but to completely realign our interests in the Middle East as a result of this, when for instance the Russians kill journalists ... Turkey imprisons journalists?' asked Adam

Kinzinger, a Republican Congressman from Illinois. 'It's not a sinless world out there.'[4]

Nevertheless, senators were determined to be in full possession of the facts on the Khashoggi case. Leaks to the press from the CIA's assessment weren't good enough. Their request for CIA Director Gina Haspel to answer questions about the journalist's death had been turned down, in what looked like a further attempt by the Trump administration to shield the crown prince from scrutiny.

'Anything that you need for me to do to get out of town,' said Senator Lindsey Graham, 'I ain't doing it until we hear from the CIA.'

Haspel was said to be furious about the leaks, which risked damaging her relationship with President Trump, who might have concluded that his own spies were briefing against him. After all, in January 2017, Trump had compared the US intelligence community with 'Nazi Germany' after press stories appeared about the president-elect's allegedly improper links with the Putin regime in Russia. A rift between Trump and Congress was one matter; but another rift between the CIA and Trump was best avoided.

As it was, the CIA's analysts were incandescent that their finely honed[5] 'balance of probability' judgement call on the crown prince's involvement had been set aside as politically inconvenient.[6] US intelligence hadn't been distorted so much as sidestepped. 'There is extraordinary frustration,' a US intelligence official said.

Instead of hearing from Haspel, Mike Pompeo and the defence secretary, Jim Mattis, gave the Senate a ninety-minute classified briefing about the importance of the US–Saudi relationship – warning that censuring Riyadh now could jeopardise a ceasefire being brokered in the Yemen war.

After the briefing, Mattis told reporters outside the Pentagon that 'we have no smoking gun the crown prince was involved, not the intelligence community or anyone else. There is no smoking gun.' Mike Pompeo, who had previously served as CIA director, chose his words rather more carefully, claiming there was 'no direct reporting connecting the crown prince to the order to murder . . . that's all I can say in an unclassified setting.'

'No direct reporting', because there was no kill order, either in document or audio form; but there was a wealth of damning circumstantial evidence nonetheless.

'There is not a smoking gun, there's a smoking saw,' Senator Graham replied in blunt disbelief.

'As to whether the crown prince was involved in this killing, it's my belief that he was,' said Senator Bob Corker. 'It's my belief that he ordered it.'[7]

This lack of a specific order to murder kept alive other possible explanations which would help protect the crown prince. It could be argued that plan A may have been to kidnap Khashoggi from the consulate and return him to the kingdom, and that the Rapid Intervention Group bungled the task by using excessive force. However, the preparedness of the hit squad to dismember him also suggested that a plan B, to kill him, had also been authorised.

In early December, senators were finally given the briefing by Gina Haspel, the CIA director, which they had been asking for, on the condition that the hour-long meeting was confined to a small and senior group of lawmakers behind closed doors. Unsurprisingly, given what they already knew about the CIA's assessment, it only confirmed them in their view that the crown prince had given the order to have Khashoggi killed.

'The crown prince is a wrecking ball,' Senator Lindsey

Graham told reporters afterwards. 'I think he's complicit in the murder of Mr Khashoggi to the highest level possible . . . I think he's crazy, I think he's dangerous.'

The senator pointed out that he had defended the Saudi royal family when it was accused of complicity in the 11 September attacks. Turning a blind eye now would, he argued, give the green light to other Middle Eastern despots to commit human rights abuses with the confidence that America would look the other way.

'If the crown prince went in front of a jury, he would be convicted in thirty minutes,' said Senator Bob Corker, adding that in twelve years he'd never heard intelligence testimony anything like the CIA's presentation.

Of course, MbS would not be in the dock in front of a jury at all. Instead, he was due to appear at a G20 summit in Argentina – and no leader inside or outside the kingdom would dare suggest he shouldn't go. Saudi Arabia's economy ranked at eighteenth in the list of the world's biggest – ironically just ahead of Turkey. What could be a better way of demonstrating that it was business as usual for the crown prince, than by posing in the summit's annual 'family' photograph, alongside the most powerful people on the planet?

18

THE CROWN PRINCE
COMEBACK TOUR

'The man can scream "I didn't do anything" all day
long but at the back of everybody's mind will be: "The
crown prince. Is he the killer?"'

— Adviser to President Erdoğan

At the end of November, the crown prince embarked on what
was quickly dubbed the 'comeback tour'. It was not a surprise
that he was welcome in the United Arab Emirates and Egypt.
After all, Abu Dhabi had never had an Arab Spring revolution,
while Cairo's brief flirtation with democracy under the Muslim
Brotherhood had ended with a return to a form of elected
dictatorship.

In Tunisia, however, the birthplace of the Arab uprisings,
protesters made it clear that the scion of a royal family which had
given shelter to their former dictator was not welcome. Saudi
Arabia had given Zine al-Abidine Ben Ali immediate refuge in
Jeddah seven years earlier.

The headquarters of the Journalists' Syndicate in Tunis was
adorned with a banner, two storeys high, showing a robed
Saudi figure holding a large chainsaw. 'No to the desecration of
Tunisia, the land of the revolution', the banner read.[1]

The Women's Association in Tunis was fronted by a poster of a figure carrying a whip with the slogan 'No welcome to the flogger of women'.

Hundreds marched down the capital's main avenue, chanting not just against the crown prince but also the war he was prosecuting in Yemen.

Many in the crowd waved saws. The crowds weren't huge, but had Jamal Khashoggi been alive to see them, he would surely have been moved beyond measure. In his last and posthumously published column, the journalist had noted that Tunisia was the 'one country in the Arab world that has been classified as free'. Tunisians were also still thankfully at liberty to condemn the murder of a man who so admired what they had achieved.

The crown prince's next stop was the G20 summit in the Argentinian capital, Buenos Aires, where he led a delegation of 400 Saudis, many of them booked into the luxury Four Seasons hotel.[2] MbS stayed at the fortified Saudi embassy, after an Argentinian prosecutor began an inquiry into potential criminal charges against him, brought on behalf of Human Rights Watch, for 'indiscriminate and disproportionate air strikes on civilians' in Yemen, 'serious allegations of torture and other ill treatment of Saudi citizens', as well as responsibility for Jamal Khashoggi's murder.

Angela Merkel, the German chancellor, refused to see him. The then British prime minister, Theresa May, said she had informed him of the importance of a full, transparent and credible investigation into the terrible murder. While the French president, Emmanuel Macron, told him international investigators should be part of efforts to establish the truth surrounding Khashoggi's death. President Macron's supposedly private confrontation with the crown prince was captured by a television camera.

'Don't worry,' MbS told the French leader.

'I do worry. I am worried. I told you,' a clearly angry Macron replied.

'Yes, you told me. Thank you very much,' the prince said, bowing respectfully.

'You know what I mean . . . you never listen to me,' Macron continued, in the tone of an adult scolding a naughty child.

'I do listen to you. It's okay. I can deal with it,' the prince said.

What had Macron told him? Was it a generalised warning to curb his behaviour, or was it more specific? Perhaps the French president was referring back to the kidnapping of the Lebanese prime minister in Riyadh the year before. Macron had taken a lead role in negotiating his release; but Khashoggi's death, coupled with the ongoing arrests of Saudi activists and dissidents, hardly suggested that the wayward prince had heeded the Frenchman's advice.

At the 'family photo', the prince was at the end of the back row of the podium, as far away as he could be from the rest. He did not mingle afterwards, as if he knew many fellow leaders would not want to be seen with him. Especially President Erdoğan, who had been standing in the front row at the very opposite end.

Before flying back to Washington, President Trump blamed a busy schedule for not having arranged his own meeting with MbS. 'I mean, I would – I would have met with him, but we didn't set that one up,' he said. There were, however, what the White House called 'exchanged pleasantries' in Buenos Aires. 'We had no discussion. We might, but we had none,' the president said. It was as if his 'maybe he did, maybe he didn't!' prevarication over the murder even extended to whether he and the crown prince had spoken to each other or not.

If this politest of Trump rebuffs was the only price the prince would pay for his alleged involvement in the murder of a US resident, then no serious damage was done. Besides, another leader could still be counted upon to give him an unabashedly warm welcome.

As the group was sitting down for a round-table discussion, Vladimir Putin found himself next to the crown prince. It was a photo opportunity other G20 leaders had deliberately avoided, but Putin looked delighted, stretching out his right hand in greeting for a high-five. The crown prince happily returned the gesture and then affectionately slapped the back of the Russian leader's hand. Both men laughed, with Putin grinning from ear to ear. The Russian leader's spokesman said Putin frequently greeted friendly leaders in this way — though no other meeting like this was filmed in Buenos Aires; and the pictures quickly went viral, as Putin may have intended that they should.

This breezy encounter between two autocrats towards the end of 2018 seemed to symbolise the relative impunity of the world in which they lived. Here on display was the defiance of men who had both torn up the so-called 'rules-based order' by allegedly ordering the murder of dissidents on foreign soil.

Donald Trump had frequently expressed admiration for Putin, as he had for the crown prince. There was a sense in which the high-five in Buenos Aires was actually of the American president's making — or at least a consequence of his stewardship of world affairs.

The jovial greeting between Putin and MbS also recalled how Jamal Khashoggi had compared them in an article for the *Washington Post* during the Ritz-Carlton affair the previous November: 'Saudi Arabia's crown prince is acting like Putin,' the headline read.

The similarities between their behaviour were indeed striking. On 3 October, the day after Khashoggi's death, Putin had lambasted as a 'traitor to the motherland' Sergei Skripal, the former double agent who had fallen ill after a nerve-agent attack by Russian military intelligence operatives in the English city of Salisbury.

Putin had also made clear what fate would befall traitors in a television interview eight years earlier. 'Traitors will kick the bucket, believe me,' he had said. 'Whatever they got in exchange for it, those thirty pieces of silver they were given, they will choke on them.'

The remark seemed to echo the crown prince's own alleged comment in 2017 that he would use 'a bullet' against Khashoggi. Another common thread was discernible in President Trump's approach to both the Skripal and Khashoggi cases. Although he was persuaded to expel Russian spies after the Salisbury attack, the *New York Times* reported that he was sceptical at first. 'He had initially written off the poisoning as part of legitimate spy games,' the paper reported.[3]

Nevertheless, it was clear from the cold shoulders of many in Buenos Aires that the crown prince was regarded as 'damaged goods' on the international stage. President Erdoğan unsurprisingly avoided him, after complaining that the Saudi side was neither co-operating nor admitting that the murder was premeditated. 'They think the world is dumb,' Erdoğan said in mid-December. 'This nation isn't dumb and it knows how to hold people accountable.'

Turkey's leader was himself emerging from this crisis no less isolated from the West than before. US backing for Kurdish forces in Syria – regarded by Ankara as terrorists – had begun to cast an even bigger shadow over the Ankara–Washington relationship. Trump tweeted that the US 'will devastate Turkey economically if they hit Kurds', after he announced that American troops would be leaving Syria; when it came to the Kurdish issue, the agendas of these two NATO allies were wildly at odds.

Erdoğan was also determined to press ahead with the purchase of a Russian S-400 anti-aircraft missile system instead of its American rival, the Patriot. So just at the moment when US sanctions on steel and aluminium had been lifted, there was a risk that new American sanctions would be imposed.

Washington feared that if the Russian missile system's radar learned how to spot and track the new F-35 Lightning fighter jet due to join in the Turkish air force, then the aircraft's stealth would be seriously compromised. Around a thousand components, including fuselage and landing-gear parts, were built in Turkey. However, the Americans were now considering removing Turkish factories from the production line. Turkey did not cancel the Russian purchase. Washington did not hold back its response.

In June 2019, the Pentagon ordered forty-two Turkish pilots to stop training in America and return home. Then Turkey's order for 116 of the planes was cancelled. It was the biggest crisis in US–Turkey relations since America imposed an arms embargo, following the invasion of northern Cyprus in 1974. Although Erdoğan had spoken to Trump at the G20 summit, too much else had got in the way of their relationship to let Jamal Khashoggi's murder form the bridgehead to better relations. The White House was continuing to shield the crown prince; the Turks were still hinting darkly that he was involved without actually saying it.

If any positive outcome was to emerge from this gruesome murder, it would not be in Turkey, where the crime took place. The death of one man might just ease the suffering of millions – some 2,000 miles away, in Yemen.

19

ONE TRAGEDY EXPOSES ANOTHER

'The death of one man is a tragedy, the death of millions is a statistic.'

— Attributed to Joseph Stalin

On 9 November, news emerged that the US was halting its in-air refuelling of aircraft from the Saudi-led coalition waging war in Yemen. The announcement came not from the Americans but from the Saudi embassy in Washington, which said the kingdom had requested the move. The Saudis said they could now handle their fuelling needs on their own.

Only a fifth of coalition aircraft required in-air refuelling, so the announcement — a rare public rebuke of Saudi Arabia, dressed up as an agreement — was more symbolic than significantly punitive. It seemed that both countries were co-ordinating the move in order to placate the US Congress, which had demanded action not just over Jamal Khashoggi's death but over alleged war crimes in Yemen too. Congress had previously permitted the US air force to refuel Saudi aircraft after seeking assurances that the Saudis were taking significant steps to avoid civilian casualties. Yet US diplomats were increasingly anxious that this was not the case.

Jamal Khashoggi had himself called for an end to the Yemen

conflict in his *Washington Post* column, estimating that it was costing his country $200 million per day. Given that MbS had launched the offensive, the article must have been read in Riyadh as a highly personal attack on the prince's reputation.

'When Saudi Arabia's war in Yemen erupted in March 2015, there was widespread Saudi popular support for it – including by me,' the journalist wrote in 2017: 'Today, Yemen is teetering on the verge of a humanitarian disaster . . . My country's reputation has been badly damaged and our credibility weakened. Images of starving children should overwhelm even the most stalwart defender of the Saudi security interests that led us to destroy the poorest, most illiterate country in the Arab world.'[1]

In June 2018, the conflict had taken a significant turn. Emirati forces within the Saudi coalition launched a siege of the port city of Hodeidah, which quickly failed to make much progress. The port was the entry point for over 80 per cent of food and aid to Yemen. The UN warned that if the battle disrupted food supplies, it could threaten the lives of 300,000 children in the immediate area and prevent delivery of humanitarian aid to millions more – 8.4 million Yemenis were one step away from famine, according to the World Food Programme.

The aid agency Save the Children warned that 85,000 children under the age of five may have died of hunger since Saudi Arabia's air war had begun. The UN had stopped counting the dead, but estimated that on average 100 civilians were either killed or injured during every week of 2018. Human Rights Watch documented some ninety strikes by the Saudi-led coalition which had hit homes, markets, hospitals, schools and mosques.

In August 2018, opposition in Congress to the war increased after some forty children were among those killed when a Saudi jet dropped an American laser-guided bomb, an MK82, on a Yemeni school bus.

Although the US and British governments, which armed the Saudis, had tried to avoid conflating Yemen and Khashoggi's death, many American lawmakers took a far more holistic view. An attempt in the Senate to stop arms sales to Saudi Arabia the previous year had only just fallen short. Negative media coverage of the Khashoggi's case, combined with a deteriorating humanitarian situation in Yemen, rendered the status quo increasingly intolerable. The furore over the tragic killing of one journalist would help bring into sharp focus a statistically far greater tragedy – the war crimes being perpetrated in Yemen.

'Senators are looking for some way to show Saudi Arabia the disdain they have for what has happened, with the journalist, but also concerns about the way Yemen has gone,' said Senator Bob Corker, the Republican chairman of the Senate Foreign Relations Committee.[2]

'The Saudis will keep killing civilians and journalists as long as we keep arming and assisting them,' tweeted Senator Rand Paul, a Republican from Kentucky. US and UK policy had long been to persuade all parties in Yemen of the need for dialogue and a political solution. A new UN envoy, a Briton named Martin Griffiths, was breathing new life into a peace process whose best hope lay in all sides realising that the conflict was unwinnable. But the killing in the Saudi consulate, combined with the threat of famine and the Saudis' refusal to limit air strikes, had rendered those talks even more urgent. As important as arms sales were, the paradox of bombing Yemen and feeding millions of starving people had become unsustainable, and to many lawmakers and policymakers in both Britain and America it was now downright reprehensible.

On 15 November, six senators – three Republican and three Democrat – proposed the Saudi Arabia Accountability and Yemen Act of 2018, requiring the president to suspend arms sales and impose sanctions on all those found responsible for Khashoggi's death, including anyone who ordered it.[3] It was certainly a sign of congressional displeasure, even if months of political wrangling would be required before the bill was to stand a chance of becoming law.

Both the Yemen conflict and the Khashoggi probe were discussed by the crown prince and Jeremy Hunt, then British foreign secretary, in Riyadh a few days earlier.

'I talked very frankly about our concerns,' Hunt said of the murder, 'and how important it is for Saudi's strategic partners to know that this cannot and will not happen again.'[4]

Any British criticism of Saudi Arabia and its notoriously volatile crown prince was always in the context of the UK's trading relationship, even if the weapons it was supplying continued to be associated with attacks that killed or injured civilians in Yemen. In London only six months before Khashoggi's murder, the Saudi crown prince had signed a memorandum of understanding to begin further talks on buying forty-eight more Eurofighter Typhoon jets from BAE Systems, which had previously laid off 2,000 staff due to a slowdown in sales.

British arms deliveries to Saudi Arabia were worth an estimated $1.4 billion in 2017. The Typhoon project was worth several times that, with at least 5,000 jobs depending upon it. The Saudis had already bought seventy-two of the Typhoons, while their Qatari neighbours had recently placed an order for twenty-four.

There was, of course, nothing new in controversy over British arms sales to Riyadh. The al-Yamamah ('dove of peace') arms deal, agreed by Margaret Thatcher in 1985, included seventy-two jets and was the largest weapons contract in British history, worth $86 billion. A criminal investigation into alleged kickbacks was later halted by Tony Blair's government, partly on the grounds that it would jeopardise sales of the new Typhoons.

Nevertheless, Khashoggi's murder was also an opportunity for British diplomats to make use of Saudi Arabia's new-found vulnerability to international criticism to press home the need for talks to end Yemen's war – even if Typhoon sales were once again at stake. In reality, London and Washington were pushing at a half-open door: the Saudis admitted privately that they were bogged down in a Yemeni quagmire. The question was how to leave, without handing victory to Iran-backed Houthi rebels and without Riyadh losing face.

In mid-November, Emirati forces suspended their offensive on the port of Hodeidah – a sign that the Saudi-led coalition was beginning to respond to a diplomatic environment more uncomfortable than it had been before.

Then in Washington the following month, the US Senate voted, by fifty-six to forty-one, to end American support for the war in Yemen. The president said he would veto it – it would also require a majority in the House of Representatives to become law – but it was the first time since the War Powers Act of 1973 that either legislative chamber had tried to clip the wings of a president's power to involve US forces in conflict.

Senator Lindsey Graham was among those who opposed the Yemen resolution, on the grounds that the relationship with Saudi Arabia was bigger and more important than solely its crown prince; but he supported a second resolution, which was passed unanimously a few moments later. It held the crown prince 'responsible for the murder' of Jamal Khashoggi and insisted Saudi Arabia 'ensure appropriate accountability' for all those involved.

'What the Khashoggi event did was to demonstrate, hey, maybe this isn't a regime that we should just be following that eagerly into battle,' was how Senator Mike Lee, a Republican from Utah, summed up both votes.

With MbS now widely reviled in the American media, which had given him the nickname 'Mr Bone Saw', the Senate vote confirmed the biggest rupture in US–Saudi relations since the 11 September attacks of 2001. As senators saw it, their silence on the murder of a journalist, who had recently moved to Virginia, could not be bought with lucrative arms sales.

The Saudi foreign ministry, apparently unchastened, criticised what it called the 'esteemed legislative body of an allied and friendly government' for 'unsubstantiated claims and allegations' and 'blatant interference'. As for weapons transfers, the foreign minister, Adel al-Jubeir, hinted darkly that the Saudis could buy from elsewhere. 'We prefer to be armed by our allies,' he said, 'but Saudi Arabia's commitment to defend its land and its people obligates it to obtain the weapons it needs from any source.'[5]

The votes in the Senate also marked a highly unusual bipartisan rebuke of Donald Trump, who had sent his secretaries of defence and state back to Capitol Hill to lobby against it. Secretary of State Pompeo warned that without US involvement in Yemen, the humanitarian crisis there would be 'a hell of a lot worse – that Iran, ISIS and al-Qaeda in the Arabian peninsula would only grow stronger'.

'Try defending that back home,' he said.[6]

The Americans had helped draw up a no-strike list of hospitals, schools and other targets the Saudis should avoid in Yemen. They had trained pilots and their commanders in human rights and posted military advisers to the operation's command centre. Yet still Yemeni civilian deaths from air strikes continued – at least 4,800 of them, according to one study, which didn't include the first year.[7]

In the same week as the Senate vote on ending US support for the war, Yemen's warring parties met in Sweden under UN auspices to agree a fragile truce. Amid smiles and the shaking of hands, the Saudi-led coalition and Houthi rebels also agreed a mass prisoner swap and withdrawal of troops from the port city of Hodeidah, Yemen's gateway for humanitarian aid.

The need to push for the ceasefire was chiefly motivated by impending famine, with UNICEF claiming a Yemeni child was dying every ten minutes; but the fact remained that the furore over Jamal Khashoggi's death had helped intensify diplomatic efforts to secure peace talks for the first time since 2016. The fighting in Hodeidah stopped for the first time in six months, though this did not ease concerns on Capitol Hill that US weaponry might have been used in war crimes.

The Senate wasn't just concerned about the sale of conventional American weaponry; it feared that Washington might be helping Saudi Arabia to become a nuclear-armed power too.

'Saudi Arabia does not want to acquire any nuclear bomb,' the crown prince had told CBS in March 2018, 'but without a doubt, if Iran developed a nuclear bomb, we will follow suit as soon as possible.'[8]

Since November 2017, the time of the Ritz-Carlton detentions, the US energy secretary, Rick Perry, had issued seven approvals for US companies to take part in the country's civilian nuclear programme; but lawmakers complained that too many of the details were kept secret. They were worried that America was fueling a nuclear arms race in the Middle East, despite Saudi protestations that the eighteen nuclear reactors they envisaged building were purely for non-military purposes.

Two of the nuclear technology transfers were signed off by the US Department of Energy after Khashoggi's murder, one of them just sixteen days later. The Saudis were planning to invite bids for two nuclear power reactors; if the Americans didn't win the contracts, the Russians, Chinese, French or South Koreans would.

'President Trump's eagerness to give the Saudis anything they want, over bipartisan congressional objection, harms American national security,' said Senator Tim Kaine. 'The alarming realisation that the Trump administration signed off on sharing our nuclear knowhow with the Saudi regime after it brutally murdered an American resident adds to a disturbing pattern of behaviour.'

Having already linked ending US involvement in the Yemen war to investigating Khashoggi's death, senators now added the need to curb the prince's nuclear ambitions too. Lawmakers from both parties proposed the No Nuclear Weapons for Saudi Arabia Act, which required the Saudis to release more details about the Khashoggi case.

In March 2019, the US Senate voted once again, this time by fifty-four to forty-six, to end America's participation in the Yemen war. The House of Representatives, with a newly installed Democratic Speaker, then followed the Senate's lead, voting 247 to 175, the first time both chambers had voted to cease US military engagement in a foreign conflict.[9]

The majority leader, Senator Mitch McConnell, had urged his colleagues to reject the resolution, but seven Republican senators defied him. The shaky ceasefire in Hodeidah was not in itself enough to persuade American lawmakers that logistical support for Saudi-led coalition forces could be justified any longer: Saudi-led air strikes on a school and a hospital in the Yemeni capital, Sana'a, were reported to have left at least twenty-one civilians dead, twelve of them children, in the week leading up to the vote on Capitol Hill.

'No blank cheques any more,' said Congressman Eliot Engel, the Democratic chair of the Foreign Affairs Committee. 'No more war in which we're complicit where a wholesale population is starving.'

Jamal Khashoggi's death had in its own way created history, as Capitol Hill finally found its voice to defy the Trump White House over Saudi Arabia's war. It therefore seems entirely fitting that the last of the journalist's columns to be published in his lifetime was also on the subject of Yemen. It appeared on 11 September 2018, seventeen years on from the terrorist attacks on America which plunged US–Saudi relations to their previous crisis point.

'The longer this cruel war lasts,' Khashoggi had written, 'the people of Yemen will be busy fighting poverty, cholera and water scarcity . . . the crown prince must bring an end to the violence and restore the dignity of the birthplace of Islam.'[10] It was as direct an attack on his country's de facto leader as any he had made. To imply that the birthplace of Islam had been sullied under MbS's stewardship seemed guaranteed to provoke rather more than indignation in the royal court.

The US Congress also seemed to have listened, even if only after the author of the *Washington Post* article was dead.

However, less than a fortnight after the bipartisan measure to cease American military engagement, President Trump carried out his threat to wield his veto for only the second time in his presidency. The first time it had been to uphold his declaration of a national emergency along the Mexican border.

'We cannot end the conflict in Yemen through political

documents,' Trump said in his veto message. 'Peace in Yemen requires a negotiated settlement.'

Senator Tim Kaine, Democrat from Virginia, Khashoggi's home state, said the veto was 'part of an alarming pattern of Trump turning a blind eye to Saudi Arabia's actions that fly in the face of American values'; but the president said he had put a stop to an attempt to limit his constitutional powers as commander-in-chief. Even though Trump had been elected in part for his determination to end America's involvement in foreign wars, with plans for troop drawdowns from Syria and Afghanistan, logistical and intelligence support for Saudi Arabia would continue.

Khashoggi's murder certainly helped focus minds on the Yemen conflict, but how much had really changed on the ground? In May 2019, the Houthis began to withdraw from Hodeidah, which was described as the most significant progress in attempts to end four years of war, though fighting erupted again shortly afterwards.

The contents of the port's main grain store began to rot, as aid agency access to it was denied by Houthi fighters. Mark Lowcock, the UN's humanitarian affairs co-ordinator, warned that famine still loomed and 300,000 individuals had been struck by cholera.[11] A UN Development Programme report reached the appalling conclusion that even if the conflict were to finish by the end of 2019, it would have killed around 233,000 people, most of them children under the age of five.[12]

In Britain, the Campaign Against Arms Trade, backed by other pressure groups, sought to overturn a High Court ruling in 2017 which upheld that weapons transfers to Saudi Arabia had not breached international humanitarian law. Five opposition parties had also called on the Conservative government to halt sales.

Not only did the then British foreign secretary, Jeremy Hunt, refuse to budge, he lobbied the Germans to resume their exports to benefit Britain. The Eurofighter Typhoon and the Tornado fighter jet both contained German-made components: so without the German parts, the British would not be able to fulfil several contracts with Riyadh[13] and the UK's sale of forty-eight Typhoons, worth some £10 billion, was at risk of being delayed.

'I am pleased the German government has listened to our request to ensure the spares for the existing Typhoon and Tornado aircraft in Saudi Arabia may now continue to be licensed,' Hunt wrote to a British parliamentary committee.[14]

It was in Berlin's interests to carry on licensing, too. The German government is a shareholder in Airbus, a member of the consortium that makes the Typhoon. In its first quarter results for 2019, Airbus said it had lost €19 million ($213 million) 'as a consequence of the prolonged suspension of defence export licences to Saudi Arabia by the German government'.[15]

However, both British and American arms sales would continue to run into opposition. In the summer of 2019, the UK said it would suspend the approval of new export licences after the High Court ruled that British ministers had failed to determine whether the Saudi-led coalition in Yemen was violating international law.

By coincidence, on the same day in June, the US Senate blocked the fast-tracking of $8.1 billion of arms sales to Saudi Arabia, the United Arab Emirates and Jordan – twenty-two deals in all. The weapons package included 120,000 precision-guided bombs, with the assembly of some bomb parts to take place in Saudi Arabia itself.

Congress is usually given the opportunity to review such sales, but the previous month the Trump administration announced it was planning to bypass the legislature, citing a rarely used clause in the Arms Export Control Act. The clause permits exports in what the president deems an emergency situation, 'which requires the proposed sale in the national security interest of the United States'.[16]

So what was this national security emergency? Not Yemen, but Iran and the threat it could pose to energy supplies passing through the Persian Gulf. However, many senators believed this was just a pretext to carry on selling to the Saudis as usual, and voted against the weapons transfers accordingly.

'President Trump is only using this loophole because he knows Congress would disapprove of this sale,' Democratic Senator Chris Murphy said in a statement. 'There is no new "emergency" reason to sell bombs to the Saudis to drop in Yemen and doing so only perpetuates the humanitarian crisis there.'[17]

In the aftermath of Jamal Khashoggi's murder, America's relationship with Saudi Arabia – and specifically arms sales – had created the greatest foreign policy rift between the Trump administration and Capitol Hill. Only the president's veto would allow him to carry on selling weapons. On the day of their vote to block sales in June 2019, leading lawmakers explained that their underlying grievance was Khashoggi's killing itself. 'This is the moment to stand up for some moral clarity,' explained Senator Bob Menendez. 'This is the moment to send a global message you cannot kill journalists with impunity.'

Once again, Senator Lindsey Graham was more explicit than most: 'There is no amount of oil you can produce that will get me and others to give you a pass on chopping somebody up in a consulate,' he said.

Even if senators thought they were being duped by a White

House hell bent on arms sales, they also knew the president would use his veto to override their votes; and much as the Saudis actually wanted the war to stop in Yemen, they hadn't worked out how, continuing to view Iranian involvement there as an existential threat. Moreover, the Trump administration's declaration of an emergency situation involving Iran was fast becoming a self-fulfilling prophecy.[18]

2 0

THE FAUSTIAN BARGAIN

In the spring of 2019, the USS *Abraham Lincoln* was ordered to the Arabian sea earlier than planned amid escalating tensions in America's relationship with Iran. With a complement of over 3,000 sailors and almost as many air crew, the aircraft carrier was accompanied by three destroyers and a cruiser, all armed with guided missiles. The 'Super Hornet' fighter jets on board conducted daily flying missions, carrying out joint exercises with B-52 bombers which had been deployed to the Al Udeid air base in Qatar.

It therefore came as no surprise that when Donald Trump had a 'great conversation' with the Saudi crown prince on 21 June, Jamal Khashoggi's murder, in the president's words, 'really didn't come up'.

'I think it's been heavily investigated,' he said in a television interview the same day, admitting he had never even raised the subject and rejecting calls for an FBI investigation:

INTERVIEWER: What about the FBI?
TRUMP: Here's where I am. Are you ready?
INTERVIEWER: Uh-huh.
TRUMP: Iran's killed many, many people a day . . . the Middle East, this is a hostile place. This is a vicious,

hostile place. If you're going to look at Saudi Arabia . . . they spend $400 to $450 billion over a period of time, all money, all jobs, all buying equipment . . . Take their money. Take their money![1]

It wasn't just the president's fondness for arms sales that eclipsed the murder in Istanbul of a US resident. Iran had risen to the top of Trump's foreign policy agenda. Five hundred American troops would be deployed to Saudi Arabia for the first time since 2003, as part of a strengthening of US forces across the Middle East; but the USS *Abraham Lincoln* was the most visible projection of the 'big stick' against Iran now being carried by America's commander-in-chief.

In fact, the night before his phone call with the Saudi crown prince, Trump had approved and then called off air strikes on Iranian targets, in retaliation for the downing of an unmanned US surveillance drone by a surface-to-air missile. It was only when one of his generals informed him that 150 Iranians would be killed in the pre-dawn attack that the president suddenly changed his mind.

Two days earlier, the UN special rapporteur on extra-judicial executions, Agnes Callamard, had accused Saudi Arabia of a 'deliberate premeditated execution' and claimed that there was 'credible evidence' that MbS himself should be investigated for Jamal Khashoggi's murder. 'The people directly implicated in the murder reported to him,' she said, querying how much the crown prince knew, whether he had directly or indirectly incited the killing or could have prevented it.

'Every expert consulted', she wrote, 'finds it inconceivable that an operation of this scale could be implemented without the crown prince being aware, at a minimum, that some sort of mission of a criminal nature, directed at Mr Khashoggi, was being launched'.

In her report, she listed all the evidence she could find for premeditated murder. There was little plausible explanation for the presence of Dr Tubaigy other than disposal of the body; he had discussed cutting up Khashoggi thirteen minutes before the journalist walked into the consulate; the hit squad had discussed the arrival of a 'sacrificial animal'; Brigadier General al-Madani, the 'body double', was there to cover up an enforced disappearance. Killing the journalist was either the primary intention or the second option authorised by Riydah, given that it was very unlikely that a special operations team leader would kill without permission from his superiors.

The Frenchwoman had begun investigating the crime at her own initiative, after noticing that no international body or state had offered to mediate between Turkey and Saudi Arabia on access to the crime scene – and that there was no sign of any international criminal investigation. The office of the UN Secretary General, António Guterres, indicated that he did not have the power to launch a criminal inquiry without a mandate from an intergovernmental body, or a UN Security Council resolution, or a request from a member state.

The UN's own rapporteur disagreed, urging Guterres to establish an international criminal inquiry. 'The secretary general could have set a more proactive process for himself and the UN and he chose otherwise,' Callamard complained. 'Inaction and silence and hoping that it is going to disappear is just not going to work.' The rapporteur also urged the FBI to open an investigation, leading to prosecutions in the United States. After all, Khashoggi had lived there and applied for a 'green card' of permanent residence. Turkey's reputation for holding unfair trials would make any internationally supported prosecution in Istanbul virtually impossible. Although if Saudi Arabia and Turkey continued to refuse to co-operate with each other in providing evidence, then the rapporteur's suggestion of a trial or inquiry was highly unlikely to succeed anywhere. If the crown prince's brother, Prince Khalid, really had spoken to Khashoggi in Washington and advised him to visit the Saudi consulate in Istanbul – which he denied – then prosecutors could argue that part of the crime had transpired in the United States; but the CIA's assessment of Khalid's alleged role remained classified.[2]

In the absence of much international will to act, justice was being pursued in a federal court in New York. The Open Society Justice Initiative, a non-governmental organisation funded by the billionaire financier George Soros, was trying to force seven US government departments, including the CIA, to produce all records related to the killing, including the spies' conclusions on the crown prince's role.

The US State Department was asked under the Freedom of Information Act to produce 7,500 pages of documents per month for the case; it replied that 300 pages a month was a more realistic objective, given 'current limited resources and competing obligations' and the need to hold back classified information. It could be decades before the relevant documents are published, while the judge, Paul Engelmayer, accused the government of 'not behaving' over the delays.[3]

In the meantime, as the crisis with Iran continued to escalate, the Saudi crown prince could be confident that it would drown out the issue of one dead journalist. An interviewer from the *Asharq Al-Awsat* newspaper asked MbS about anti-Saudi feeling in America over the Khashoggi case.

'I am confident that our strategic relations with the US will not be affected by any media campaigns,' he said, describing the journalist's death as 'a very painful crime that is unprecedented'.

'Unfortunately,' he added, 'the suspects are government employees and we seek to achieve full justice.'

Full justice it certainly was not. Although Jared Kushner had advised his friend MbS to be 'as transparent as possible',[4] when the first hearing opened at the Criminal Court of Riyadh in January 2019, it was held behind closed doors and none of the eleven suspects was publicly named. Brigadier General Mutreb and Dr Tubaigy were among five Saudis understood to be facing murder charges and the death penalty. Yet one media report claimed the doctor was living in a villa in Jeddah with his family; and not under formal arrest, as the Saudis had claimed.[5]

The UN rapporteur drew up a list of the eleven men she believed to be on trial, but at least four of the squad who travelled to Istanbul – Naif Hassan al-Arifi, Mishal Saad al-Bostani, Thaar Ghaleb al-Harbi and Badr Lafi al-Otaibi – were mysteriously absent from that list.

Arifi and Bostani, a special forces soldier and air force lieutenant respectively, were among the five deployed to the consul's residence on 2 October; but Otaibi (a major in foreign intelligence) and Harbi were among the ten hit squad members identified at the consulate itself.

Harbi had served as a guard at one of the crown prince's palaces and travelled to America ahead of MbS's visit there in 2015. Turkish intelligence had let it be known that his voice was identified as one of those trying to put his hand over Khashoggi's mouth during his final moments. Could it really be true that he wasn't on trial? Saudi officials had earlier claimed that he was. With the press denied access to court, it was hard to tell.

Despite the veil of secrecy, all eleven defendants reportedly claimed through their lawyers that they were state employees who could not object to the orders of their superiors; it was understood that some protested that they didn't even know Khashoggi would be killed. Three of the accused said they had covered Jamal Khashoggi's mouth to stop him from screaming, which resulted in his accidental death. Major General Asiri, who had never left Riyadh, reportedly conceded that he had ordered the fifteen men to return the journalist home, but claimed he had never ordered the use of force. Farhad al-Balawi, a member of the royal guard, said Brigadier General Mutreb had ordered him to dissect the body. Brigadier General Mustafa al-Madani, the 'body double', told the court it 'was his duty' to do what he did.

The disclosure of these fragments of information suggested it would not be as easy to silence the eleven accused men as the Saudi authorities might have hoped. Foreign access to the trial was limited to diplomats from the permanent members of the UN Security Council: the USA, Britain, France, Russia, China – along with Turkey. These observers were summoned to court with little notice and not allowed to bring interpreters.[6]

Astonishingly, diplomats who arrived in court were also understood to have committed to non-disclosure agreements, preventing them from leaking any details to the press, although the scope and duration of this agreement remained unclear; and some details, outlined above, have come to light. The choice the diplomats faced may have been a stark one: be an eyewitness to the trial and agree to disclose nothing, or witness nothing at all. Not that there was much to see, with only five hearings held in six months. The UN rapporteur, Agnes Callamard, claimed the diplomats' involvement in such a questionable legal process meant that 'they are allowing themselves to be made complicit in what is, by all appearances, a miscarriage of justice'.

Unsurprisingly, she concluded that the trial was 'clouded in secrecy and lacking in due process' and recommended that it should be suspended. She never received a reply to her own request to visit to the kingdom at the start of her probe and her written questions were ignored.

Callamard called on the Saudi government to make a public apology to Jamal Khashoggi's loved ones and friends as well as the Turkish and American governments. So that the event should not be forgotten, she suggested that Turkey erect a memorial to the journalist and his commitment to press freedom outside the Saudi consulate in Istanbul. 'There is sufficient space for this purpose,' she concluded, having seen for herself the small patch of grass in front of the building.

However, her words about the heir to the Saudi throne seemed bound to cause the most offence. Foreign sanctions against individual Saudis might act as a 'smokescreen', she concluded, by diverting attention away from those who were actually responsible: so she recommended additional sanctions on the crown prince's 'personal assets abroad' until sufficient evidence cleared him of responsibility – although she didn't name his château in France or the $450 million Leonardo da Vinci painting which was reported to be on board his yacht.

'She was biased from the beginning,' said Adel al-Jubeir, minister of state for foreign affairs, during a visit to London. He accused Callamard of making baseless allegations and finding out nothing new. 'She didn't have a mandate . . . let the trial play out, see the verdict and then judge it,' he concluded.[7]

It was already possible to judge Saudi justice by who wasn't standing in the dock; and that included Saud al-Qahtani, the crown prince's media adviser and close aide. A representative of Khashoggi's family reportedly asked for him to be brought before the court; but six months after the killing, this had still not happened. What's more, he had not been charged with any crime.

A senior Saudi official had said the prince's aide was sacked 'based on dereliction of duty and participation in the sequence of events' which led to the murder.[8] Yet, although it was claimed that Qahtani was under house arrest and a travel ban, the *Wall Street Journal* reported in February 2019 the concerns of American officials that Qahtani was still working as an informal adviser to the royal court.

'We don't see that Saud al-Qahtani is very constrained in his activities,' a senior US State Department official told the newspaper. That was an understatement. Saudi officials said the aide had been spotted in the Emirati capital Abu Dhabi, making a mockery of his supposed confinement.

A member of the royal family said MbS was furious that his father, King Salman, had officially fired Qahtani – and had assured him he could return when the Khashoggi case had blown over. He'd even been spotted at the royal court, twice.

Sources told Reuters that although he'd abandoned Twitter on 23 October 2018, the prince's media adviser was continuing to dictate the court's editorial line to journalists by using WhatsApp messages. The prince's brother, Prince Khalid, had reportedly explained that there was no point taking Qahtani's mobile phone away from him as he would find other ways of communicating.[9] It was reported that Qahtani's media operation, the Centre for Studies and Media Affairs, had been renamed the Centre for Communication and Knowledge Foresight, under which title it was still monitoring the activities of Saudi dissidents.[10]

In April 2019, Qahtani was listed by the US State Department as one of sixteen Saudis banned, along with their immediate family members, from travelling to the United States. Bizarrely, Mohammed al-Otaibi, the former consul general in Istanbul, was not on the list.[11]

'We have basically withdrawn the visas of the assassination team, which means they can't come here and go to Disneyland,' Bob Jordan, a former US ambassador to Saudi Arabia, told me. 'It is feeble. It needs a much more robust response.'

Instead, business was resuming as usual. In Washington, MSL, the parent company of the lobbying firm Qorvis Communications, reported receiving $18.8 million from the Saudi government since Khashoggi's murder; although the company said the money was for lobbying work carried out over several previous years. Six months on from the killing in the consulate, the chief executives of HSBC and BlackRock flew back to Riyadh, having previously pulled out of the 'Davos in the Desert' conference the previous autumn.

'We are excited about the role that we can play here,' John Flint, HSBC's CEO, said on a panel alongside JP Morgan's co-president, Daniel Pinto, adding that the future was bright for the Saudi economy.[12]

The American cinema chain AMC pressed ahead with plans to roll out at least forty new theatres in the next five years, pointing out that, otherwise, ordinary Saudis would be deprived of a form of entertainment which had previously been banned for decades.

Even if the US was set to become a net exporter of energy by 2020, Saudi Arabia also remained a vital supplier of oil to the global economy. Although the flotation of a chunk of the state oil company, Aramco, had been indefinitely postponed in the summer of 2018, the inaugural bond sale the following year was vastly oversubscribed and raised $12 billion; Aramco was the world's most profitable company, with a net income of over $111 billion, and therefore too good a prospect for many financial institutions to ignore.

A senior member of the Saudi royal family summed up the prospects for foreign investment to the *Wall Street Journal*. 'Time heals. And when the verdict is out, when justice is done, when a few heads get chopped off, it will come back.'[13]

It wasn't just Iran and arms sales weighing on the mind of President Trump, but family too. His son-in-law, Jared Kushner, was counting on the Saudi crown prince's endorsement of his peace plan for Israel and the Palestinians, which was said to be nearing publication after months of delay.[14]

A leak of the plan to an Israeli newspaper suggested that Arab Gulf states would be asked to provide 70 per cent of the cost – $30 billion over five years.[15] If the peace plan was to stand any chance of working, Kushner would need Saudi Arabia's money.

The president was even considering Riyadh's request to designate the Muslim Brotherhood, the organisation Khashoggi had joined as a young man, as a foreign terrorist organisation, no better than the Iranian Revolutionary Guard.

President al-Sisi of Egypt had urged him to do it at a meeting in the White House. The Saudi crown prince spoke to Trump by phone the same day, and the crown prince of Abu Dhabi called the president three days before that, in what was presumed to be a co-ordinated attempt to persuade Trump to outlaw Islamist political opposition groups.[16]

Jamal Khashoggi would surely have been appalled at America's attempt to impose economic and travel sanctions on loose-knit groups of Islamists opposed to authoritarian Arab rule. But maybe that was to underestimate the genuine threat that a mass social movement with millions of members, more illiberal than it often likes to appear, poses to what passes for stability in much of the Middle East.

The deal at the heart of the Saudi relationship had survived the Khashoggi murder pretty much intact. It remains a modified version of the same deal as that struck in 1945 in a meeting on the USS *Quincy* between President Franklin Delano Roosevelt and the nation's founding king, Ibn Saud: America would gain access to newly discovered Saudi Arabian oil fields, in exchange for guaranteeing to defend the country's security, forming the basis for what remains the US's oldest alliance in the Middle East.

This Faustian bargain has frequently been open to question – because, in the words of the former CIA officer Bruce Riedel, 'the two countries have shared interests but no shared values'.

'We don't rely on them for petroleum any more,' a senior White House adviser told me, 'but we have longstanding alliances and they are a very good ally against Iran.'

He continued to explain:

'We tried to restore relations after Obama. We thought it was important to bring these guys round. They are a very good ally against radicalism; I can't go into it, but they have been doing things with us to stop terrorism. They are modernising. They want jobs, entertainment. The options on the president's desk are not a good option or a bad option; but a bad option or a less bad option. [Khashoggi] was an awful situation. We condemned it. We put some sanctions on individuals and [Secretary of State] Pompeo pledged to get to the bottom of it. But we also have to protect our national interests.'

Those national interests included intelligence co-operation for the sake of American security, with the threat from al-Qaeda and later ISIS entering its fourth decade, along with commercial benefits including arms sales. At the end of 2018, Saudi Arabia signed acceptance documents for the purchase of forty-four Lockheed Martin missile launchers worth $15 billion. Simply put, the killing of Jamal Khashoggi was not the 'red line' or turning point in relations with America that many of his friends hoped for.

However, a sixty-year-old Saudi journalist, who always disliked being labelled as a dissident, had become more famous in death than in life; not just for speaking what he saw as truth to power and then being killed for it – but for prompting from beyond the grave the toughest questions about the US–Saudi relationship since the 11 September attacks.

At the end of 2018, Jamal Khashoggi was named by *Time* magazine as one of a group of journalists, which it collectively called 'guardians of the truth', who had won the magazine's annual 'person of the year' award. The other recipients included Wa Lone and Kyaw Soe Oo, two Reuters journalists imprisoned in Burma after reporting on the massacre of Rohingya Muslims in 2017; and four journalists killed by a gunman in the newsroom of the *Capital Gazette* in Maryland.

The award reflected a dramatic shift in the threats faced by members of the press. The good news was that the number of media workers killed globally in conflict in 2018 had fallen to its lowest level in seven years. The bad news was that the numbers targeted for murder in reprisal for their reporting had almost doubled in a year, to thirty-four. Khashoggi's killing inside the Saudi consulate had become the most brazen and gruesome emblem of a much bigger problem.[17]

Time argued that Khashoggi's death had exposed the 'utter absence of morality in the Saudi–US alliance' and 'laid bare the true nature of a smiling prince'. If the award was a disappointment to President Trump, who had said he couldn't imagine anyone other than himself winning it, it also reflected a glaring absence of international leadership on the issue of press freedom in an era when 'shooting the messenger' was in danger of becoming an unchallenged norm.

When it came to the press, Trump had a reputation for aiming at the press himself. A study by the Committee to Protect Journalists in 2019 showed that since he began his run for president, he had sent 1,339 tweets about the media that were critical, insinuating, condemning or threatening. In the year of Khashoggi's murder, he used the moniker 'enemy of the people' twenty-one times to describe the press, nearly all of them after the killings of American journalists in Maryland. One of Trump's favourite phrases, 'fake news', casts doubt on the credibility of journalists and journalism in general. The human rights lawyer Amal Clooney accused him of 'making honest journalists all over the world more vulnerable to abuse'.

'This is still a developing set of facts,' said Mike Pompeo, the US Secretary of State, when asked at the end of 2018 about the crown prince's alleged involvement in Khashoggi's murder. 'The direct evidence isn't available. It may show up tomorrow.'[18] The Secretary of State must have been hoping that it would not.

The previous month, both Republican and Democratic leaders of the Senate Foreign Relations Committee sent the White House a letter demanding that the president report back in 120 days on 'whether Crown Prince Mohammed bin Salman is responsible for Mr Khashoggi's murder'.

On 8 February 2019, 120 days later, the administration refused, pointing out that it had already sanctioned individual Saudis involved. Instead, Mike Pompeo wrote a letter back committing to 'use relevant authorities as appropriate to promote accountability' for the killing. He made no mention of the crown prince.

The case against MbS has appeared throughout this book.

It includes the composition of the fifteen-man hit squad from royal guard units who protected the crown prince, as well as from the media department of the royal court; the squad's commander, Brigadier General Mutreb, allegedly informing the crown prince's media aide, Saud al-Qahtani, to 'tell your boss' after the killing; the attempt by the Saudi government to erase the evidence afterwards; and MbS having talked about using 'a bullet' against Khashoggi more than a year before he was killed. The CIA itself concluded with 'medium to high confidence' that the crown prince 'probably ordered his death'.

It is possible that Khashoggi was captured and then murdered in part because the crown prince believed he was a member of the Muslim Brotherhood. Although MbS reportedly made this claim of Brotherhood membership to the White House afterwards, it seems unlikely to be the underlying motive. The journalist's youth and his friendships with the group's members and sympathisers do not to my mind amount to anything like as strong a case for a murderous grievance in Riyadh as the journalist's articles and speaking engagements. After all, the rift deepened when Khashoggi was ordered by the prince's adviser to stop all media appearances in 2016. The journalist fled to Washington the following year and then started writing for the *Washington Post*. However, the CIA's assessment cited evidence of a desire to capture the journalist dating back as far as August 2017, before his employment at the paper started and before his controversial text exchanges with a dissident in Canada, Omar Abdulaziz, about setting up a social media campaign inside the kingdom itself.

It seems Jamal Khashoggi was a marked man for more than a year before his death. We know the Saudis' moment of opportunity to strike against him was his visit to their consulate in Istanbul. We don't know precisely when the targeting of him began and, crucially, no specific 'kill order' from the crown prince has come to light at the time of writing.

'We don't know what led to the final decisions,' David Ignatius, Khashoggi's *Post* colleague, told me. 'But I think that when Jamal decided that he wanted to be an international journalist writing from the platform of the *Washington Post*, something changed in the kingdom and he came to be viewed as a threatening person.' Perhaps the best way of explaining a motive for the journalist's murder is to put it down to the paranoia of one man, who could not tolerate direct criticism from a fellow Saudi he regarded as a traitor, residing far too close to the heart of American power.

Will Khashoggi's body ever be found? That seems unlikely, unless the crown prince dramatically reverses course and takes responsibility for the murder, prompting unprecedented Saudi co-operation. The body could have been flown out of Turkey on one of the hit squad's private jets; if it is at the bottom of a well in the consul general's residence, Turkish police would need to regain access to investigate. At the time of writing, the Turks have not released the audio recording of the murder itself. It seems as if the potential drawbacks of an even deeper schism with the Saudis outweigh any possible benefits. Not that the Turks won't stop demanding answers and accountability. 'I cannot understand America's silence when such a horrific attack took place, and even after members of the CIA listened to the recordings we provided,' President Erdoğan said.[19]

Yasin Aktay, one of his advisers, told me the crown prince was a 'natural suspect' who should be prosecuted. 'If you keep him out of this prosecution and trial process, it is not justice,' he said.

Another adviser to the Turkish leader told me the element of doubt against MbS was so strong that he was 'damaged goods' on the world stage and would remain so for years. However, Turkey's indignation did not seem in danger of translating into a real threat to the Saudi heir's position; Donald Trump still had the prince's back. The president had weighed up who could replace him and decided he should stay put.

In an interview with the *Washington Post* just a few weeks after the killing, the president said he did not want MbS to be replaced because he had read about other possible candidates and the prince was 'considered by far the strongest person'. It was an endorsement Trump would apparently not withdraw unless the evidence forced him to – and the evidence remained classified at CIA headquarters.[20]

The crown prince himself was reported by his friend Bernard Haykel, professor of Near Eastern studies at Princeton University, to be 'deeply shocked by the reaction in the West', and focusing on developing relations in Asia as a result.[21]

In February 2019, MbS flew to Pakistan, on the first leg of a trip that included India and China. Amid much fanfare, he was greeted at an airbase by the Pakistani prime minister, Imran Khan, where he was accorded a 21 gun salute.

Saudi Arabia's de facto leader was pivoting eastwards until the storm died down and Western leaders agreed to shake his hand again in public.

He didn't have to wait long.

Eight months after being sidelined to the edge of the G20 'family photo' in Buenos Aires, MbS was centre stage of the leaders' next gathering in Japan, standing in the front row in conversation with Donald Trump, who said it was a 'great honour' to be with him.

It was as bold a statement of the crown prince's impunity as could be imagined, apart from if he had hosted the G20 himself.

'Saudi Arabia is a good purchaser of American products,' Trump said at their bilateral meeting, congratulating MbS on opening up the kingdom in recent years.

'We are trying to do our best for our country, Saudi Arabia, and it's a long journey,' the crown prince replied.

The president said he had mentioned the murder to him 'very strongly' but Trump refused to comment on the CIA's assessment of the prince's involvement.

'I'm extremely angry and unhappy about a thing like that taking place,' the president said of Khashoggi's death. 'They've taken it very, very seriously. They will continue to.'

At the end of the summit in Kyoto, it was announced that Saudi Arabia (and therefore MbS) would indeed be hosting the event the following year. The UN rapporteur Agnes Callamard was horrified. 'He [the crown prince] is pretending to be one of them, and the rest of the G20 community is pretending that he is one of them,' she said. 'Political accountability for Mr Khashoggi will mean that it [the summit] doesn't happen, or it's moved.'

At a conference on press freedom in London the following month, the then British foreign secretary, Jeremy Hunt, claimed the Saudis had 'paid a big reputational price' with 'profound diplomatic consequences'.[22] What those were, he didn't say. If anything, Western nations confining their response to financial sanctions and travel bans on named individuals only underpinned the Saudi narrative that the killing was a rogue operation. Hunt's judgement stood in stark contrast to that of the woman he had appointed as the Foreign Office's special envoy on media freedom – Amal Clooney.

'When Jamal Khashoggi, *Washington Post* columnist, was tortured to death and dismembered by Saudi Arabian officials in Istanbul, world leaders responded with little more than a collective shrug,' she said. 'States must ensure that when a journalist is attacked, this crime is investigated and those responsible held to account.'

~

The House of Saud has witnessed far greater internal turmoil in the past than the furore caused by Jamal Khashoggi's death.

Take the kingdom's second king, Saud, who was deposed by his own family in 1964 after a power struggle with his half-brother, Prince Faisal. President John F. Kennedy was so worried about the monarchy's potential collapse in the run-up to this palace coup that he persuaded Faisal to implement internal reforms, including the abolition of slavery and the introduction of free education.

In Donald Trump's case, reforming Saudi Arabia was never on his agenda. The murder of Jamal Khashoggi did not in his mind warrant any substantial US intervention in his ally's internal affairs. An opportunity to push for political as opposed to social reforms, at a moment of potential weakness, was simply not taken. Though there was nothing new in that.

Bruce Riedel, the former CIA officer who has written a history of US–Saudi relations, claims that no US president, before or since Kennedy, has convinced a Saudi leader of the need for major internal change.[23] Donald Trump was no exception to the rule.

With Trump firmly in the prince's corner, perhaps the greatest threat to MbS came from within his own family. Would the thirty-four members of the so-called 'Allegiance Council' in Riyadh dare to block his eventual accession to the throne?

It is the council's job to confirm the new monarch, either when the king dies or his capacity to govern is irredeemably lost. Introduced by King Abdullah in 2007, the council was supposed to provide stability by making the succession the subject of more formal agreement across several branches of the royal family. It comprises sons of the kingdom's founder, Ibn Saud, along with his grandsons whose fathers are deceased. A son of the present king and a son of the crown prince are also included.

This meant that in 2017, MbS had the opportunity to vote for himself as crown prince, though he may not have done so, simply because he may not have needed to: the council's authority had been sufficiently weakened over the years by the deaths of elder princes that it was under pressure to 'rubber-stamp' King Salman's choice.

Prince Ahmed, King Salman's only surviving full brother, was reported to be one of only three princes on the council to have voted against his nephew's appointment in 2017. Yet the chances of Ahmed's fellow Allegiance Council members rallying around the 77-year-old as heir in the event of King Salman's death seemed remote, given the unprecedented degree of military authority MbS has already accrued.

The crown prince's two predecessors, Muqrin and Mohammed bin Nayef, were removed from power and effectively neutralised by MbS. Organising against him now would be both difficult and dangerous, given the prince's previous purges of several potential rivals from government and his tight grip on internal security.

'If there is any kind of challenge, there will be a massacre,' Professor Madawi al-Rasheed, a Saudi expert, told me, claiming the majority of princes preferred to keep a low profile and accept their generous monthly living allowances rather than challenge the status quo.

However, it is worth recalling the assassination of King

Faisal in 1975. A nephew of the king appears to have been seeking revenge for the death of his brother, shot dead years earlier during demonstrations against Faisal's decision to introduce television.

There is probably no shortage of candidates who would like revenge on MbS. He has made many enemies among his cousins and uncles in the House of Saud, as well as across the border in Yemen; the prince accused of ordering the assassination of Jamal Khashoggi is one of the world's most heavily protected men and a prime target for assassination himself.

Assuming he survives, MbS's rise may prove irreversible; unless King Salman listens to the prince's critics and turns against his favourite son.

'My sense is that he is very secure in his position, that he controls all the levers of power,' said Bernard Haykel. 'There is absolutely no daylight between him and his father.'[24]

However, in March 2019, *The Guardian* reported rumours of just such a rift. The newspaper claimed that a new security team was flown out to join King Salman during his visit to Egypt, in case of a possible move against him by MbS loyalists within his existing guards. During the king's absence, MbS signed off on the appointment of his younger brother, Khalid, formerly ambassador to Washington, as minister of defence. The king reportedly found out about it by watching television and believed Khalid's appointment was premature.[25]

The Saudi embassy in Washington dismissed the article, pointing out that it was customary for the king to delegate power to the crown prince whenever he travelled abroad. However, the story then took a dramatic turn. The two journalists on *The Guardian* story were warned by an unnamed source that their email accounts were being targeted by hackers based in Saudi Arabia.

The newspaper obtained a single-page internal memo, dated two days after the article appeared, which was addressed to the cybersecurity directorate within the crown prince's private office. The order was to 'carry out the penetration of the servers of *The Guardian* newspaper and those who worked on the report . . . with complete secrecy'.

It was signed in the name of Saud al-Qahtani, the crown prince's media adviser, whom the king had supposedly fired during the kingdom's Khashoggi investigation. Saudi diplomats queried the memo's authenticity and claimed that they were trying to find out more, but the newspaper said the authorities in Riyadh repeatedly declined to comment on the record.[26]

It wasn't just journalists apparently still at risk. Several prominent critics of MbS living outside the kingdom felt compelled to adopt a higher state of vigilance after Khashoggi's death.

The *Financial Times* reported that, more than nine months after the murder, Saudi Arabia was still trying to lure home critics by assuring them of a safe return. A study on political dissidents, commissioned by the royal court, estimated that the number of political asylum seekers outside the kingdom would reach 50,000 by 2030.

'Someone close to the leadership or another mediator would typically contact you and say: "I have a personal message from the crown prince," promising there would be no harm or jail time if you decide to take up the offer,' said one Saudi who had been approached.[27]

In spite of this softly-softly approach, the CIA warned four Western countries of what the UN rapporteur Agnes Callamard described as 'foreseeable and immediate threats' to dissidents from Saudi Arabia and other Arab states. In fact, Callamard was so worried about the Saudis spying on their critics abroad that she called for a moratorium on the sale of surveillance technology to Riyadh in her report on the murder.

The dissidents at risk were understood to include Khashoggi's friends Omar Abdulaziz in Canada and Iyad el-Baghdadi, a Palestinian living in Norway. The concern for el-Baghdadi arose from the help he had given an investigator working for Jeff Bezos, the *Washington Post* owner and Amazon CEO, who reached the incredible conclusion that the Saudis had hacked the billionaire's mobile phone in the aftermath of Khashoggi's murder.[28]

'Some Americans will be surprised to learn that the Saudi government has been very intent on harming Jeff Bezos since last October, when the *Post* began its relentless coverage of Khashoggi's murder,' said the investigator, Gavin de Becker.[29]

If even the world's richest man was being targeted, who could call themselves safe?

After the killing in Istanbul, police in London issued Ghanem al-Dosari, a Saudi satirist, with a portable alarm and a panic button for use at his home. Dosari had a long history of run-ins with supporters of the House of Saud, who were frequently outraged by his denunciations of the royal family on his YouTube channels, which have been viewed around 230 million times across the Arab world.

In 2017, Dosari recorded a threatening phone call from MbS's brother-in-law, Prince Abdulaziz bin Mashhur al-Saud, claiming the prince had his 'file' and that he would be returned to the kingdom, where his head would be placed under the feet of MbS. The satirist's Facebook, Instagram and Twitter accounts have either been hacked or spammed; and a few months before Khashoggi was killed, Dosari received three text messages which surveillance experts believe installed spyware on his mobile phone.

One of them was received on 23 June 2018 — the same day Khashoggi's friend in Canada, Omar Abdulaziz, received virtually the same malicious text. Dosari's British lawyers have notified the Saudi government that he intends to take them to the High Court for alleged harassment and misuse of his private information.

'I want them to apologise, to stop acting like a rogue regime – going crazy, hacking people's privacy,' he told me, adding that he was still receiving daily threats from Saudi Arabia in messages, voicemails and through social media.

The counterpoint to Dosari's story is the fervent support which exists for the Saudi crown prince. A regional survey of Arab youth conducted in May 2018 showed a 91 per cent approval rating for the prince's appointment, with 97 per cent considering him a strong leader. Over 90 per cent of young Saudis were in favour of his anti-corruption drive and his Vision 2030 economic development plan.[30] His crackdown on the super-rich at the Ritz-Carlton hotel was wildly popular, according to interviews conducted in Riyadh. For many young people, MbS also embodies their hope that the power of Salafist clerics will be rolled back, making their country a less stifling place in which to live. 'A younger generation is taking power; a once-joyless country is learning to have fun and be creative,' was how David Ignatius put it. 'The yearning for change is unmistakeable.'

Ironically, it echoed what Jamal Khashoggi believed should happen and might have written himself.

Saudis must weigh up the tangible benefits of greater cultural freedoms (cinemas, open-air music, women driving) against the House of Saud's ruthless determination to remain an absolute monarchy and stifle dissent. The execution of thirty-seven Saudis for alleged terrorism-related crimes in April 2019, including three who were minors at the time of their alleged offences, signalled that the kingdom's justice system would continue on its own defiant path. One of the beheadings was followed by a crucifixion. It was the single biggest day of executions in over three years.[31]

Protected by President Trump, arguably unassailable at home and with his critics still fearful of him abroad – how much had life for the heir to the Saudi throne really changed?

THE STORY HE DID NOT COMPLETE

'I am the one story Jamal did not complete.'

– Hatice Cengiz, *Washington Post*, 2 November 2018

In May 2019, Jamal Khashoggi's fiancée, Hatice Cengiz, wandered around the monuments and museums of Washington DC on her first visit to America, thinking about what might have been.

The journalist had told her about his friends there, about how he would introduce her to them after their marriage the previous October in Istanbul, had it gone ahead.

'Trust me, you will love it here,' he had told her on the phone. As she walked the streets of the US capital without him, she could hear the excitement in his voice and see his smiling, absent face.

'We dreamed of living together in this town,' she wrote. 'And then suddenly, Jamal was taken from us in an unthinkable manner, something that could only happen in a horror movie. Yet that is the life I now live.'[1]

After the murder she postponed her doctorate in Istanbul and tried to work out how to recover from the ordeal, but also how to grieve – with no body to bury and no prospect of all those involved in the plot to kill Jamal Khashoggi being held accountable in an open trial.

However, if there was to be the public face of a campaign for justice, Cengiz knew it might have to be hers, in the absence of anyone else's. Khashoggi's son, Abdullah, was quoted as saying, 'I want the da Vinci', not long after his father's death – referring to the *Salvator Mundi* painting owned by the crown prince[2] – but while the journalist's relatives were undoubtedly angry, they chose not to show it, preferring to say as little in public as possible. Two weeks after the killing, a brief written statement said the Khashoggi family 'yearns to be together during this painful time'. It was a plea to the Saudi authorities to let the columnist's eldest son, Salah, who lived in Jeddah, leave the kingdom in order to join his mother, brother and sisters at his father's home in Virginia. He was only allowed to fly after he had shaken the crown prince's hand in a televised meeting three weeks after the murder.

The family statement also called for an 'independent and impartial international commission' to investigate, but as long as Salah chose to carry on living in Jeddah with his wife and child, that might be as far as the family dare go in its demands for accountability. Not only might it be too dangerous to speak out, but the question arose as to whether the Khashoggis were being paid for their silence.

In April 2019, the *Washington Post* reported that all four of the journalist's children had received houses worth up to $4 million each in a shared compound in Jeddah, plus monthly payments of at least $10,000, as part of a compensation deal with the Saudi government. The paper also reported that the siblings had received initial payments of about $266,000 and that the deal had been agreed by King Salman.[3] These payments were confirmed to me by a friend of the family who suggested they were in lieu of a public apology for what had happened. 'Things are run differently in our country,' the friend explained.

After the story was published, Salah Khashoggi issued a statement on Twitter, offering his wholehearted support to the king and crown prince, describing them as 'guardians of all Saudis'.

'Acts of generosity,' he wrote, are 'not admission of guilt or scandal. We, Jamal Khashoggi's family, were brought up by our parents to thank acts of good, not to disavow them.'

It sounded as if the money had been accepted purely as a 'gift'.

'The trial is taking place and no settlement discussion had been reached or is discussed,' Salah claimed. 'The people who committed and were involved in this crime will all be brought to justice and face punishment.'

The House of Saud's negotiations with the Khashoggis were reportedly led by Prince Khalid bin Salman, the crown prince's brother and US ambassador at the time of the killing, who had denied personally encouraging the journalist to visit the consulate in Istanbul. Prince Khalid may have left Washington under a cloud of scandal, but he was welcomed back in March 2019, this time as deputy defence minister, discussing with Secretary of State Pompeo further sanctions on Iran.

'The secretary congratulated the minister on his new role and looked forward to continuing to work together to advance the US–Saudi partnership,' the State Department said, as if Khashoggi's death had never happened.

The money the Khashoggi family has received so far might be only the beginning. 'Blood money' payments could also be expected as part of the Saudi criminal justice system. Eleven people had been charged with involvement in Khashoggi's killing, with five of them facing possible execution. Khashoggi's relatives could be given the opportunity to grant clemency to those facing the death penalty, in exchange for potentially tens of millions of dollars.

A clemency deal might also suit the crown prince. It arguably might be easier for him if his former employees were pardoned or given suspended prison sentences – otherwise their relatives could complain that they were being made scapegoats and had only obeyed orders.

Hanan el-Atr, the Egyptian air stewardess Khashoggi married in Virginia in the summer of 2018, was also hoping for a share of whatever financial compensation became available. 'I will have whatever sharia law gives me,' she told me in an interview. 'I don't know how she can expect anything,' was the response of a friend of the Khashoggi family, who said a Saudi court had dismissed her claim to part of the journalist's estate.

One of Khashoggi's ex-wives, Alaa Naseif, was quoted by Al Arabiya television shortly after the murder as claiming that no dissidents had ever been harmed in Saudi Arabia's history and that 'everyone has to keep silent' until the truth of the journalist's disappearance was established.

She also appeared to discredit Hatice Cengiz, who had been the first to raise the alarm. 'If Hatice was in Jamal's life, I would be the first to know,' she reportedly said. 'But she was never in his life.'[4] However, a friend of Naseif's told me the words were not her own, implying she had come under pressure from the Saudi authorities as part of a disinformation campaign against Cengiz following the murder.

Khashoggi's eldest son, Salah, had also questioned the Turkish woman's status as his partner, telling Al Arabiya: 'I do not know this woman and I have never heard of her except through the media.'

In fact, Jamal Khashoggi had introduced Cengiz to his youngest son, Abdullah, in Istanbul, a few weeks before their wedding was due to take place. Further family introductions would have followed; and the journalist talked of starting a new family with Cengiz, dividing his time between Turkey and Washington DC. At the time of writing, Khashoggi's relatives have expressed no wish to meet her following his murder.

The story of her waiting alone outside the consulate doors for a lover who never returned had struck an emotional chord around the world. At the same time, she was uncomfortable with becoming the centre of global media attention, particularly when she had not recovered from the ordeal herself.

After the Saudis first admitted her fiancé had been killed, she accepted the Turkish government's offer of two police bodyguards. She was unable to walk down a street in Istanbul without being recognised, and of course, as the only eyewitness to both his entry and failure to exit, she felt in potential danger herself.

During her wait for news in the weeks after his disappearance, and unable to eat or sleep much, she would repeatedly scroll back to the last text message she received from him: 'The house is beautiful, like its owner,' Khashoggi had written of their new home in Istanbul.

There had been no sorrow in her goodbye to him on 2 October; just the conviction that she was happier to be alive than she had ever been, after a whirlwind romance lasting barely five months. She had taken two of his shirts to the dry-cleaner's that morning, while he slept off the fatigue of his flight from London in their new apartment. In her mind, they were almost married already. She planned to organise a late lunch or dinner to celebrate their engagement and she had begun texting friends to arrange it.

'If he thought something was going to happen to him, he wouldn't have gone in there,' she told me later, reminding herself that he had always said he felt safe in Turkey.

Later, a psychologist told her she was suffering from

'survivor's guilt'. 'What did he not notice? What did *we* not notice?' she constantly asked herself, telling friends she would rather have entered the consulate in her fiancé's place.

'I wonder if he was angry with me,' she admitted tearfully to the *Washington Post*. 'During his last moments, after he went inside, I wonder what did he go through, was he angry with me? What did he feel at the end? I really wonder whether he felt a lot of pain.'

All he had wanted was what she referred to in her diary as 'that goddamned document' to get married to her. Instead, in her words, her lover was 'writhing in agony' while she waited in blissful ignorance outside.

She had wanted to bring his loneliness to an end, to ease his longing for his homeland. The only consolation she could find was knowing that the Saudi journalist ended his life having met someone he loved and who loved him back.

'Maybe that crossed his mind in his last minutes,' she said, describing herself as 'the one story Jamal did not complete'.[5]

At a memorial event in London on 29 October, she talked of her disappointment at the international community's response, and she took aim at the US in particular.

'President Trump should help reveal the truth and ensure justice be served. He should not pave the way for a cover-up of my fiancé's murder,' she said. 'Let's not let money taint our conscience and compromise our values. I believe the Saudi regime knows where his body is.'

In the spring of 2019, Hatice Cengiz moved to London for several months, renting a flat with her two sisters and enrolling in an intensive English language programme. Some Arab tourists, seeing her in the street, remembered her headscarfed face from the TV news coverage and occasionally asked her for selfie photographs, which she declined; but for the most part she revelled in the anonymity of the new city, a place where she could attempt to pick up the pieces of her shattered life.

Her first trip to Washington DC would not be easy. Not just because her fiancé had lived there, but because she reckoned he would have been most disappointed of all at America's response to his murder and what she called the Trump administration's 'cynical prism of self-interest'.

On an emotionally difficult visit to Khashoggi's employer, the *Washington Post*, she confirmed that the Saudi government had not contacted her to offer either compensation or condolences. She also testified before the House Foreign Affairs subcommittee on human rights.

'This act – this murder – was a great brutality,' she told members of Congress, 'and the last seven, eight months, we see that nothing has been done.'

The man she loved had walked into a building and never returned to the life they both dreamed of; but there was a lot more to the story of Jamal Khashoggi than that. He was a complicated man with a tangled private life, from the radical Islamism of his youth, to Saudi government insider, to outspoken critic of the kingdom's young crown prince in the pages of a leading American newspaper; and it was surely this final incarnation as a brave journalist that his killers could not forgive.

'It wasn't just Jamal that was killed,' his heartbroken fiancée told the congressional committee. 'It was also what we're talking about here – it was the values that the United States represents.'

'Didn't they get murdered as well?'[6]

ACKNOWLEDGEMENTS

This book would not have been possible without the help and testimony of many of Jamal Khashoggi's friends and loved ones in London, Washington DC, Istanbul and beyond. Some of them preferred to speak anonymously, given the sensitivity of the case and the fear of reprisals, but most of them are quoted in this book. I thank them all for trusting me to tell his story, especially Jamal's fiancée, Hatice Cengiz, who has been remarkably brave in the most appalling circumstances.

The report of the UN special rapporteur on extrajudicial executions was published on 19 June 2019. The work of the rapporteur, Agnes Callamard, and her team was of enormous value to this book and I have used information from her report throughout. The report can be found at: https://www.ohchr.org/EN/HRBodies/HRC/RegularSessions/Session41/Pages/ListReports.aspx.

I am indebted to the reporting teams of the *New York Times* and *Washington Post*, whose work is quoted throughout. Their determination to get to the bottom of what happened to Jamal Khashoggi has served as a reminder of what great news organisations they are, and of how journalists must look out for one another in dangerous times.

At the *Washington Post*, the chief executive, Fred Ryan, the opinion page editor, Fred Hiatt, and the associate editor (and Jamal's friend), David Ignatius, were good enough to see me and be interviewed when the shock of Jamal's loss remained all too real. Frances Sellers helped make the introductions. The *Post*'s Istanbul bureau chief, Kareem Fahim, was full of good advice over beers in a bar there.

In Turkey, several old friends came to my rescue. Murat Yetkin, one of the country's finest journalists and the former editor of the *Hurriyet Daily News*, made some important introductions. The Ottoman historian Caroline Finkel has been teaching me about Istanbul for over twenty-five years, as has her husband, Andrew – their love and understanding for the place knows few equals. Yavuz Harani helped translate and Serpil Karacan translated even more. Nothing happens in Istanbul without Serpil knowing about it and she accompanied me to two important interviews.

The Istanbul police department provided insight into their investigation into Jamal Khashoggi's disappearance and death, as well as many of the photographs reprinted here. I would also like to thank Ferhat Unlu of the *Sabah* newspaper, Hami Aksoy, spokesman at the Turkish Foreign Ministry, Umit Yalcin, Turkey's ambassador to London, and all those current or former officials who spoke to me anonymously .

My *Channel 4 News* friends and colleagues Michael French and Stephen Hird accompanied me on my first trip to the Saudi consulate in the aftermath of Jamal Khashoggi's disappearance, when none of us knew this would result in a book.

In Washington DC, Dani Isdale and Toby Holder were generous and welcoming hosts. Allan Thornton and Polly Ghazi housed me comfortably in their basement and Polly gave me valuable feedback on my writing too.

At the International Bar Association's Human Rights

Institute, Baroness Helena Kennedy QC provided expert insight into the case for which I am particularly grateful. Professor Madawi al-Rasheed of the London School of Economics and Sir John Jenkins, formerly the Foreign Office's chief Arabist, were thoughtful readers who made plenty of good suggestions, ensuring that a pacy read did not entirely run away with itself. Karin von Hippel, director-general of the Royal United Services Institute, was generous with her contacts in Washington DC. Ian Kelly, Kate Colquhoun, Julian Granville, Alec Russell, Sophie Clarke Gervoise, Beth Mendelson, Ian Sherwood and Peter Everington gave me advice or morale-boosting support when I needed it.

I'd like to thank Lindsey Hilsum and Jonathan Miller, my *Channel 4 News* stable mates, for their encouragement over many years; and my editors Ben de Pear, Nevine Mabro, Liliane Landor and Rob Hodge for granting me book leave and their forbearance while I was writing it. At Simon & Schuster, Ian Marshall, Kaiya Shang and Melissa Bond gently steered this book towards publication in double quick-time.

My agents, Martin Redfern and James Carroll at Northbank Talent, first suggested that I should write *The Killing in the Consulate* and were always at hand when I needed them. My wife, Rachel Lewis, was not only remarkably patient during the whole process, but helped with the editing and transcription. My greatest thanks go to her, as they have ever since we were married in Istanbul.

NOTES

INTRODUCTION

1 'Jamal Khashoggi's fiancée Hatice Cengiz: the international community must bring my fiancé's killers to justice', *Washington Post*, 2 November 2018

1 THE FINAL JOURNEY

1 *Jamal Khashoggi: His Life, Struggles and Secrets*, Hatice Cengiz, Sinan Onus and Mehmet Akif Ersoy, Kopernik, Inc., April 2019
2 *Ibid.*

2 WALKING THE TIGHTROPE

1 'By blaming 1979 for Saudi Arabia's problems, the crown prince is peddling revisionist history', *Washington Post*, 3 April 2018
2 'Adnan Khashoggi obituary', *The Guardian*, 7 June 2017
3 'Inside the fabulous world of Donald Trump where money is no problem', *Washington Post*, 9 October 2015
4 '"I like them very much": Trump has long-standing business ties with Saudis, who have boosted his hotels since he took office'; 'Jamal Khashoggi's long road to the doors of the Saudi consulate', *Washington Post*, 11 and 12 December 2018
5 'By blaming 1979 for Saudi Arabia's problems, the crown prince is peddling revisionist history', op. cit.
6 *The Looming Tower*, Lawrence Wright, Alfred Knopf, 2006
7 *The Osama bin Laden I Know*, Peter Bergen, Free Press, 2006
8 Ibid.
9 'Murdered journalist should not be forgotten in his college', *Tribune-Star*, 15 December 2018
10 *Inside the Kingdom*, Robert Lacey, Arrow, 2009

11   *The Osama Bin Laden I Know*, op. cit.

12   *Jamal Khashoggi: His Life, Struggles and Secrets*, op. cit.

13   *The Osama bin Laden I Know*, op. cit.

14   'From travels with bin Laden to sparring with princes: Jamal Khashoggi's provocative journey', *Washington Post*, 7 October 2018

15   *The Looming Tower*, op. cit.

16   'Jamal Khashoggi's long road to the doors of the Saudi consulate', op. cit.

17   'The Saudi royal family circles its wagons in the Khashoggi crisis', *Washington Post*, 24 October 2018

18   'Osama: the Sudan years', *The Guardian*, 17 October 2001

19   *The Looming Tower*, op. cit.

20   WikiLeaks, October 1998, US diplomatic cable

21   *Daily Star* (Beirut), 18 June 2002

22   *Kings and Presidents: Saudi Arabia and the United States since FDR*, Bruce Riedel, Brookings Institution Press, 2017

23   'Who was Jamal Khashoggi?', *USA Today*, 19 October 2018

24   'Saudi newspaper head resigns after run-in with conservatives', AFP, 17 May 2010

25   'I know Jamal Khashoggi personally and I fear for his safety', Al Jazeera, 4 October 2018

26   'Jamal Khashoggi's long road to the doors of the Saudi consulate', op. cit.

27   'The US is wrong about the Muslim Brotherhood – and the Arab world is suffering for it', *Washington Post*, 28 August 2018

28   'Jamal Khashoggi's long road to the doors of the Saudi consulate', op. cit.

29   Ibid.

3   MEET THE CROWN PRINCE

1   'Saudi Arabia is playing an increasingly destabilising role in the Middle East', *Independent*, 4 December 2015

2   'Saudi Arabia's heir to the throne talks to *60 Minutes*', CBS, 19 March 2018

3   'Trump meets Saudi prince as US and kingdom seek warmer relations', *New York Times*, 14 March 2017

4   'The Saudi regime's other victims', *New York Times*, 13 December 2018

5   'Jamal Khashoggi's long road to the doors of the Saudi consulate', op. cit.

6   'Saudi Arabia vs Iran: is the Cold War heating up?', Al Jazeera, 16 January 2016

7   'Kidnapped: Saudi Arabia's missing princes', BBC, 15 August 2017

8   *Jamal Khashoggi: His Life, Struggles and Secrets*, op. cit.

9   'Two princes: Kushner now faces a reckoning for Trump's bet on the heir to the Saudi throne', *Washington Post*, 14 October 2018

10   'A Saudi prince's quest to remake the Middle East', *New Yorker*, 9 April 2018

11 'Who are the Houthis and why are we at war with them?', Brookings Institution, 18 December 2017

12 'Rise of Saudi prince shatters decades of royal tradition', *New York Times*, 15 October 2016

13 'Saudi royal calls for regime change in Riyadh', *The Guardian*, 28 September 2015

14 Madawi al-Rasheed, *New York Times*, 18 October 2018

15 'Saudi reshuffle empowers prince in generational shift', *Financial Times*, 22 June 2017

16 'How a chilling Saudi cyberwar ensnared Jamal Khashoggi', *Washington Post*, 7 December 2018

17 'Uproar over dissident rattles Saudi royal family', *New York Times*, 19 October 2018

18 Quoted in *Kings and Presidents: Saudi Arabia and the United States since FDR*, op. cit.

19 *Fire and Fury: Inside the Trump White House*, Michael Wolff, Henry Holt and Company, 2018

20 'The wooing of Jared Kushner: how the Saudis got a friend in the White House', *New York Times*, 8 December 2018

21 '"I was ordered silent": how Jamal Khashoggi fell out with bin Salman', *Vanity Fair*, 16 October 2018

22 'The wooing of Jared Kushner: how the Saudis got a friend in the White House', op. cit.

23 'Young Saudis celebrate as reach of religious police is reined in', *Financial Times*, 14 October 2017

24 'What Saudi Arabia can learn from *Black Panther*', *Washington Post*, 17 April 2018

25 'Rise of Saudi prince shatters decades of royal tradition', op. cit.

26 'World's most expensive home? Another bauble for a Saudi prince', *New York Times*, 16 December 2017

27 'A Leonardo made a $450 million splash. Now there's no sign of it', *New York Times*, 30 March 2019

28 'Where in the world is "Salvator Mundi"? Kenny Schachter reveals the location of the lost $450 million Leonardo', artnet.com, 10 June 2019

29 'Saudi Arabia's heir to the throne talks to *60 Minutes*', op. cit.

4   THE FALL FROM GRACE

1 Washington Institute website, 15 November 2016

2 '"It's not a citizen": Trump telegraphs a soft line on Jamal Khashoggi – even as evidence becomes more damning', *Washington Post*, 12 October 2018

3 '"I was ordered silent": how Jamal Khashoggi fell out with bin Salman', op. cit.

4   Conversation as relayed by Khashoggi to his friend Wadah Khanfar

5   'Crown prince sought to lure Khashoggi back to Saudi Arabia and detain him, US intercepts show', *Washington Post*, 10 October 2018

5   FLIGHT TO WASHINGTON

1   '"I was ordered silent": how Jamal Khashoggi fell out with bin Salman', op. cit.

2   'Behind Prince Mohammed bin Salman's rise, two loyal enforcers', *New York Times*, 14 November 2018

3   'How a chilling Saudi cyber war ensnared Jamal Khashoggi', op. cit.

4   'US seeks accountability for former Saudi aide in Khashoggi killing', *Wall Street Journal*, 12 February 2019

5   'How the mysteries of Khashoggi's murder have rocked the US–Saudi partnership', *Washington Post*, 29 March 2019

6   'The Khashoggi killing had roots in a cutthroat Saudi family feud', *Washington Post*, 27 November 2018

7   'The Saudi royal family circles its wagons in the Khashoggi crisis', op. cit.

8   '"I was ordered silent": how Jamal Khashoggi fell out with bin Salman', op. cit.

9   'The Saudi regime's other victims', op. cit.

10 'We Saudis will never be silent about Jamal Khashoggi's death', *Washington Post*, 24 October 2018

11 'In a book proposal, Khashoggi outlined a US-inspired vision for a new Saudi Arabia', *Washington Post*, 5 April 2019

12 'Jamal Khashoggi's long road to the doors of the Saudi consulate', op. cit.

13 'The silencing of Saudi journalist Jamal Khashoggi', *Washington Post*, 3 October 2018

14 'Karen Attiah, Jamal Khashoggi's editor, on the writer and his work', *New York Times*, 18 October 2018

15 'Jamal Khashoggi: the emergence of a Saudi dissident, and his potentially tragic end', *Independent*, 9 October 2018

16 'The silencing of Saudi journalist Jamal Khashoggi', op. cit.

17 'Jamal Khashoggi's long road to the doors of the Saudi consulate', op. cit.

18 'The silencing of Saudi journalist Jamal Khashoggi', op. cit.

19 'For Khashoggi, a tangled mix of royal service and Islamist sympathies', *New York Times*, 14 October 2018

6   THE RITZ-CARLTON AFFAIR

1   'The crown prince of Saudi Arabia is giving his country shock therapy', *Washington Post*, 27 February 2018

2   'The Saudi crown prince just made a very risky power play', *Washington Post*, 5 November 2017

3   'Alwaleed bin Talal says life is back to normal', Bloomberg, 19 March 2018

4   BBC News website, 29 November 2017

5   'A year after the Ritz-Carlton round-up, Saudi elites remain jailed by the crown prince', *Washington Post*, 5 November 2018

6   '"I was ordered silent": how Jamal Khashoggi fell out with bin Salman', op. cit.

7   'Saudi Arabia's crown prince is acting like Putin', *Washington Post*, 5 November 2017

8   'How a Saudi royal crushed his rivals in a "shakedown" at the Ritz-Carlton', NBC News, 3 November 2018

9   'Saudi Arabia concludes sweeping anti-corruption campaign', *Financial Times*, 30 January 2019

10 'Saudi Arabia's heir to the throne talks to *60 Minutes*', op. cit.

11 'A Saudi prince's quest to remake the Middle East', op. cit.

12 'What Saudi Arabia could learn from South Korea about fighting corruption', *Washington Post*, 8 January 2018

13 'Why Saad Hariri had that strange sojourn in Saudi Arabia', *New York Times*, 24 December 2017

14 'Praying for Jamal Khashoggi', *New York Times*, 8 October 2018

15 'What Saudi Arabia's crown prince can learn from Queen Elizabeth II', *Washington Post*, 28 February 2018

16 'America's dilemma: censuring MbS and not halting Saudi reforms', *New York Times*, 16 October 2018

17 'A Saudi prince's quest to remake the Middle East', op. cit.

18 '"I was ordered silent": how Jamal Khashoggi fell out with bin Salman', op. cit.

19 'Saudi prince's reform: car race, concerts, but no criticism', Associated Press, 22 December 2018

20 'Saudi Arabia's women can finally drive. But the crown prince needs to do much more', *Washington Post*, 25 June 2018

21 'Saudi crown prince's brutal drive to crush dissent began before Khashoggi', *New York Times*, 17 March 2019

22 'Story of disappeared Saudi power couple spotlights dissident crackdown', CNN, 8 January 2019

23 'ALQST confirms new details of torture of Saudi women activists as British MPs seek access to prison to investigate', alqst.org, 1 March 2019

24 *Channel 4 News*, 17 April 2019

25 'Supporters of missing Saudi columnist call for US investigation into his disappearance', *Washington Post*, 10 October 2018

26 'Saudi Arabia's crown prince already controlled the nation's media. Now he's squeezing it further', *Washington Post*, 7 February 2018

27 'How to work with Mohammed bin Salman', Al Arabiya, 8 April 2018

28 'Saudi Arabia's reformers now face a terrible choice', *Washington Post*, 21 May 2018

29 'The crown prince of Saudi Arabia is giving his country shock therapy', op. cit.

30 'Why the Arab world needs democracy now', *New York Times*, 22 October 2018

31 'Saudi Arabia cannot afford to pick fights with Canada', *Washington Post*, 7 August 2018

32 'Israeli software helped Saudis spy on Khashoggi, lawsuit says', *New York Times*, 2 December 2018

33 'In death, Saudi writer's mild calls for reform grew into a defiant shout', *Washington Post*, 20 October 2018

34 'Jamal Khashoggi's private WhatsApp messages may offer new clues to killing', CNN, 4 December 2018

35 'Jamal Khashoggi's long road to the doors of the Saudi consulate', op. cit.

7   A WOMAN IN ISTANBUL

1 *Jamal Khashoggi: His Life, Struggles and Secrets*, op. cit.

2 'Khashoggi's fiancée seeks answers and justice: it is a moral duty', *New York Times*, 3 May 2019

3 'My fiancé Jamal Khashoggi was a lonely patriot', *New York Times*, 13 October 2018

4 *Jamal Khashoggi: His Life, Struggles and Secrets*, op. cit.

8   LAST WEEKEND IN LONDON

1 *Jamal Khashoggi: His Life, Struggles and Secrets*, op. cit.

2 'The US is wrong about the Muslim Brotherhood – and the Arab world is suffering for it', op. cit.

3 *Jamal Khashoggi: His Life, Struggles and Secrets*, op. cit.

4 'Khashoggi's fiancée seeks answers and justice: it is a moral duty', op. cit.

9   THE KILLING IN THE CONSULATE

1 'Jamal Khashoggi's final months as an exile in the long shadow of Saudi Arabia', *Washington Post*, 21 December 2018

2 'Khashoggi murder one step closer to resolution with striking new findings', *Daily Sabah*, 28 December 2018

3 Ibid.

4 'CIA concludes Saudi crown prince ordered Jamal Khashoggi's assassination', *Washington Post*, 16 November 2018

5 *Jamal Khashoggi: His Life, Struggles and Secrets*, op. cit.

6 'Jamal Khashoggi's killers carried syringes, electro-shock devices and cutting tools as they left Istanbul, says report', *Independent*, 13 November 2018

7 Ibid.

8 'Aide to Saudi crown prince, suspect in Khashoggi case, is shown walking into consulate', *New York Times*, 18 October 2018

9 'Jamal Khashoggi, Saudi journalist, detained in consulate in Istanbul', *New York Times*, 2 October 2018

10 'Friends fear for safety of prominent Saudi writer Jamal Khashoggi', *Washington Post*, 2 October 2018

11 'Saudis are said to have lain in wait for Jamal Khashoggi', *Washington Post*, 9 October 2018

10 AFTERMATH

1 'The silencing of Jamal Khosshogi', *Washington Post*, 3 October 2018

2 'What happened to Jamal Khashoggi? Conflicting reports deepen a mystery', *New York Times*, 3 October 2018

3 Ibid.

4 'Saudi crown prince discusses Trump, Aramco, arrests: transcript', *Bloomberg*, 5 October 2018

5 '5-year jail, 3 million fine for rumormongers', *Saudi Gazette*, 13 October 2018

6 'Saudi Arabia opens up consulate after journalist vanishes', Reuters, 6 October 2018

7 'Please, President Trump, shed light on my fiancé's disappearance', *Washington Post*, 9 October 2018

8 'CIA concludes Saudi crown prince ordered Jamal Khashoggi's assassination', op. cit.

9 'Turkish officials say Khashoggi was killed on order of Saudi leadership', *New York Times*, 9 October 2018

11 INVESTIGATION

1 'How the man behind Kashoggi's murder ran the killing via Skype', Reuters, 22 October 2018

2 'Audio offers gruesome details of Jamal Khashoggi killing, Turkish official says', *New York Times*, 17 October 2018

3   '"I can't breathe." Jamal Khashoggi's last words disclosed in transcript, source says', CNN, 10 December 2018

4   'One killing, two accounts: what we know about Jamal Khashoggi's death', *New York Times*, 20 October 2018

5   'Khashoggi murder one step closer to resolution with striking new findings', op. cit.

6   Al Arabiya tweet, 11 October 2018

7   'Surveillance footage shows Saudi "body double" in Khashoggi's clothes after he was killed, Turkish source says', CNN, 23 October 2018

8   'What we know about the 15 Saudis said to have played a role in Jamal Khashoggi's disappearance', *Washington Post*, 19 October 2018

9   'Turkish officials accuse Saudi Arabia of lack of co-operation in Khashoggi probe', *Washington Post*, 10 October 2018

10 'Trump says it appears that missing journalist Khashoggi is dead', *Washington Post*, 18 October 2018

11 'A Saudi agent discussed hiding Khashoggi's remains before his death, prosecutors say', *Washington Post*, 26 November 2018

12 'Trump vows "severe punishment" if US determines Saudi Arabia killed Khashoggi', *Washington Post*, 13 October 2018

13 'Turkish officials accuse Saudi Arabia of lack of co-operation in Khashoggi probe', op. cit.

14 'Turkish investigators search Saudi consulate where journalist was last seen', *Washington Post*, 15 October 2018

15 Ibid.

16 'Turkish TV shows purported transfer of Khashoggi remains', Reuters, 31 December 2018

17 'Saudi king stands by crown prince as outrage over Khashoggi killing spreads', *New York Times*, 19 November 2018

18 'Recep Tayyip Erdoğan: Saudi Arabia still has many questions to answer about Jamal Khashoggi's killing', *Washington Post*, 2 November 2018

19 'Khashoggi's last words were "I can't breathe"', CNN, 10 December 2018

20 'Prince Salman backed into tight corner as links to Khashoggi murder become clearer', *Yeni Safak*, 22 October 2018

21 'Saudi-commissioned report contests US finding about Khashoggi's killing', *Wall Street Journal*, 7 February 2019

22 Ibid.

23 Ibid.

24 'Bolton says tape doesn't link Saudi prince to critic's death', Associated Press, 13 November 2018

25 'Year before killing, Saudi prince told aide he would use a "bullet" on Jamal Khashoggi', *New York Times*, 7 February 2019

26 'CIA intercepts underpin assessment Saudi crown prince targeted Khashoggi', *Wall Street Journal*, 1 December 2018

27 'Despite stigma of Khashoggi killing, crown prince is seen as retaining power', *New York Times*, 1 November 2018

28 'CIA intercepts underpin assessment Saudi crown prince targeted Khashoggi', op. cit.

29 'How the mysteries of Khashoggi's murder have rocked the US–Saudi partnership', op. cit.

30 'Jamal Khashoggi: Saudi murder suspect had spy training', BBC, 19 October 2018

31 'Suspects in disappearance of Khashoggi linked to Saudi security services', *Washington Post*, 16 October 2018

32 'It wasn't just Khashoggi: a Saudi prince's brutal drive to crush dissent', *New York Times*, 17 March 2019

33 'Khashoggi's fiancée criticises Trump's response to killing of Saudi journalist', *Washington Post*, 15 May 2019

12   TRUMP AND THE HOUSE OF SAUD

1 'US raises pressure on Saudi Arabia over missing journalist', Reuters, 10 October 2018

2 CBS, *60 Minutes*, 15 October 2018

3 'Saudi Arabia is the top US weapons buyer – but it doesn't spend as much as Trump boasts', CNBC, 15 October 2018

4 'Trump's claim of jobs from Saudi deals grows by leaps and bounds', *Washington Post*, 22 October 2018

5 'Bomb that killed 40 children in Yemen was supplied by the US', CNN, 17 August 2018

6 'Fox News fact-checks Donald Trump on Saudi Arabia business deals', *Newsweek*, 16 October 2018

7 'Jamal Khashoggi's fate casts a harsh light on Trump's friendship with Saudi Arabia', *Washington Post*, 10 October 2018

8 '"I like them very much": Trump has long-standing business ties with Saudis, who have boosted his hotels since he took office', op. cit.

9 'Amid global outrage over Khashoggi, Trump takes soft stance toward Saudis', *Washington Post*, 17 October 2018

10 'Trump vows "severe punishment" if US determines Saudi Arabia killed Khashoggi', op. cit.

11 'Trump criticises rush to condemn Saudi Arabia over Khashoggi', Associated Press, 17 October 2018

12 'Jamal Khashoggi: what the Arab world needs most is free expression', *Washington Post*, 17 October 2018

13 'In shift on Khashoggi killing, Trump edges closer to acknowledging a Saudi role', *New York Times*, 18 October 2018

14 'In *Post* interview, Trump calls Saudi Crown Prince Mohammed a "strong person" who "truly loves his country"', *Washington Post*, 20 October 2018

15 'Trump says it appears that missing journalist Khashoggi is dead', op. cit.

16 'Air strikes take toll on civilians in Yemen war', *New York Times*, 12 September 2015

17 'Saudi Arabia says Jamal Khashoggi was killed in consulate fight', *New York Times*, 19 October 2018

18 'Turkey's Erdoğan says Khashoggi recordings "appalling", shocked Saudi intelligence', Reuters, 13 November 2018

19 'Saudi Arabia fires 5 top officers, arrests 18 Saudis, saying Khashoggi was killed in fight at consulate', *Washington Post*, 19 October 2018

20 'Turkey's president vows to detail Khashoggi death "in full nakedness"', *New York Times*, 21 October 2018

21 'Saudi Arabia modifies intelligence service following Khashoggi's murder', Reuters, 20 December 2018

22 'Saudi electric army floods Twitter with insults and mistruths after Khashoggi's disappearance', *Washington Post*, 19 October 2018

23 'Saudi attempts to distance crown prince from Khashoggi killing haven't quieted uproar', *Washington Post*, 21 October 2018

24 'Amid scepticism, Saudi official provides another version of Khashoggi death', Reuters, 21 October 2018

25 'Khashoggi murder one step closer to resolution with dramatic findings', op. cit.

13 ERDOĞAN AND THE HOUSE OF SAUD

1 'Jamal Khashoggi body double created false trail in Turkey, surveillance images suggest', *New York Times*, 22 October 2018

2 'Uproar over dissident rattles Saudi royal family', op. cit.

3 *Osman's Dream: The Story of the Ottoman Empire 1300–1923*, Caroline Finkel, John Murray, 2006

4 'Egypt's Islamists warn Turkish PM over regional role', Reuters, 14 September 2011

5 'Saudi prince says Turkey part of "triangle of evil" – Egyptian media', Reuters, 7 March 2018

6 'The Gulf divided: the impact of the Qatar crisis', Jane Kinninmont, Chatham House, May 2019

7 'Saudi Arabia is misusing Mecca', *New York Times*, 12 November 2018

8 'Khashoggi fiancée criticises Trump's response to killing of Saudi journalist', op. cit.

14   THE LONELY TURK

1   'Erdoğan says order to kill Khashoggi came from highest levels of Saudi government', *Washington Post*, 2 November 2018

2   'Turkey acted responsibly with Skripal poisoning stance – Russia', Ahval News, 29 March 2018

3   'When it comes to defending the press, President Erdoğan is the world's biggest hypocrite', *Washington Post*, 13 December 2018

4   'Black sites: Turkey', https://correctiv.org, 11 December 2018

15   DAVOS IN THE DESERT

1   'Despite Khashoggi case, US firms and Saudi prince show up at "Davos in the Desert"', *Washington Post*, 23 October 2018

2   'Saudi crown prince calls Khashoggi's slaying a "heinous crime", vows perpetrators will be brought to justice', *Washington Post*, 25 October 2018

3   'The buck stops with Mohammed bin Salman', *The Week*, 29 October 2018

4   'Saudi crown prince calls Khashoggi's slaying a "heinous crime", vows perpetrators will be brought to justice', *Washington Post*, 24 October 2018

5   'Khashoggi killing overshadows Saudis' grand economic ambitions', *New York Times*, 25 October 2018

6   'The Saudi royal family circles its wagons in the Khashoggi crisis', *Washington Post*, 24 October 2018

7   'Senior Saudi prince returns to kingdom as royals confront Khashoggi crisis', *New York Times*, 30 October 2018

8   'Mnuchin meets with Saudi Crown Prince Mohammed bin Salman despite outcry over journalist's death', *Washington Post*, 22 October 2018

9   *Riyadh Daily*, 25 October 2018

10 'Bolton says tape doesn't link Saudi prince to critic's death', op. cit.

11 'Turkish prosecutor says Saudis strangled Khashoggi', *New York Times*, 31 October 2018

12 'Khashoggi sons issue emotional appeal for the return of their father's body', CNN, 5 November 2018

13 'Saudi Arabia tells UN it will prosecute Khashoggi killers', Reuters, 5 November 2018

14 'Erdoğan presses for answers from Saudi prince in Khashoggi killing', *New York Times*, 13 November 2018

16   THE SAUDIS VS THE CIA

1   'Saudi Arabia's public prosecution briefing on the Jamal Khashoggi murder investigation', *Arab News*, 15 November 2018

2   'US, Saudi steps in Khashoggi case don't go far enough, lawmakers say', *Washington Post*, 15 November 2018

3   'Intercepts solidify CIA assessment that Saudi prince ordered Khashoggi killing', *New York Times*, 2 December 2018

4   'Why bring a bone saw to a kidnapping, Your Highness?', *Washington Post*, 18 November 2018

5   'Khashoggi family receives condolences after Riyadh proffers murder culprits', Reuters, 16 November 2018

6   'Funeral prayers for Jamal Khashoggi ring out in absentia', *The Guardian*, 16 November 2018

7   'Hatice Cengiz: the international community must bring my fiancé's killers to justice', *Washington Post*, 2 November 2018

8   'Trump says "I don't want to hear the tape" of purported Khashoggi killing', Fox News, 18 November 2018

9   US Treasury website, 15 November 2018, https://home.treasury.gov/news/press-releases/sm547

10   US Treasury press release, 15 November 2018

11   'How the mysteries of Khashoggi's murder have rocked the US–Saudi partnership', op. cit.

12   'US, Saudi steps in Khashoggi case don't go far enough, lawmakers say', op. cit.

13   'CIA intercepts underpin assessment Saudi crown prince targeted Khashoggi', op. cit.

14   'US seeks accountability for former Saudi aide in Khashoggi killing', op. cit.

15   'CIA concludes Saudi crown prince ordered Jamal Khashoggi's assassination', op. cit.

16   'Trump speaks with CIA about Khashoggi killing, says there will be a report by Tuesday', *Washington Post*, 17 November 2018

17   'Trump says "I don't want to hear the tape" of purported Khashoggi killing', op. cit.

17   'MAYBE HE DID, MAYBE HE DIDN'T!'

1   'Washington Post Publisher and CEO Fred Ryan statement on Jamal Khashoggi', *Washington Post*, 20 November 2018

2   'MbS has a toxic record of recklessness. The Trump administration doesn't need him', *Washington Post*, 19 November 2018

3   'Trump says he won't listen to Khashoggi suffering tape', *Washington Post*, 18 November 2018

4   'Senate votes to condemn Saudi crown prince for Khashoggi killing, end support for Yemen war', *Washington Post*, 13 December 2018

5   'Gap continues to widen between Trump and intelligence community on key issues', *Washington Post*, 11 December 2018

6   'Trump accuses US spy agencies of Nazi practices over "phony" Russia dossier', Reuters, 11 January 2017

7   'Senators, furious over Khashoggi's killing, spurn President on war in Yemen', *New York Times*, 28 November 2018

18   THE CROWN PRINCE COMEBACK TOUR

1   'Alone in the Arab world, Tunisians can protest visit by Saudi crown prince', *Washington Post*, 27 November 2018

2   '"We don't want him here": Saudi crown prince is protected pariah at G-20 summit', *Washington Post*, 1 December 2018

3   'Gina Haspel relies on spy skills to connect with Trump. He doesn't always listen', *New York Times*, 16 April 2019

19   ONE TRAGEDY EXPOSES ANOTHER

1   'Saudi Arabia has devastated Yemen – but a lesson from 1965 can help fix the mess', *Washington Post*, 22 November 2017

2   'US lawmakers expect votes on steps to crack down on Saudi Arabia', Reuters, 13 November 2018

3   'Senate lets Bahrain weapon sale proceed; Yemen unease grows', Associated Press, 15 November 2018

4   'Hunt sees prospect for Yemen talks, news on Khashoggi inquiry', Reuters, 12 November 2018

5   'Mattis says US must balance rights concerns with "strategic" Saudi ties', *Washington Post*, 21 November 2018

6   'Rebuking Trump, senators back effort to suspend US support for Saudi-led war in Yemen', *Washington Post*, 28 November 2018

7   'Saudi warplanes, most made in America, still bomb civilians in Yemen', *New York Times*, 22 May 2019

8   'Saudi Arabia's heir to the throne talks to *60 Minutes*', op. cit.

9   'With vote to end US involvement in Yemen's war, House sets up Trump's second veto', *Washington Post*, 4 April 2019

10 'Saudi Arabia's crown prince must restore dignity to his country – by ending Yemen's cruel war', *Washington Post*, 11 September 2018

11 'Yemen: ceasefire broken as fresh fighting breaks out in Hodeidah', *The Guardian*, 15 May 2019

12 'Yemen war dead could hit 233,000 by 2020 in what UN calls humanity's greatest preventable disaster', *Independent*, 30 April 2019

13 'German halt in Saudi arms sales hurting UK industry – Hunt', Reuters, 19 February 2019

14 'UK negotiates loophole in Saudi export ban to sell planes for use in Yemen', *The Guardian*, 23 May 2019

15 'How the murder of Jamal Khashoggi made the income of Boeing's competitor Airbus plummet', *Washington Post*, 30 April 2019

16 'Trump officials prepare to bypass Congress to sell weapons to Gulf nations', *New York Times*, 23 May 2019

17 'Donald Trump bypasses Congress on Saudi, UAE arms sales', *Financial Times*, 24 May 2019

18 'Senate votes to block Trump's arms sales to Gulf nations in bipartisan rebuke', *New York Times*, 20 June 2019

20 THE FAUSTIAN BARGAIN

1 NBC 'Meet the Press', 23 June 2019

2 'How the US could prosecute Jamal Khashoggi's killers', *Washington Post*, 31 March 2019

3 'Federal court presses Trump administration to release Khashoggi documents', *Washington Post*, 21 May 2019

4 'Kushner says he has urged Saudi prince to be transparent about killing', Reuters, 23 April 2019

5 'Khashoggi murder one step closer to resolution with striking new findings', op. cit.

6 'Royal adviser fired over Khashoggi murder absent from Saudi trial – sources', Reuters, 24 March 2019

7 Jubeir interview, RUSI.org website, 20 June 2019

8 'Saudi aide fired over Khashoggi murder still wields influence: sources', Reuters, 15 January 2019

9 'US seeks accountability for former Saudi aide in Khashoggi killing', op. cit.

10 'How the mysteries of Khashoggi's murder have rocked the US–Saudi partnership', op. cit.

11 https://www.state.gov/public-designation-of-sixteen-saudi-individuals-under-section-7031c

12 'Wall Street returns to Saudi Arabia as biggest deals entice CEOs', Bloomberg, 23 April 2019

13 'In Khashoggi murder trial, absence of Crown Prince Mohammed's aide stands out', *Wall Street Journal*, 22 June 2019

14 'Trump vetoes measure to force end to US involvement in Yemen war', *New York Times*, 16 April 2019

15 'Israeli newspaper reveals leaked document of Trump's "deal of the century"', *Middle East Eye*, 7 May 2019

16 'On Muslim Brotherhood, Trump weighs siding with autocrats and roiling Middle East', *New York Times*, 6 May 2019

17 'More journalists killed on the job as reprisal murders nearly double', Committee to Protect Journalists, 19 December 2018

18 'Pompeo challenges accuracy of reports that CIA is confident of Saudi crown prince's involvement in Khashoggi death', *Washington Post*, 12 December 2018

19 'Erdoğan slams US silence over Khashoggi, demands Saudi answers', Al Jazeera, 4 February 2019

20 'In *Post* interview, Trump calls Saudi Crown Prince Mohammed a "strong person" who "truly loves his country"', op. cit.

21 'A Middle Eastern studies professor on his conversations with Mohammed bin Salman', *New Yorker*, 8 April 2019

22 'UK Foreign Secretary says Saudi Arabia has paid the price for Khashoggi killing', *Time*, 11 July 2019

23 *Kings and Presidents: Saudi Arabia and the United States since FDR*, op. cit.

24 'A Middle Eastern studies professor on his conversations with Mohammed bin Salman', op. cit.

25 'Rumours grow of rift between Saudi king and crown prince', *The Guardian*, 5 March 2019

26 '*Guardian* told it was target of Saudi hacking unit after Khashoggi killing', *The Guardian*, 19 June 2019

27 'Saudi Arabia revives efforts to draw dissidents home', *Financial Times*, 15 July 2019

28 'Arab activist in Norway details his Saudi work before threat', Associated Press, 13 May 2019

29 'Saudis hacked Amazon chief Jeff Bezos's phone, says company's security adviser', *The Guardian*, 31 March 2019

30 'Saudi crown prince wildly popular among Arab youth, survey shows', *Arabian Business*, 8 May 2018

31 'Saudi Arabia executes 37 citizens over alleged terrorism offences', Associated Press, 23 April 2019

21 THE STORY HE DID NOT COMPLETE

1 'Jamal Khashoggi was my fiancé. His killers are roaming free', *New York Times*, 19 June 2019
2 'Khashoggi children have received houses in Saudi Arabia and monthly payments as compensation for killing of father', *Washington Post*, 1 April 2019
3 Ibid.
4 'Khashoggi ex-wife: I do not know Khadijah, why is she handling his social media?', *Al Arabiya English*, 14 October 2018
5 *BBC Newsnight* interview, 30 October 2018
6 '"I am asking for justice": Khashoggi's fiancée urges Congress to put more pressure on Saudi Arabia in the wake of journalist's killing', *Washington Post*, 16 May 2019

BIBLIOGRAPHY

Al-Rasheed, Madawi (ed.), *Salman's Legacy: The Dilemmas of a New Era in Saudi Arabia* (Hurst & Co., 2018)

Bergen, Peter L., *The Osama bin Laden I Know: An Oral History of al Qaeda's Leader* (Free Press, 2006)

Cagaptay, Soner, *The New Sultan: Erdoğan and the Crisis of Modern Turkey* (I. B. Tauris, 2017)

Finkel, Caroline, *Osman's Dream: The Story of the Ottoman Empire 1300–1923* (John Murray, 2005)

Kandil, Hazem, *Inside the Brotherhood* (Polity Press, 2015)

Lacey, Robert, *Inside the Kingdom: Kings, Clerics, Modernists, Terrorists and the Struggle for Saudi Arabia* (Hutchinson, 2009)

Onus, Sinan; Ersoy, Mehmet Akif; Cengiz, Hatice, *Jamal Khashoggi: His Life, Struggles and Secrets'* (Kopernik, 2019)

Riedel, Bruce, *Kings and Presidents: Saudi Arabia and the United States since FDR* (Brookings Institution Press, 2018)

Unlu, Ferhat; Simsek, Abdurrahman; Karaman, Nazif, *Diplomatik Vahset: Cemal Kasikci, Cinayetinin Karanlik Sirlali* (Turkuvaz Kitap, 2018)

Wright, Lawrence, *The Looming Tower: Al Qaeda's road to 9/11* (Allen Lane, 2006)

INDEX

Key: HC= Hatice Cengiz; JK = Jamal Khashoggi; MbS = Mohammed bin
Salman; SA = Saudi Arabia; *WP = Washington Post*

A Haber, 177
Abahussain, Mansour Othman, 172–3
Abdul Aziz, Prince Abdulaziz bin Saud
  bin Nayef bin, 32, 174
Abdulaziz , Prince (interior minister),
  32, 174
Abdulaziz , Prince (MbS's brother-in-
  law) 306
Abdulaziz, Omar, 100–2, 298, 306, 307
Abdulaziz, Prince Ahmed bin, 49,
  238–9
Abdulaziz, Prince Mohammed bin
  Nawwaf bin, 2
Abdullah, Daud, 123, 127
Abdullah, King, 35, 52, 61, 303
  assassination attempt of, 64
  death of, 44, 48
Abdullah, Prince Miteb bin, 88–9
Abraham, 15, 19
Abraham Lincoln, USS, 285, 286
Abu Dhabi, 57, 62, 266, 292, 294
Abu Dis, 124
Abu Salah, *see* Khashoggi, Jamal bin
  Ahmad
Adams Center, 85

Afghanistan, 231, 281
  bin Laden in, 28, 32
  Soviet invasion of (1979), 24, 25,
    26–8
  US-led invasion of (2001), 26
agnatic seniority, 49
Ahmed, Prince, 49, 238–9
Ahmet (police guard), 106–7
Aiban, Bandar al-, 244–5
Airbus, 282
AK Parti (Justice and Development
  Party), 141
Akar, Hulusi, 175, 178
Aktay, Yasin, 117, 141–4, 185, 222–3,
  250, 260, 299
al-Aiban, Bandar, 244–5
Al-Arab, 36–7
Al Arabiya, 97, 158, 169, 182, 312
al-Arifi, Naif Hassan, 186, 289
al-Asiri, Gen. Ahmed, 121, 205–7,
  213, 246, 248, 251–2, 290
Assad, Bashar al-, 59, 219
Al-Baqi cemetery, 244
al-Faisal, Prince Turki, 27, 32, 33, 34,
  49, 72–3, 77, 89, 215, 238

al-Harbi, Lt Thaar Ghaleb, 12, 186, 289
al-Hathloul, Alia, 96
al-Hathloul, Lina, 96
al-Hathloul, Loujain, 94–6
Al Hayat, 26, 29, 37, 60, 79
Al-Hiwar, 128–30
al-Jabhah al-Islāmiyah lil-Inqādh (Islamic Salvation Front), 30
Al Jazeera, 34, 62, 65–7, 124, 129, 145, 225
al-Jubeir, Adel, 212, 240, 246, 249, 277, 291
al-Junabi, Ahmad Abdulaziz, 173
al-Khereiji, 143–4
Al Medina, 220
al-Mujeb, Saud, 214, 240, 241–2, 246
al-Nasr, Prince Saud bin Saif, 45–6
al-Nimr, Sheikh Nimr Baqir, 44, 45
Otaibi, Maj. Badr Lafi al-, 290
al-Otaibi, Mohammad, 120–2, 138, 148–9, 152–3, 165, 179, 198, 247, 251, 289, 293
al-Qaeda, 26, 28, 29, 31–2, 44, 50, 64, 107, 277, 295
al-Qahtani, Maj.-Gen. Ali, 89
al-Qahtani, Saif Saad, 139–40, 147, 170
al-Qahtani, Saud, *see* Qahtani, Saud al-
al-Qani, Abumayan ('Saad'), *see* Saad
al-Qaradawi, Sheikh Yusuf, 64
al-Rasheed, Prof. Madawi, 33, 78, 303, 319
al-Salam Palace, 12
al-Saud, Prince Abdulaziz bin Mashhur, 306
al-Saud, Abdullah bin Abdulaziz, *see* Abdullah, King
al-Saud, Bader bin Abdullah bin Mohammed bin Farhan, 57
al-Saud, King Faisal bin Abdulaziz, 61, 65, 303–4
al-Saud, Prince Khalid bin Salman bin Abdulaziz (MbS's brother), 82, 150, 156–7, 253–4, 288, 292, 304, 311
al-Saud, Crown Prince Mohammed bin Salman ('MbS'), *see* MbS
al-Saud, Murqin bin Abdulaziz, 49, 303
al-Saud, Salman bin Abdulaziz, *see* Salman, King
Al Sharq Forum, 106
Al-Sharq TV, 223
al-Tubaigy, Lt-Col Dr Salah Mohammed, *see* Tubaigy, Lt-Col Dr Salah Mohammed al-
al-Tunisi, Rawiya (wife), *see* Tunisi, Rawiya al-
Al Udeid air base, 63, 285
Al Watan, 32, 34, 35, 61, 94
al-Yamamah ('dove of peace') arms deal, 275–6
al-Zamil, Essam, 75, 77, 93–4, 126, 128
al-Zahrani, Khaled Yahya, 173
al-Zahrani, Muhammad Saad, 186
AlAhli Bank *see* National Commercial Bank
Alawwad, Awwad, 72
Aldakhil, Turki, 182–3
Aleppo bombardment, 220
Algeria, 28, 68, 127, 129
civil war in, 30
Algumizi, Abdulaziz Soliman, 172
Ali, Zine al-Abidine Ben, 266
Allegiance Council, 302–3
Altun, Fahrettin, 168
Alwaleed, Prince, 21, 36, 49, 88–9, 194, 222, 238
Alzheimer's disease, 49, 200
Amanpour, Christiane, 75–6
Ambler, Eric, 161
AMC, 41, 293
America First!, 258, 259, 260

Amnesty International (AI), 95, 231–2
Ankara, 2, 4, 66, 116, 141–3, 146–7,
    150, 154, 160, 167, 168, 180, 202,
    215, 218, 220–1, 230, 270
Anatolia News Agency (Turkey), 224
Apple, 40, 135, 214
The Apprentice, 240
Arab News, 25
Arab Peace Initiative, 218
Arab revolt (1916 and 1919), 217
Against the Arab Spring, 98
Arab Spring (2011), 4, 23, 35, 38, 43–4,
    48, 60, 64–7, 85, 98–9, 107, 127,
    142, 183, 203, 219–24, 231, 266
Aramco, 49, 55–6, 75, 89, 235, 293–4
Arasta bazaar, 141
Argentina, 265, 267
Arifi, Naif Hassan al-, 186, 289
Arms Export Control Act (1976) (US),
    283
arms trade, 190–3, 197, 229, 240,
    274–7, 281–3, 286, 294–6
Army of Conquest, 219–20
Arzu (HC's best friend), 140
Asharq Al Awsat, 288
Asiri, Gen. Ahmed al-, 121, 205–7,
    213, 246, 248, 251–2, 290
Assad, Bashar al-, 59, 219
Assiri, Yahia, 78–9
Associated Press (AP), 95, 199
Atatürk airport 7, 219, 221
Atatürk, 7, 140, 165
Atr, Hanan el- (wife), 111–14, 150,
    212, 312
Attiah, Karen, 76, 79–81, 145, 204,
    236
audio recordings, 3, 153, 172, 179, 196,
    202, 208–9, 213–14, 227, 241,
    243, 248, 255, 299
  CIA assessment of, 137
  transcripts, i, 13–14, 117–21, 131–2,
    134–7, 172–3

Australia, 13
Awad, Nihad, 29–30, 66, 84, 104–5,
    184
Awdah, Salman al-, 128
Azerbaijan, 232
Azzam, Abdullah, 24

Badawi, Raif, 99
Badawi, Samar, 99
Bader, Prince, 57
BAE Systems, 275
Baghdadi, Abu Bakr al- 65
Baghdadi, Iyad el-, 306
Bahrain, 45, 63, 88, 211, 225
  anti-government protests in, 36–7
Balawi, Farhad al-, 290
Bandar, Prince (ambassador) ('Bandar
    Bush'), 33, 34
Bandar, Prince (newspaper owner),
    32
Bandar, Prince Turki bin (reformist),
    45
BBC, i, 125, 126, 186
Becker, Gavin de, 306
Bel Air 40
Belgrad Forest, 172
Bergen, Peter, 22
Bezos, Jeff, 306
bin Abdulaziz, Prince Ahmed, 49,
    238–9
bin Abdulaziz, Prince Mohammed bin
    Nawwaf, 2
bin Abdullah, Prince Miteb, 88–9
bin Bandar, Prince Turki, 45
bin Laden, Osama, 4, 22–9, 31–2, 65,
    88
  JK interviews, 25
  US finances, 28
  as US's 'most wanted' 28
bin Nayef, Crown Prince Mohammed,
    49, 50–51, 60, 63, 87, 303
bin Saud, Emir Abdullah, 217

bin Talal, Prince Alwaleed, 21, 36, 49, 88–9, 194, 222, 238
bin Turki, Sultan, 45
bin Zayed, Crown Prince Mohammed ('MbZ'), see MbZ
Black Panther, 54
#TheBlacklist, 70
BlackRock, 293
Blair, Tony, 276
'blood money' payments, 311
Bloomberg News, 126, 151, 209
Blue Mosque, 139, 141, 170, 214
BND, 42
body double, 139, 141, 147, 170, 214, 287, 290
Bolton, John, 167, 183, 195
   audio tape dismissed by, 182
Bostani, Mishal Saad al-, 186, 289
Bouazizi, Mohamed, 35
Branson, Sir Richard, 235
Broadcasting House, 125
Brotherhood see Muslim Brotherhood
Brunei, 21
Brunson, Pastor Andrew, 216, 233
Bundesnachrichtendienst (BND) 42
Burma (Myanmar), 222, 296
Bush, Bandar (Prince Bandar bin Sultan), 33, 34
Bush, George W., 33
Butairi, Fahad al-, 95

Cairo, 36, 45, 107, 144, 170, 211, 219, 266
Çalışkan, Mustafa, 170, 178
Call of Duty, 46–7
Callamard, Agnes, 104, 163–4, 286, 287, 290–1, 301, 305–6, 317
caller ID phone app, 170
Camp David, 12
Campaign Against Arms Trade, 281
camera footage, see CCTV footage
Canada, 99–101, 229, 298, 306–7

Capital Gazette, 296
CBS, 91, 191, 197, 278
CCTV footage, 116, 118, 139, 141, 152–3, 155, 158, 169–70, 172, 176–9, 187, 189, 242
Cengiz, Hatice (fiancée), 3, 5, 7–8, 9–10, 16, 20,
   background of, 106–7
   consulate vigil of, i, 147
   frantic phone calls made by, 141
   as guardian of JK's memory 107
   JK first meets, 106–8, 110
   JK first meets father of, 108–10
   JK's last few hours with, 9–11, 15, 118
   Missing Person report filed by, 178
   moves to London following JK's death, 314
   pleas made to Trump by, 188–9
   police guard attached to, 106–7
   proposed marriage of, 3, 5, 8, 107, 108, 110, 112, 131, 132, 141, 147, 148, 151
   Trump criticised by, 189, 250, 314, 315
   Trump invites to White House by, 189
   waits outside consulate, 16–17
   WP interviews with, 148, 188–9, 309
Cengiz, Mr (father-in-law-to-be), 10, 108–9, 115
Cengiz, Zeynep (sister-in-law-to-be), 140, 148, 314
Center on International Cooperation, 27
Central Intelligence Agency (CIA), see CIA
Centre for Communication and Knowledge Foresight, 292
Centre for Studies and Information Affairs, 69

Centre for Studies and Media Affairs, 293

Centre for Studies and Media Affairs (CSMARC), 118, 184, 292

Channel 4, 2

Channel 4 News, 1, 318, 319

chemical attacks, 256

'chemo' against corruption, 87

China, 190–3, 258, 279, 290, 300
   pro-reform demonstrations in, 29

Christie's, 57

CIA, 8, 26, 43, 50, 72, 137, 152, 157, 166–7, 181–5, 196, 201–9 *passim*, 214, 246–57, 259–60, 263–4, 288, 295, 298–302, 305

Citizen Lab, 100

Clinton, Hillary, 59

Clooney, Amal, 301

closed-circuit camera footage, *see* CCTV footage

CN Tower, 100

CNBC, 235

CNN, 75, 170, 236, 239, 243

Cold War, 161

Committee for the Promotion of Virtue and the Prevention of Vice, 54

Committee to Protect Journalists (CPJ) 297

Constantinople, Ottoman conquest of, 15

Cook, Steven, 209

Cook, Tim, 40

Corker, Bob, 196, 261, 264–5, 274

corruption, 20, 86, 91–2, 203, 307

Council on American–Islamic Relations, 104

CPJ (Committee to Protect Journalists) 297

Crown Prince's office, 170

CSMARC, 118, 184, 292

Cumhuriyet, 232

Custodian of the Two Holy Places (Khadim al-Haramayn al-Sharifayn), 218, 221, 230

cyber-attacks, 224

'cyber bees', 102

cyber crime 152, 224

cybersecurity directorate, 305

Cyprus, 37, 271

da Vinci, Leonardo, 57, 291, 310

Daily Sabah, 164–5, 169, 318

Daily Star, 31

Damascus, 219

Dar al-Hijrah Islamic Centre, 85

Davos in the Desert, 205, 234–45, 293

DAWN, 104, 105, 130

death penalty, 128, 248, 289, 311

Decisive Storm, 47

'Defending Muslim Lands' declaration, 24

democracy, Trump's zero interest in, 98

Democracy for the Arab World Now (DAWN), 104, 105, 130

'desert wisdom', 48

diplomatic immunity, 149, 176, 178

diplomatic passports, 147, 178

Diriyyah, 217

Djebbar, Saad, 46–7, 68–9, 72, 75, 90, 127–8

Doha, 37
   Riyadh's relationship with, 64–5, 66

Dosari, Ghanem al-, 306–7

double agents, 171, 228, 270

Douglas, Michael, 40

'dove of peace' (al-Yamamah) arms deal, 275–6

Downing Street, 11, 240

Dundar, Can, 232

The Economist, 52

editorial independence, 37
E5, 9, 115
Egypt:
  intelligence, 224
  Mamluk rule in, 217
  Muslim Brotherhood deposed in,
    35, 191
  parliament-in-exile, 220
  Saudi $5-billion aid package to, 36
  2011 revolution in, 218–19
  2013 coup in, 220
Eid al-Fitr Ramadan, 19, 187
Eight Investment Company, 56–7
el-Atr, Hanan (wife), 111–14, 150,
  212, 312
el-Baghdadi, Iyad, 306
Elliott, Laurie, 23
embassy bombings, 28
Engel, Eliot, 280
Engelmayer, Paul, 288
Entertainment Authority (Saudi
  Arabia), 54
Erdoğan, Recep Tayyip, 3, 30, 37, 117,
  128, 141, 144, 149, 153
  accusations levelled against, 160
  audio tape obtained and released by,
    165, 180
  authoritarian rule exercised by, 162
  electronic eavesdropping obsession
    of, 161
  and House of Saud, 215–27
  King Salman's relationship with,
    218, 220
  MbS's relationship with, 220–2, 226
  Muslim humanitarian causes
    championed by, 221–2
  neo-Ottomanism alleged of, 218
  newspaper articles penned by, 179,
    227, 230
  press conferences held by, 155, 158
  religious piety of, 222
  Trump's G20 meeting with, 271

  US visit of, 232–3
  WP piece by, 227, 230
Eurofighter Typhoon, 275–6, 282
Europe Apartments, 9, 115
European Union (EU), 43, 129, 229
  Turkey bribed by, 231
exile(s):
  'Arab revolt', 217
  Egyptian parliament-in-, 220
  in Istanbul, 249–50, 223
  JK's self-imposed, 7, 68–86, 94, 98,
    105, 109, 114, 129, 157, 182
extrajudicial executions, 104, 163–4,
  189, 286, 317

Facebook, 12, 40, 152, 186, 223, 306
Faisal, King, 61, 65, 303–4
Faisal, Prince Bandar bin Khalid al-, 32
Faisal, Prince Khalid al-, 215, 216
Faisal, Prince (MbS's half-brother),
  46, 302
Faisal, Prince Turki al-, 27, 32, 33, 34,
  49, 72–3, 77, 89, 215, 238
fake evidence, 141, 170, 187
'fake news', 152, 158, 193, 297
'family photo' at G20, 300
Fatih mosque, 249
Fatih Sultan Mehmet University, 115
the Fatiha, 109
FBI, 285, 287
Federal Intelligence Service (BND)
  (Germany) 52
Feierstein, Gerald, 48, 55, 192
Fidan, Hakan, 144, 162–3, 167
Fidan, Irfan, 242–3
Financial Times (FT), 305
Fire and Fury (Wolff), 52
First World War, 217
Fleming, Ian, 161
Flint, John, 293
Four Seasons, 267
  MbS books all rooms in, 40

Fourth of July celebrations
  (Independence Day) (US), 102
Fox & Friends, 201
Fox News, 189, 190, 212, 238, 256
France, 56, 93, 229, 290, 291, 318
  joint statement issued by, 208
Freedom of Information Act (FOIA)
  (1966) (US), 288
freedom of the press, 204, 232, 291,
  297, 301
freedom of speech, 4, 60, 127
Freeland, Chrystia, 99
Freeman, Morgan, 40
Friedman, Thomas, 93, 94
Friends of Democracy in Algeria, 30,
  129
FT, 305

Gabon, 232
Gaddafi, Col Muammar Mohammed
  Abu Minyar, 64
Gandhi, Mahatma, 57
Gates, Bill, 40
Gaza Strip, 1, 65, 129, 218
General Intelligence Directorate
  (GID), 207
Germany, 43, 229, 232
  intelligence (BND), 42
  joint statement issued by, 208
  Nazi 231, 263
getaway planes (HZSK-1; HZSK-2), 8,
  140, 143
Glasgow University, 13
Global Center for Combating
  Extremism, 191
Global Magnitsky Act (2016) (US),
  189
Global Opinions (*WP*), 7, 39–40, 76
Golden Horn, 15
Graham, Lindsey, 195, 201–2, 260,
  263–5, 276, 283
Grand Hyatt, 106

Grand Mosque, Mecca, 24
Griffiths, Martin, 274
G20 265–7, 269, 271, 300–1
Guardian, The, 304, 305
'guardians of the truth' journalists
  296
Gülen, Fethullah, 226, 233
Guterres, António, 228, 287

Haberturk, 189
Haci Baba, 220
Hamas, 33–4, 63, 65, 129
Haqqani, Jalaluddin, 26
Harbi, Lt Thaar Ghaleb al-, 12, 186,
  289
Hariri, Saad, 92–3, 145, 237
Haspel, Gina, 166, 255, 256, 263–4
Hathloul, Alia al-, 96
Hathloul, Lina al-, 96
Hathloul, Loujain al-, 94–6
Haykel, Prof. Bernard, 300, 304
Hezbollah, 48, 92
Hiatt, Fred, 145, 153–4, 318
Hitler, Adolf, 42
Holland, 231
Hollywood, 39, 40, 54
Hollywood Reporter, 40
Horn of Africa, 222
House Foreign Affairs (US), human-
  rights subcommittee, 315
House Intelligence Committee (US),
  209, 262
House of Saud, 52, 93, 138, 262, 304,
  306
  al-Dosari and, 306–7
  attempted overthrow of, 24
  and cultural freedom, 307
  dissent stifled by, 304
  Erdoğan and, 215–27
  factions within, 302
  Prince Faisal agrees to Kennedy's
    reforms of, 302

House of Saud – *continued*
  Khashoggi family's negotiations
    with, 311
  Trump's association with, 188–14
HSBC, 293
human rights, i, 5, 40, 43, 95, 104,
    152, 265, 267, 273, 278, 297 (*see*
    also human-rights organisations
    by name)
  and the Global Magnitsky Act, 189
  House Foreign Affairs
    subcommittee on, 315
  International Bar Association on,
    319
  in Middle East generally, 40, 104,
    265
  Obama briefly highlights, 192
  in Saudi Arabia, 99–100, 192,
    243–4, 251
  treaties, 211
  Trump's lack of support for, 98,
    190–1, 250, 299
  in Turkey, 231, 243
Human Rights Institute (HRI), 319
Human Rights Watch (HRW), 95,
    267, 273
Hunt, Jeremy, 275, 282, 301
Hurricane Harvey, 11
Hurriyet Daily News, 318
Hussa-al-Sudairi, 50
HZSK-1; HZSK-2, *see* getaway planes

Ibn Saud, 20, 41, 50, 138, 295, 303
Ignatius, David, 32, 35, 37, 69, 79, 99,
    160, 185, 299, 307, 318
Independence Day (July 4) (US), 102
Independent, 78
Indiana State University, 23
'information space', 70
Instagram, 306
Interpol, 134
intra-Arab disputes, 219

Iran, 46, 91, 149, 197–8, 262, 274–5,
    277, 283, 289, 294, 308
  escalating tensions with, 286–7
  Islamic Revolution of (1979), 24
  nuclear programme, 43, 278
  Obama's deal with, 43
  Revolutionary Guard, 294
  sham trials in, 146
  Trump's foreign-policy agenda
    towards 286
  Trump's loathing of 41, 42
Iraq, 1, 47–8, 64, 231
ISIS, 63, 65, 107, 154, 277, 295
Islamic elite, 129
Islamic Salvation Front, 30
Isler, Emrullah, 143
Israel, 34, 42–3, 53, 54, 101, 198, 210,
    255, 294
  intelligence (Mossad), 31
  MbS does business with, 101
  Turkish activists killed by 218
Istanbul, i, 1–4, 66, 96, 104–22
  Atatürk airport, 7, 219, 221
  caliphate governed from, 217
  espionage reputation of, 161
  Europe Apartments in, 9, 115
  JK in, 7–17, 21, 30, 40–1, 46, 52,
    63, 70, 79, 82, 90, 98, 101,
    102, 103, 123
  political crisis in, 66
  'safe house' story, 213
  Zeytinburnu district, 9
Istanbul University, 107
Izmir textile markets, 20

Jeddah, 12, 22, 24, 27, 29, 36, 57, 60,
    66, 72, 83, 96, 100, 101, 105, 111,
    237, 243, 249, 266, 289, 310
Jenkins, Sir John, 43–4, 319
jihad, 23–8, 262
@JKhashoggi, 84, 152
Jordan, 65, 95, 107, 172, 282

Jordan, Bob, 42, 49, 90, 293

journalistic independence 37–8, 67, 71–2, 80, 126, 310

Journalists' Syndicate, 266

JPMorgan, 293

Jubeir, Adel al-, 212, 240, 246, 249, 277, 291

Junabi, Ahmad Abdulaziz al-, 173

Justice and Development Party (AK Parti), 141

KAICIID, 61

Kaine, Tim, 252, 279, 281

Kalın, İbrahim, 149, 168

Kamel, Saleh, 89, 249

Kaplan, Hilâl, 222

Karman, Tawakkol, 158

Kasikci ('spoon maker'), 20

Kemerburgaz landfill site, 170

Kennedy, Baroness Helena, QC, 165, 179, 319

Kennedy, John F. (JFK), 302

Kereeiji, Walid bin Abdul Karim al-, 150

Kerry, John, 46

Khadim al-Haramayn al-Sharifayn (Custodian of the Two Holy Places), 218, 221, 230

Khalid, Prince (governor), 215, 216

Khalid, Prince (MbS's brother), 82, 150, 156–7, 253–4, 288, 292, 304, 311

Khamenei, Ayatollah, 42

Khan, Imran, 235, 300

Khanfar, Wadah, 62, 71, 73–4, 82, 124, 239

Khartoum, bin Laden moves to, 28, 29

Khashoggi, Abdullah (son), 33, 83, 110, 112–13, 124, 310

Khashoggi, Adnan (second cousin), 20–1

death of, 21

extradition threat to, 21

Khashoggi, Ahmed (father), 19, 20

Khashoggi, Emad (cousin), 56

Khashoggi, Esaaf (mother), 19

Khashoggi, Jamal bin Ahmad, 221, 280

'Abu Salah' sobriquet of, 19

al-Qaeda connections of, 26

Al Watan sacks, 31–2

at BBC, 125–6

bin Laden interviewed by, 25

body double of, see main entry

book proposal by, 75

Brotherhood membership of, 21–4, 27, 34, 38, 294

cat video of, 212

CIA concludes killing of, see main entry

depression suffered by, 61, 85, 111

education of, 21, 23–4

enters consulate, 17

in exile, 7, 68–86, 94, 98, 105, 109, 114, 129, 157, 182

father-in-law-to-be first met by, 108–10

53rd birthday of, 38

final social-media posting of, 60

green card of, 287

HC first meets, 106–8, 110

HC travels to consulate with, 15–17

HC's last few hours with, 9–11, 15–17, 118

HC's Missing Person report filed for, 178

as head of Al-Arab, 36

investigation into death of, 160–87

in Istanbul, see main entry

last birthday meal of, 19

last breakfast taken by, 10

London weekend of, 123–32

MbS criticised by, 47, 107–8, 126

MbS's potential motive for killing, 183

Khashoggi, Jamal bin Ahmad – *Continued*
  memorial event in honour of, 314
  mystery surrounding disposal of
      body of, 13, 138, 172–80, 187,
      207, 214, 287
  'O' visa obtained by, 75
  online trolling operation against,
      105
  Ottoman descent studies by, 15
  Palestinians supported by, 125–6
  patrons of, 18–21, 34, 72, 77, 238
  'pre-planned murder' of, 153
  precarious career of, 37–8
  proposed marriage of, 3, 5, 8, 107,
      108, 110, 112, 131, 132, 141,
      147, 148, 151
  Qahtani moves against, 51–2, 61, 66
  Reuters footage of, 152–3
  SA forced to admit death of, 206–
      14, 215
  as Saudi envoy sent to bin Laden,
      28–9
  'Saudi gets out of Medina' life, 23
  on Saudi payroll, 33
  Saudi rulers' silent witness to
      murder of, 137–8
  self-imposed exile of, *see* in exile
      subentry, above
  60th birthday of, 111
  sons praise, 244
  spying accusations levelled at, 95–6
  student years of, 23–4
  Time honours, 296–7
  timeline to consulate, 8, 14–17
  Trump criticised by, 59, 70, 93
  'Turkish model' argued by, 223
  TV station run by, 21, 88
  on Twitter (@JKhashoggi), 32, 60,
      72, 74, 83, 84, 95, 117, 128,
      183
  UN rapporteur's investigation into
      death of, 104, 163, 165, 179,

      287, 289, 290, 301, 305–6, 317
  US citizenship sought by, 75–6
  Wali al-Amr ruling against, 62
  wives of, *see also* by name
  as *WP* Global Opinions columnist,
      7, 39–40, 76
  WP 'online pulpit', 95
Khashoggi, Mohammed (first cousin),
      20
Khashoggi, Noha (daughter), 18, 33,
      68, 83, 310
Khashoggi, Razan (daughter), 18, 33,
      68, 83, 310
Khashoggi, Salah (son), 33, 83, 105,
      128, 210, 236, 243–4, 249,
      310–11, 312
Khosrowshahi, Dara, 235
King Abdullah bin Abdulaziz
      International Centre for
      Interreligious and Intercultural
      Dialogue (KAICIID), 61
King Saud University, 46
Kislakci, Turan, 21, 23, 27, 31, 37, 46,
      108–10, 115, 143, 154, 158
Koran, 15, 109
Korea, 195, 279
Kosovo, 232
Kremlin, 160, 228
Kurds, 220, 232–3, 270–1
Kushner, Jared, 87, 101, 183, 191, 205
  MbS's relationship with, 39, 42,
      52–3, 124, 149–50, 195, 203,
      239, 255, 289, 294
  as White House 'princeling', 53,
      87–8
Kuwait 47–8
Kyaw Soe Oo, 296

Laden, Osama bin, *see* bin Laden,
      Osama
Landmark, 71
Law, Bill, 34–5

Lebanon, 33, 92, 93, 145
Lee, Mike, 277
Liberty for the Muslim World, 30, 129
Libya, 35, 44, 64
Lillian Court, 72
'local collaborator' claim, 207, 214,
    215, 241, 249
London:
    Dosari given police protection in,
        306
    HC moves to, 314
    JK's last weekend in, 123–32, 193,
        313
    JK's memorial event in, 314
    MbS signs memorandum of
        understanding in, 275
    press-freedom conference held in,
        301
    Prince Ahmed in retirement in, 238
    Prince Turki Saudi ambassador to,
        238
    Saudi embassy in, 32, 134, 185, 248
    Yalcin Turkish ambassador to, 318
London School of Economics (LSE),
    78, 319
The Looming Tower (Wright), 28
Lopez, Eli, 146
Louisville University, 186
Louvre Abu Dhabi, 57
Lowcock, Mark, 281
LSE, 78, 319
Luxembourg, 56

Mabahith, 153
McConnell, Mitch, 279
McKinsey Global Institute (MGI), 55
Macron, Emmanuel, 93, 267–8
Madani, Brig.-Gen. Mustafa
    Mohammed al-, see al-Madani,
    Brig.-Gen. Mustafa Mohammed
Maduro, Nicolás, 226
Magnitsky, Sergei, 189

Maha, Mr ('commission') 132
Maha (wife), 61
Mandela, Nelson, 57
Mar-a-Lago, `260
Marshall, Julian, 125–6
Marshall, Tim i
mass-casualty accidents, determining
    deaths in, 14
Mattis, Jim, 263–4
May, Theresa, 11, 240, 267
MBC, 69
MbS:
    alleged misdeeds roll call of, 195
    audio recordings appear not to
        mention, 181
    autocratic behaviour of, 93
    BAE contract signed by, 275
    Bloomberg interviews, 151
    BND briefs journalists on, 42
    CIA concludes involvement of,
        252–4
    'comeback tour' of, 52, 266–71
    commission chaired by, 211
    consigliere of, 68
    'crisis committee' of advisers
        formed by, 205
    critics of, fear own safety, 171–2
    crown prince deputy elevation of,
        49
    crown prince elevation of, 50, 52
    '007' licence of, 227
    Erdoğan's relationship with, 220–2,
        226
    on freedom of speech, 127
    French château bought by, 56
    as 'guardian of all the Muslim
        nations' 222
    global PR exercise of, 80–1
    at G20, 265, 267
    Ignatius interviews, 98–9
    inward/outward investment
        promoted by, 41

MbS – *continued*
  JK's criticisms of, 47, 107–8, 126
  Kushner's relationship with, 39, 42,
    52–3, 124, 149–50, 195, 203,
    239, 255, 289, 294
  media czar of, *see* Qahtani, Saud al-
  memorandum of understanding
    signed by, 275
  as Minister of Defence, 44
  Mr Bone Saw sobriquet of, 277
  New Yorker profile of, 46–7
  'PlayStation king' description of, 46
  prosecutor makes no mention of,
    297
  Putin comparison made of, 90
  Putin's G20 meeting with, 269
  Qahtani *consigliere* to 69
  Ritz-Carlton affair orchestrated by,
    87–103, 269
  Salah Khashoggi meets, 236
  Senate Committee reports on, 196
  sobriquets of, 46, 91, 277
  Trump lunches with, 39, 42
  Trump's 'exchanged pleasantries'
    with, 268
  US evidence against, 181–2
  US media revile, 277
  US tour of, 52, 266–71
  'Vision 2030' plan of, 55, 76, 307
  'WhatsApp ruler' description of,
    46, 52
  White House shields, 195, 234, 261,
    262, 268
  WP off-the-record briefing given by,
    39–40
  WP writes to, 149–50
  'wrecking ball' description of, 201,
    264–5
  Yemeni war launched by, 58
MbZ, 62
Mecca, 19, 24, 63, 109, 215, 217–18,
  220, 226, 249

Medina, 19, 22, 23, 28, 29, 33, 109,
  217–18, 220, 223, 244, 249
Mehmed the Conqueror (Mehmed
  II), 15
MEMO (Middle East Monitor), 123
MenoM3ay, 170
Merkel, Angela, 229, 267
Mexico, 74
MGI (McKinsey Global Institute), 55
Microsoft, 40
Middle East:
  human rights abuses in, *see main*
    entry
  Mamluk rule in, 217
  partitioning of, 217
  peace process, 40, 42, 101, 274, 294
  Trump's zero interest in democracy
    in, 98
  Western 'democratisation' of, 30
Middle East Institute, Washington,
  DC, 73
Middle East Monitor (MEMO), 123
Middle East TV, 224
mistranslations, 164, 166, 181
MIT (Millî İstihbarat Teşkilatı;
  MİT) (National Intelligence
  Organisation) (Turkey), 161, 163
Miteb, Prince, 88–9
Mnuchin, Steve, 234–5, 239, 251
Mohammed, Crown Prince ('MbZ'), 62
Mohammed, Khalid Sheikh, 63–4
Mohammed, Prince (ambassador), 2
Mohammed, Prince (King Salman's
  nephew), 49, 50–51, 60, 63, 87,
  303
Mohammed, Prince ('MbZ'), 62
Mongolia, 232
Moonlight Sonata, 46
Morocco 45, 65
Mövenpick, 3,, 9, 88, 131, 138, 141,
  143, 159
Mubarak, Hosni, 223

Muhammad, Prophet, 19, 152
mujahideen, 25–8
Mujeb, Saud al-, 214, 240, 241–2, 246
Muqrin, Crown Prince, 49, 303
Murdoch, Rupert, 40
Murphy, Chris, 155–6, 200, 283
Muslim Brotherhood, 21–5, 27, 30,
         34–6, 38, 64–5, 67, 72–5, 82,
         84, 127, 129, 183–4, 191, 211–12,
         219–24, 231, 244, 248, 259, 266,
         294, 298
'Muslims are one nation' interview, 25
Mutreb, Brig.-Gen. Maher Abdulaziz,
         8–9, 11, 12–13, 14, 17, 40–1,
         90, 96, 117–20, 134–6, 138,
         142–4, 163, 166, 180–2, 185,
         209, 213, 246–8, 251–2, 254,
         287, 289–90, 298
    'dark face' nickname attributed to
         186
mutual interest, 5
Myanmar (Burma), 222, 296

Nabila, 21
NASA, 46
Naseif, Alaa (wife), 34, 61, 71, 80,
         81–3, 312
Nasr, Prince Saud bin Saif al-, 45–6
Nasser, Col Gamal Abdel, 22, 36, 219
National Commercial Bank (NCB),
         237
National Intelligence Organisation,
    Turkey, see MIT
National Security Agency (NSA), 202,
         253
NATO, 26, 160, 202, 231, 271
Natural History Museum, 2
Nayef, Crown Prince Mohammed bin,
         49, 50–51, 60, 63, 87, 303
Nayef, Prince (interior minister), 32,
         174
Nazi Germany, 231, 263

NBC News, 90
NCB (National Commercial Bank)
         237
Nematt, Salameh, 26
neo-Ottomanism, 218
NEOM, 55
Netherlands, 231
Never Say Never Again, 21
New Broadcasting House, 125
'A New President and the Middle East'
         (Khashoggi), 59
'new world order', 191
New York Times (NYT), 43, 53, 57, 69,
         77, 93, 96, 145, 148, 159, 165,
         168, 181–3, 187, 201, 204–5,
         207, 209, 216, 248, 270, 317
New York University, 27
New Yorker, 46, 51, 91, 94
Newshour, 125
'Night of the Long Knives'
         (Khashoggi), 90
Nimr, Sheikh Nimr Baqir al-, 44, 45
9/11, 31, 43, 64, 80, 85, 99–100,
         155–6, 195, 265, 277, 280, 296
No Nuclear Weapons for Saudi Arabia
         Act (2018) (US), 279
North Africa, 106
North Korea, 195
Nour, Ayman, 223–5
NSA, 202, 253
NSO Group, 101
Number 10 see Downing Street
NYT see New York Times

Obama, Barack, 12, 43, 48, 50, 61,
         191, 192, 295
O'Donnell, Norah, 91
Oke, Fatih, 145
ohchr.org 317
Okhaz, 25
Olayan, Lubna, 235–6
Oman, 107, 112

One Franklin Square, MbS visits, 39
Open Society Justice Initiative, 288
Operation Decisive Storm, 47
'Oslo at 25: A Legacy of Broken
    Promises', 123
Otaibi, Maj. Badr Lafi al-, 290
Otaibi, Mohammad al-, 120–2, 138,
    148–9, 152–3, 165, 179, 198,
    247, 251, 289, 293
Ottoman Empire, 8, 15, 20, 216–18,
    221, 225, 318

Pakistan, 25, 31, 32, 232, 235, 300
Palestine, 24, 30, 33, 42, 66, 129–30,
    306
    Abu Dis, 124
    Erdoğan becomes loudest
        spokesperson for, 218
    Gaza Strip, 1, 65, 129, 218
    Hamas rule in, 33–4, 63, 65, 129
    journalists from, 62, 73, 114, 126,
        239
    Middle East Monitor reports on,
        123
    peace deal, 53, 54, 101, 124–5, 255,
        294
    press monitoring of, 122
    suicide bombers, 64, 128
Patriot missile system, 271
Paul, Rand, 252, 260, 274
Pearl, Daniel, 31
'Pegasus' spyware, 101
Pentagon, 164, 271
Perry, Rick, 278
Peskov, Dmitry, 228
phone-traffic recordings, Riyadh–
    Istanbul, 117 (see also audio
    recordings)
Pinto, Daniel, 293
pleasure wives, 20
political lobbying, 23, 83
political prisoners, 75

polygamy, 10, 20, 28, 50, 61, 110, 113,
    312
Pompeo, Mike, 50, 149–50, 195,
    198–203, 252, 259, 263–4, 277,
    295, 297, 311
Popular Committee for Aiding
    Martyrs, Families and Mujahedin
    in Palestine, 218
press freedom, 204, 232, 291, 297, 301
    (see also freedom of speech)
Princeton University, 300
Prisoners of Conscience, 75
Prisoners of Geography (Marshall) i
profligate lifestyles, 20
Pulp Fiction, 159
Putin, Vladimir, 90, 171, 228, 263,
    269–70

Qahtani, Maj.-Gen. Ali al-, 89
Qahtani, Saif Saad al-, 139–40, 147, 170
Qahtani, Saud al-, 51, 60, 62–3, 66,
    70–1, 74, 79, 90, 92, 96–8,
    101, 118, 164, 181–5, 207–8,
    213, 248–52, 254, 291–3, 298,
    305
    as MbS's consigliere 69
    sobriquets of, 69
Qaradawi, Sheikh Yusuf al-, 64
Qatar, 37, 63–7, 68–70, 75, 80, 84,
    95, 106, 112, 115, 126–8, 158,
    211–12, 216, 224, 225–6, 231,
    248, 275, 285
Qatar Foundation International, 80
Quincy, USS, 295
Quran (Koran), 15, 109

Rapid Intervention Group, 8, 11, 16,
    41, 71, 90, 131, 134, 139, 147,
    169, 177, 184–5, 207, 264
Ramadan, 19, 187
Rasheed, Prof. Madawi al-, 33, 78,
    303, 319

religious tolerance/intolerance, 95,
107
rendition, 46, 134, 146, 206, 214, 247,
251, 256
Reuters, 152, 164, 165, 208, 213, 214,
292, 296
Rezaian, Jason, 146
Riedel, Bruce, 43, 182, 295
    history of US–Saudi relations
    written by, 302
Riyadh:
    and bin Laden, 29
    Criminal Court, 289
    Doha's relationship with, 64–5, 66
    Egyptian coup endorsed by, 35–6
    governor of, see Salman, King
    Hariri detained in, 237
    phone traffic, 117
    Pompeo visits, 50
    Russian commerce in, 228
    social-media campaigns directed
        from, 68
    Trump visits, 63
    UK arms sales to, 275–6
    US arms sales to, 277
Riyadh Ritz-Carlton, 86, 87–103, 195,
    203, 234, 249, 269, 278, 307
    Trump stays at, 88
'rogue killers' theory, 199–200, 228,
    229
Rohingya Muslims, 222, 296
Roosevelt, Franklin D. ('FDR'), 188,
    295
Rubin, Barnett, 27, 35, 37, 44–5, 76
rules-based order, breakdown of, 4,
    228, 269
Russia, 56, 161, 189, 190–1, 228, 258,
    262–3, 279, 290
    in Afghanistan 28
    Aleppo bombardment by, 220
    at G20 summit, 269
    intelligence, 171, 228

S-400 missile air-defence system,
    193, 231, 271
    and Skripal poisonings, 228–9, 231,
    270
    as USSR (Soviet Union), 24, 25
Ryan, Fred, 146, 149, 156, 184, 209–
    10, 260, 318

Sabah see Daily Sabah
safe houses, 171, 213
'safe speech' rooms, 162
Saffuri, Khaled, 23, 83, 84, 90, 97,
    102–3, 112
Sahin, Vasip, 143
Salafism, 32, 34, 219–20, 307
Salat al-Gha'ib, 250
Salem, Maggie Mitchell, 37, 80
Salisbury Cathedral, 171
Salisbury poisonings, 171, 228–9, 231,
    270
Salman, Crown Prince Mohammed bin
    ('MbS'), see MbS
Salman, Crown Prince Mohammed bin
    Zayed al-Nahyan ('MbZ'), 62
Salman, King (MbS's father), 31, 41,
    44, 45–6, 49–52, 54, 57–8, 89,
    92, 138, 188–9, 191, 193, 197,
    199, 210, 218, 220–1, 226–7,
    230, 238, 240, 245, 292, 303–4,
    310
    accession of, 44
    Erdoğan's relationship with, 220
    HC's pleas to, 188
    Prince Ahmed 'last' surviving
        brother of, 238
    Prince Mohammed sacked by, 51,
        303
    Prince Muqrin sacked by, 49, 303
    as Prince Salman, 27
Salman, Prince Khalid bin (MbS's
    brother), 82, 150, 156–7, 253–4,
    288, 292, 304, 311

Salvator Mundi, 57, 310
Sanaa, 46, 219
Saturday Mothers, 232
Saud, Prince Abdulaziz bin Mashhur
    al-, 306
Saud, Abdullah bin Abdulaziz al- *see*
    Abdullah, King
Saud, Bader bin Abdullah bin
    Mohammed bin Farhan al-, 57
Saud, Emir Abdullah bin, 217
Saud, King Faisal bin Abdulaziz al-, 61,
    65, 303–4
Saud, Ibn, *see* Ibn Saud
Saud, Prince Khalid bin Salman bin
    Abdulaziz al- (MbS's brother),
    82, 150, 156–7, 253–4, 288, 292,
    304, 311
Saud, Crown Prince Mohammed bin
    Salman al- ('MbS'), *see* MbS
Saud, Murqin bin Abdulaziz al-, 49,
    303
Saud, Salman bin Abdulaziz al-, *see*
    Salman, King
Saudi Arabia:
    agnatic seniority in, 49
    Air Force, 186
    anti-government protests in, 36, 44
    beheadings in, 44, 308
    charities, 61
    CIA vs, 246–57
    Crown Prince office in, 169
    crucifixions in, 308
    cultural freedoms in, 307
    death penalty in, 128, 248, 289,
        311
    decadence displayed by, 20, 40, 49,
        87, 88, 90, 115, 267
    disinformation put out by, 312
    'electronic army' plan of 102
    EU arms sales to, 229
    fake evidence supplied by, 141, 170,
        187
    foreign SIM cards sent to activists
        in, 102
    as guardian of Wahhabism 218
    global credibility problem of, 211,
        240, 273
    human rights abuses in, 99–100,
        192, 243–4, 251
    intelligence, 12, 26, 27, 33, 46, 72,
        117, 120, 133–4, 162, 211,
        212, 241, 252
    inward/outward investment
        promoted by, 41
    lack of tolerance in, 19–20
    'local collaborator' claim, 207, 214,
        215, 241, 249
    Macron visits, 93
    MbS's father's accession in, 44
    Minister of Defence, 44
    National Day celebration, 2, 204–5
    National Guard, 48, 88
    national symbols of, 2, 3, 17
    Obama's visits to, 43
    official statement issued by, 212–14,
        215
    oil reserves, 56
    $100 million donation to US, 202
    paradox of, 77
    'Pegasus' spyware utilised by, 101
    Prince Ahmed afraid to return to,
        238
    profligate lifestyles in, 20
    prosecutor's final report, 246–7
    public debate banned in, 94
    Rapid Intervention Group, *see main
        entry*
    Research Council, 73
    'rogue killers' claim made by, 199–
        200, 228, 229
    Royal Guard, 12, 184, 186, 290,
        298
    sanctions against, 189, 250–2
    secret police (Mabahith), 152

Senate Committee reports on, 195, 196

snatch squads, *see* Rapid Intervention Group

social-media campaigns in, 68

spy agency, 207

state propaganda, 102

stonewalling by, 158, 200

three new departments created in, 211

Trump sides wholeheartedly with, 191

Trump visits, 52, 63, 88

Trump's early encounters with wealth and influence of, 21

Turkey fears retaliation from, 149, 180

Turkish consulate of, *see under* Turkey

UK arms sales to, 275–6, 281, 282

US arms sales to, 190–3, 197, 240, 254–5, 274–5, 277–9, 282–3, 286

US as PR agent for, 200

Vienna Convention violated by, 149

women's rights in, 34, 54, 94–6

in Yemen, *see main entry*

youth unemployment in, 55

Saudi Arabia Accountability and Yemen Act (2018) 275

Saudi Arabia First! 260

Saudi Aramco, 49, 55–6, 75, 89, 235, 293–4

Saudi embassies:
London, 32
Ottawa, 101
Washington, DC, 32

Saudi Federation for Cybersecurity, 207

Saudi Gazette, 211

Saudi paradox, 77

Saudi Rapid Intervention Group, *see* Rapid Intervention Group

Saudi Research Council, 73

Saudi Royal Guard, 12, 184, 186, 290, 298

Save the Children, 273

Scheherazade, 65

Schiff, Adam, 209, 262

Scientific Council of Forensic Medicine (Saudi Arabia), 8

Second World War, 161

secret police (Mabahith) (Saudi Arabia), 153

security-camera footage, *see* CCTV footage

Security Screening Team, 125

Sehri, Waleed Abdullah al-, 186

selfies, 40, 234, 314

11 September attacks, *see* 9/11

Serene, 56, 57

S-400 missile air-defence system, 193, 231, 271

Shaalan, Shaalan al-, 247

sham trials, 146

sharia law, 10, 312

Shefler, Yuri, 56

Shehi, Saleh al-, 203

shell companies, 56–7, 194

Silicon Valley, 39, 103

Sisi, Abdel Fattah al-, 191, 294

60 Minutes, 91

Skripal, Sergei, 171, 228–9, 231, 270

Sky Prime Aviation, 140

Skype, 164–5

smoking gun, 182, 264

snatch squads, 71 (*see also* Rapid Intervention Group)

Sochi, 228

Somalia, 222

Soros, George, 288

South Korea, 279

Soviet Union, 24, 25 (*see also* Russia)

spyware, 100, 101, 306

Stalin, Joseph, 272
state-sponsored illegallity, 146, 171 (*see also* rendition)
stonewalling, 158, 200
Sudairi Seven, 50
Sudais, Sheikh Abdulrahman al-, 226
suicide bombers/bombings, 34, 50, 64
Suleiman (friend), 23–4
Sultan of Brunei, 21
Sultan, Prince Bandar bin ('Bandar Bush'), 33, 34
Sultan, Prince (MbS's brother), 45, 46
surveillance-camera footage, *see* CCTV footage
Sweden, 278
Syria, 35, 44, 59, 172, 202, 219–20, 222, 231–2, 256, 270, 281
   Mamluk rule in, 217

Tahrir Square, 219
Taiba High School, 21
Talal, Prince Alwaleed bin, 21, 36, 49, 88–9, 194, 222, 238
'Tales from the Front Line' (Rugman), 1
Taliban, 26, 63
Tamimi, Azzam, 30, 33, 73, 77, 81, 82, 114, 129–31, 220
Tenet, George, 50
Thanksgiving (US), 85, 259, 261
Thatcher, Margaret, 55, 276
#TheBlacklist, 70
34 CC 1865, 138
Tiananmen Square, 29
Tier 1 Group, 185
Tihama bookshop, 24
Tillerson, Rex, 53, 191–2
Time, 296, 297
@tobagi1, 187
Toronto University, 99
torture, 88, 96, 155, 189, 267, 301

'Towards New Security Arrangements for the Middle East and North Africa Region', 106
Tribune, 23
trigger words, 182
Tripoli, 219
Trump, Donald, 3, 21, 41, 100, 181, 195, 227, 239, 254–7
   America First! policy of, 25, 258–60
   as *The Apprentice* host, 240
   audio tape not listened to by, 167
   becomes US president, 52, 195
   election of (2016), 52, 194
   Erdoğan's G20 meeting with, 271
   Erdoğan's 'MbS "big brother"' description of, 234
   family matters weigh on mind of, 294
   first foreign visit of, 52, 88, 191
   foreign-policy agenda of, 198
   Fox News interviews, 189–90
   HC criticises, 189, 250, 314, 315
   HC invited to White House by, 189
   HC's pleas to, 188–9
   and House of Saud, 42, 51–3, 188–214, 227
   and human rights, 42
   inauguration of, 195
   inconclusive conclusion issued by, 258
   Iran loathed by, 41, 42
   JK's criticisms of, 59, 70, 93
   JK's murder dismissed by, 158, 167, 168
   and JK's *Time* award, 296
   legislature bypassed by, 283–4
   MbS endorsed by, 89, 93
   MbS lunches with, 39, 42
   MbS's 'exchanged pleasantries' with, 268
   'new world order', 191
   Putin admired by, 269

'rogue killers' claim supported by, 228
sanctions imposed by, 216, 239,
    240, 250–1, 252, 261, 271
shell companies dissolved by, 194
Skripal response of, 270
as TV presenter, 240
on Twitter, 63, 89, 193, 203, 261,
    270, 297
US Senate rebukes, 277–9, 282
veto wielded by, 280
visits Saudi Arabia, 52, 88, 191
White House administration, *see*
    under White House
and Yemen, 240
Trump, Melania, 188
Trump Princess, 21, 195
Trump World Tower, 194
Tubaigy, Lt-Col Dr Salah Mohammed
    al-, 8, 12, 13–14, 134, 137, 143,
    146, 163–4, 166, 186–7, 201,
    209, 214, 247–8, 251, 287, 289
Tunisi, Rawiya al- (wife), 33, 35, 61, 83
Tunisia, 60, 65, 99, 266–7
Turkey:
    consulate killing, 133–47
    coup attempt (2016), 231–2
    EU bribes, 231
    foreign debts of, 215–16
    founding of, 219
    human rights abuses in, 231, 243
    intelligence, 12, 118, 125, 144, 153,
        162–7, 172–3, 179–80, 188,
        202, 232, 289
    JK's first contact with, 20
    journalists detained in, 232
    Muslim humanitarian causes
        championed by, 221–2
    Qatar supported by, 63, 66
    Russian S-400 missile air-defence
        system bought by, 231, 271
    state news agency (Anatolia), 224
    Trump imposes sanctions on, 233

Turki, Prince, 27, 32, 33, 34, 49,
    72–3, 77, 89, 215, 238
Turki, Sultan bin, 45
Turkish Airlines, 7, 16, 132, 147, 170
Turkish Arab Media Association, 154
'Turkish model', 223
Turkish soap operas, 69
Turkish Tourist Centre, 131
Twitter, 7, 154, 193, 260, 303
    Awdah's use of, 128
    Anadolu's use on, 224
    Atr's use of, 113
    Butairi's use of, 95
    Corker's use of, 261
    Dosari's use of, 306
    Freeland's use of, 99
    Graham's use of, 260
    HC's use of, 212, 250
    JK's (@JKhashoggi) use of, 32, 60,
        72, 74, 83, 84, 95, 117, 128,
        183
    Kabli's use of, 152
    Murphy's use of, 155–6, 200
    Prince Khalid's use of, 254
    Qahtani's use of, 70, 207, 208, 292
    Rand Paul's use of, 252, 260, 274
    SA's use of, 70, 99–100, 102, 127–8,
        152, 206, 211, 237
    Salah Khashoggi's use of, 311
    Trump's use of, 63, 89, 193, 203,
        261, 270, 297
    Tubaigy's use of, 186–7
    Turkey's use of, 224
Typhoon project, 275–6, 282
Tysons Corner, 72, 84, 89

Uber, 235
Ukraine, 232
UNICEF, 278
United Arab Emirates (UAE), 47, 57,
    62, 63, 65, 94, 111, 147, 183, 211,
    225, 266, 282

United Kingdom (UK):
    arms sales, 274, 281–2
    bin Salman's official visit to, 9, 11,
        41
    Foreign Office, 275, 282, 301, 319
    joint statement issued by, 208
United Nations (UN):
    al-Aiban refuses to answer questions
        from, 244–5
    Development Programme report,
        281
    General Assembly meeting, 77
    investigation called for by, 228, 287
    rapporteur's investigation, 104, 163,
        165, 179, 287, 289, 290, 301,
        305–6, 317
    Security Council, 43, 220, 287, 290
UNICEF, 278
    on Yemen, 195, 273–4, 278, 281
United States for Saudis/US Made Easy for
    Saudis (Khashoggi), 76
United States (US):
    in Afghanistan, 26
    al-Qaeda attacks on, 28–9, 30
    bin Laden financed by, 27
    bin Salman's official visit to, 9, 11,
        41
    citizenship, how to obtain, 75–6
    embassy bombings, 28
    Independence Day (Fourth of July),
        102
    intelligence, 46, 51, 182–4, 187,
        196, 255, 263
    Saudi $100 million donation to, 202
    Thanksgiving, 85, 259, 261
    UAE airbase, 62
    Yemen policy of, 275, 280–1
US Council on Foreign Relations, 209
US Foreign Affairs Committee, 280
US House of Representatives, 276, 279
US Made Easy for Saudis/United States for
    Saudis (Khashoggi), 76

US–Saudi relations, 252, 263, 277, 280
    Riedel's written history of, 302
    since 9/11 296
US Senate Armed Services
    Committee, 195
US Senate Foreign Relations
    Committee, 196, 261, 274, 297
US State Department, 150, 185, 192,
        198, 256, 288, 292–3, 311
US Treasury, 234, 239, 250, 251
USSR, 24, 25 (see also Russia)

Vanity Fair, 53, 95
@VELWYErtYVTc9cn, 187
Venezuela, 198, 226
Versailles, 56, 160
Victorian Institute of Forensic
    Medicine, 13
video footage, see CCTV footage
Vienna Convention on Consular
    Relations, 149, 176, 179, 180,
        242
Viet Cong, 48
Vinci, Leonardo da, 57, 291, 310
Virgin Group, 235
Virginia, 33, 35, 71–2, 75, 82, 85–6,
        89, 98, 104–5, 110, 112, 115, ,
        150, 195, 252, 277, 281, 310, 312
'Vision 2030' plan, 55, 76, 307
voice recordings, see audio recordings

Wa Lone, 296
Wahhabism, 54, 217, 218
Wali al-Amr ruling, 62
Wall Street Journal, 31, 181, 183, 292,
        294
War Powers Act (1973) (US), 276
Washington, DC, Saudi embassy in, 32
Washington Institute, 59
Washington Post, 1, 5, 7, 18, 20, 22, 32,
        39–40, 49, 55, 67, 71, 73
    al-Harbi's denial to, 186

CIA report published in, 252–3
Congress appeal made by, 260
Erdoğan writes in, 227, 230
Global Opinions (WP), 7, 39–40, 76
HC communicates through, 148, 188–9, 309
JK believed kidnapped by, 145–6
JK's 'abuse of its power' articles in, 91–2
JK's draft articles for, 114
JK's family speak to, 68, 184
JK's first report for, 77
JK's last reports for, 127
JK's 'online pulpit' at, 95
JK starts writing for, 76–8
Khalid allegation published by, 156
MbS headline in, 248–9
MbS letter from, 149–50
One Franklin Square HQ of, 39
posthumous final column published by, 203
reports JK's 'pre-planned murder', 153
Ritz-Carlton affair covered by, 89
Salem shares text messages with, 80
SA's official statement to, 212
'Trump effect' article, 93
Trump shell-company report in, 194
Trump speaks to, 210
Turks brief, 167, 168
unfinished work of, 309–15
Yemen report in, 273–4
Welfare Party, 30, 219
'What the Arab world needs most is free expression' (Khashoggi), 203
WhatsApp:
  Abdulaziz's use of, 100
  Aktay's use of, 144
  JK's use of, 84, 100
  Kushner's use of, 53
  MbS's use of, 46, 53, 84, 181
  Qahtani's use of, 292
White House:
  MbS shielded by, 195, 234, 261, 262, 268
  MbS visits, 43
  moonlighting, 261
  Obama, 48, 295
  'princeling', 53, 87–8
  Sisi's visit to, 294
Turkey shares consulate recordings with, 166–7, 196–8, 255
Wilson, Woodrow, 76
'wipers', defined, 173–5
wiretapping, 162
Wolff, Michael, 52
Women's Association (Tunisia), 267
women, male guardianship over 244
women's rights, 94–6
Woodrow Wilson International Center for Scholars, 76
World Cup 2022, 64
World Food Programme, 273
World Service, 125
World Trade Center, Bahrain, 36
Wright, Lawrence, 22, 28
Wyndham Grand, 16, 131, 159

X-rayed luggage, 144, 165

Yakış, Yaşar, 217
Yalova farmland, 172, 173
Yemen, 28, 44, 156, 272–84, 304
  human rights abuses in, 278
  humanitarian crisis in, 4, 48, 271, 279, 280–1
  JK writes about, 4, 272–3, 281
  limited ceasefire in, 279
  MbS launches war on, 58
  Shia control of, 47
Yeni Safak, 181
YouTube, 45, 152, 306

Zahrani, Khaled Yahya al-, 173
Zahrani, Muhammad Saad al-, 186
Zamil, Essam al-, 75, 77, 93–4, 126, 128

Zayed, Crown Prince Mohammed bin ('MbZ'), *see* MbZ
Zuckerberg, Mark, 40